Success
in
College

Success in College

The Role of Personal Qualities and Academic Ability

WARREN W. WILLINGHAM

With the assistance of
John W. Young
Margaret M. Morris

College Entrance Examination Board
New York, 1985

Editorial inquiries concerning this book should be addressed to Editorial Office, The College Board,
45 Columbus Avenue, New York, New York 10023-6917.

Copies of this book may be ordered from College Board
Publications, Box 886, New York, New York 10101.
The price is $26.95 for the hardbound edition and $16.95
for the paperbound edition.

Library of Congress Catalog Card Number: 85-72884.

ISBN 0-87447-229-6 (hardbound), 0-87447-228-8 (paperbound).

Printed in the United States of America.

9 8 7 6 5 4 3 2 1

Contents

Figures

Tables

Personal Qualities
Steering Committee

The following were members of the steering committee through the conduct of the follow-up phase of the project:

David S. Perham, Chairman
Colgate University

James M. Montoya
Occidental College

David A. Booth
Williams College

John Muyskens, Jr.
Hartwick College

Kenneth P. Goodrich
Ohio Wesleyan University

Thomas N. Pollard, Jr.
University of Richmond

John D. Kushan
Kenyon College

Richard C. Skelton
Bucknell University

Marilyn LaPlante
Kalamazoo College

The following served on the steering committee during other periods:

Paul M. Lane
Kalamazoo College

John A. Williams
Occidental College

Dwight D. Hatcher
Kenyon College

Peter Feickert
G. Gary Ripple
Douglas Steeples
Ohio Wesleyan University

Preface

What does it mean to succeed in college? Making good grades is a big part of the answer. But most readily agree that there is more to a college education than grades. Certainly college catalogs imply a lot more. One would assume that colleges are interested in the question of which students best meet the overall educational objectives of the institution and how more such students can be identified. Actually there has been remarkably little research on this question.

This book describes the outcome of a detailed study undertaken in cooperation with nine colleges: Bucknell University, Colgate University, Hartwick College, Kalamazoo College, Kenyon College, Occidental College, Ohio Wesleyan University, University of Richmond, and Williams College. It focuses on the relationship among preadmission characteristics of students, admissions policies, and different measures of success through four years of college.

In studying pre-admission characteristics, we were especially interested in personal qualities of students (e.g., background, interests, accomplishments) as well as their academic ability. For that reason the study has been known as the Personal Qualities Project. The participating colleges had a strong interest in the research questions as well as in learning more about their own practices and were willing to take on the sizable task of data collection that the study required. The sponsors, the College Board and Educational Testing Service (ETS) wanted to shed additional light on the admissions process and had a special interest in learning more about the validity of the Scholastic Aptitude Test (SAT) and its proper role in admissions.

A great strength of the SAT is that it serves as a standard academic yardstick in a highly diverse educational system. That is one reason why the test is a useful adjunct to high school rank in predicting college grades. This admissions test also adds an important element of fairness and balance, partly because it is the same measure for all, and partly because it provides an alternative to grades in identifying and encouraging academic talent.

School rank and admissions tests, however, focus on scholastic ability, narrowly defined, and that is not a trivial limitation considering the broad educational objectives that most colleges avow. Staff at the College Board and ETS as well as others concerned with college admissions have consistently maintained, of course, that selective admissions should take other types of evidence into account—that undue weight should not be placed on the SAT.

But the SAT is frequently validated, highly visible, and neatly quantified. It is widely assumed to have great influence. There is always the possibility that the test may crowd out other types of evidence—particularly evidence of personal competencies or other qualities that may well be related to success in college broadly defined. Enormous amounts of time and expense go into the preparation of detailed applications, school reports, teacher references, personal statements by students, interviews on campus, and so on. All of this activity serves more than one purpose, but one goal is to provide colleges with the broad base of information they need in order to carry out their objectives in recruiting and selecting students. How well this goal is served is another question. In contrast to the SAT and high school rank there is extremely little research on the use and validity of other information commonly used in admissions work. So one of our purposes in this study was to learn more than we presently know about the strengths and weaknesses of this mountain of data that are collected through the admissions cycle each year.

In order to get at these issues, we had to examine very carefully the different ways in which an institution might define success in light of its various objectives. The study used a number of criterion measures, all based upon the accumulated four-year record of the student. We focused especially on several broad types of success: scholarship, leadership, significant accomplishments, and the institutions' judgment as to which students were most successful overall.

The study reaffirmed that the SAT and school rank are the measures that best predict scholarship. On the other hand, our data clearly show that these colleges view success quite broadly. They put heavy emphasis on leadership and significant accomplishments, as well as on scholarship, when they identified the students they regarded as most successful.

This result raises several important issues, because these three types of success were not highly related. There are educational issues concerning what balance of academic ability and other competencies and accomplishments is proper when students are selected, trained, and judged successful. There are equity issues concerning fairness to productive individuals and to groups that may do better on important types of real-life accomplishment than on traditional grades and scholastic aptitude tests. There are programmatic issues concerning the attention and emphasis that national testing programs do and should give different indicators of talent.

After a great deal of analysis of all these data—multiple preadmission measures and multiple success criteria—we did find several measures that are useful supplements to the SAT and school rank. If I reach any one conclusion as to what personal quality is important other than the academic measures of SAT and school rank, I would say it is productivity. These colleges seemed to like producers. I suspect the broader society does as well. The data in this study suggest that it is possible to get a good idea of who will produce in college by looking carefully at what a student has done in secondary school. We even developed a measure that seems to work pretty well, though it needs a good deal more research at individual institutions.

These are complicated matters. One should be cautious not to overinterpret the results of one study. These nine institutions are reasonably representative of selective private colleges, but they do differ one from the other and they certainly do not necessarily reflect the values and practices of other types of institutions. However, I believe the study has succeeded in establishing new connections and raising useful questions.

Many have made important contributions to this project. I am especially grateful to the many students, faculty, and administrative staff who provided the data. A key role was played by the project steering committee, which consisted of a senior administrator from each institution. They are listed on page xi. These individuals supervised the work on the nine campuses. They were also responsible for policy decisions on all matters concerning student and institutional interests and for prior review and approval of all work plans and project reports. Their contribution individually and as a committee was substantial and greatly appreciated. David Perham, the chairman of the group, was especially generous with his time and with useful advice.

John Young and Margaret Morris served as senior research assistants through the second phase of the Personal Qualities Project. They did most of the data analysis and also assisted with other important aspects of the project. I am indebted to them for their fine work.

A number of other colleagues gave valuable assistance or suggestions on specific substantive or statistical questions. I want to thank especially Bernard Adler, Henry Braun, Paul Holland, Bruce Kaplan, Alfred Rodgers, Paul Rosenbaum, and Dorothy Thayer. Several people in addition to the steering committee reviewed all or parts of this report in draft: Hunter Breland, Arthur Kroll, Theodore Marchesi, Donald Rock, William Turnbull, Philip Smith, and Kenneth Wilson. My appreciation to each of them for many helpful comments and suggestions.

Bernice Gall typed the manuscript and deserves much credit for her competent work. Joseph Morsicato did his usual fine editorial job. Linda Johnson and Debra Smolinski provided much useful assistance throughout the study. I am grateful to each for their help.

Warren W. Willingham
Personal Qualities Project Director

1

A Brief Overview

Four years of college constitute a life-forming event. It is a maturing and socializing experience that should open the mind and help a young person prepare for adult responsibilities. Achieving success in that experience is highly individual and is manifested in many ways. From the standpoint of higher education generally, success in college can also mean many things because higher education serves many purposes. This volume reports the findings of a study addressed to these questions: Which students are most successful in the eyes of the college and what qualities in an applicant for admission can best show promise of such success?

This first chapter has three aims. One is to explain briefly the background and rationale of the study, which started seven years ago. This is the second major report of the findings; the first, published in 1982, was *Personal Qualities and College Admissions*, by Willingham and Breland, referred to throughout this book as *Personal Qualities*. The second aim is to review a few highlights of the earlier report in order to provide a better framework and jumping-off point for this report. Finally, because this study tackles some complex research questions and the report is loaded with data, the third aim is to ease the reader's task somewhat by describing briefly the main features of the study, the content of successive chapters, and the most important findings.

In 1978 when this study was planned, the College Board and Educational Testing Service thought it was time for a careful study of college admissions—a different and much more detailed study than had been undertaken to date. Looking to the 1980s, there was concern that increasing pressure to maintain enrollment in the face of a shrinking age cohort could pressure colleges to look for bodies rather than the most promising and deserving students. One need, then, was a better understanding of the relevance of other talents that might broaden the pool of admissible applicants. Another concern was the social imperative to broaden educational opportunity for minorities, women, the handicapped, and adults beyond the traditional college age. An altered mix of college students requires greater attention to a wider range of student characteristics and goals. There were also legal concerns as to what characteristics are permissible for use in admissions. In the mid-1970s, race was the characteristic most hotly debated, but the question extended to other qualities as well. The influential Powell (1978) opinion in *Regents of the University of California v. Bakke* underscored the appropriateness, even desirability, of institutionally determined admissions policy based on multiple characteristics of students. That legal analysis also made clear the institution's accountability for sound policy and fair practice. (See Willingham 1980 for a detailed discussion of these issues.)

These social pressures and trends all called for better understanding of the role and the validity of "other" characteristics of applicants in college admissions—characteristics other than high school rank (HSR) and test scores, the admissions measures most heavily used and frequently studied. Understanding the validity of other measures meant understanding not only their relevance but how well they actually worked. It soon became apparent that this straightforward question had many sides. What features should a study include in order to examine carefully the validity of other measures in admissions? The following were considered to be especially important.

- A variety of preadmissions measures are necessary: different types of skill and achievement that might be relevant to success in college, various background characteristics of possible interest to a college when it constitutes a class, student goals and interests that might also have a bearing on admissions or later performance.
- Specific knowledge of the institution's admissions policy is another desirable feature. Some admissions criteria reflect institutional objectives that are not necessarily related to anticipated performance in college.
- Since a measure is valid only if it works the way it is expected to

work, it is desirable to examine admissions decisions for individual candidates to determine whether that is the case. A measure may be valid in principle and statistically related to success but have no relation to actual selection decisions.

- If there are multiple admissions criteria reflecting different institutional objectives, it is necessary to have multiple measures of relevant success for the admissions measures to shoot at.
- It is also necessary to know how important different types of success are to the college so that an appropriate value can be placed on preadmissions measures that are related to that success.
- Measures of success should be based on the full four undergraduate years, partly because the upper division may be different from the lower division and partly because some types of success are simply not manifested early.
- It is important to have at least several colleges represented to lend stability and some sense of the generality of the results.

The study here reported was designed to include all seven of these features. There were, of course, a number of other aspects that proved particularly interesting—admissions staff evaluations of applicants, the students' view of success, the role of academic majors—but the seven listed above are the most critical. Including all greatly complicated the work. This study was possible only because of the extensive efforts of the nine cooperating institutions: Bucknell University, Colgate University, Hartwick College, Kalamazoo College, Kenyon College, Occidental College, Ohio Wesleyan University, University of Richmond, and Williams College.

The admissions stage (Phase I) of the Personal Qualities Project was addressed to such questions as these: How did the colleges choose among their applicants? What student characteristics influenced admissions decisions over and above school rank and test scores? Did admissions decisions accurately reflect policy? How did the students do in the freshman year?

The follow-up portion of the project reported here (Phase II) emphasized these questions: In what ways did students succeed over four years, and on what bases did the colleges nominate the seniors they regarded as most successful? What preadmissions measures were associated with what types of success? Can a college select students it regards as most successful by looking only at school rank and test scores? Before examining the latter questions, we briefly review the Phase I results reported earlier in *Personal Qualities*.

THE MAIN FINDINGS OF PHASE I

Phase I of this study was mainly concerned with admissions, but in *Personal Qualities* we did try to provide a broader context. The book examined the relevant literature and argued the case for the use of personal qualities in admissions—both from the institution's perspective and on broader educational and social grounds. The following paragraphs excerpt from *Personal Qualities* the most important findings from the earlier work that have a bearing on the follow-up study.

To what extent were personal and academic factors important in deciding who was admitted? The proportion of applicants accepted varied widely at these nine institutions, but each college placed primary emphasis upon academic factors, as was its stated policy intention. Overall the colleges' *academic* ratings of the applicant folders received about three times as much weight as did their *personal* ratings. The two main academic factors—high school rank and test scores—were weighted about equally. These two measures predicted admissions decisions fairly well, but it was evident that a number of other measures also came into play. Furthermore, there was no indication that any of these colleges were using a cutoff score on academic measures.

To examine the effect of personal qualities on selection decisions, we computed *residual selection rates* for a number of different characteristics (i.e., the actual selection rate for a particular type of student minus the selection rate that would be expected on the basis of high school rank and test scores alone). A number of interesting facts emerged from this analysis.

At the most selective institutions various personal qualities played a preferential role in selection decisions. At colleges that rejected fewer applicants there was much less preferential admission based on personal qualities. Strong affirmative action in selection was confirmed by the fact that, on the average, minority status had the largest residual selection rate of any characteristic. Other background characteristics with positive residuals were those that tended to denote some degree of affiliation with the college (e.g., alumni children). Our findings contradicted, however, any assumption that socially or economically privileged groups received preference in selection decisions.

It is widely assumed that students can enhance their chances of admission to a selective institution through noteworthy extracurricular accomplishments. To our surprise, the data offered little support for that assumption. Students with unusual accomplishments received some preference in admissions, but the advantage was small and affected relatively few applicants. This result attracted considerable attention in the public media. It also has special relevance to what we later found and here report.

The campus interview was especially interesting. Coming to the campus for an interview did not necessarily enhance the likelihood of admission, but in some colleges, those few applicants who succeeded in having an "outstanding" interview did clearly get preference. This is another result worth remembering as we examine later performance.

One of the most provocative analyses came from separating the applicants in each college into three groups: those who were not likely to be accepted, those who were likely to be accepted, and a middle group for whom admission was uncertain. The data confirmed our suspicion that the selection process is very different for these three groups and that personal qualities come into play mostly when admission is uncertain or unlikely. It appears that background characteristics (e.g., alumni ties, minority status) form a basis for affirmative admissions preference in the unlikely or uncertain categories. On the other hand, evidence of personal achievement (e.g., leadership, outstanding school references) appears to be used mainly as a tie breaker among students with similar academic credentials where the student's likelihood of admission is about fifty-fifty.

Our data indicated that admissions practices did not always correspond to policy intentions of institutions. In particular, these institutions gave much less weight to personal achievement than their policy statements would indicate, and there was often lack of agreement between the amount of weight a college intended to put on a particular measure and the degree of emphasis it received in actual selection decisions.

Once the students were on campus, we addressed this question: How do the characteristics and experiences of these freshman classes differ from college to college? Overall the profile of personal characteristics of the 4,814 entering freshmen was strikingly similar to the profile of the 25,000 applicants. It appears that the particular personal qualities of the freshmen who enroll at these institutions are determined to a considerable extent by the self-selection process that creates the original applicant pool.

These nine freshman classes varied far more in academic achievement than in other measures of personal achievement—confirming again that self-selection and institutional selection primarily reflect stratification on academic achievement. There were, however, clearly discernible differences among the freshman classes in such personal orientations as intellectual and practical goals, creative and athletic skills, and social and leadership interests. In the spring of the first year, the freshmen were more often satisfied than not with their progress toward educational goals, although there were significant differences from college to college with respect to particular goals. Two were a frequent source of disappointment: the development of intellectual skills and the exploration of career options.

How were personal qualities related to success and persistence in the freshman year? Our measures of personal achievement in secondary school were only slightly associated with earning higher college grades than would be expected from rank and test scores. Typically these personal measures were better predictors of which students were nominated by their peers as successful freshmen. Two measures that appeared to hold promise were the quality of a student's personal statement and "follow-through" in areas of personal accomplishment.

Freshmen rated very high as applicants by colleges often received substantial preference in admissions, but students so identified were not likely to achieve much higher grades than would be expected from school rank and test scores, nor were they more likely to persist to the sophomore year. High ratings by admissions staff were consistently related, however, to nomination as successful freshmen by peers.

There were variations from college to college, but overall the validity of high school rank and test scores for predicting grades was about equal and corresponded quite closely to their relative weight in selection decisions. Personal achievement measures were neither a useful substitute for, nor a supplement to, rank and test scores in predicting grades. Within individual colleges persistence to the sophomore year was only slightly related to academic performance in college and was remarkably unpredictable on the basis of any preadmissions measure. Since the persistence rate varied widely from college to college, the best way to predict the likelihood of dropping out was to know where the student enrolled.

When the freshmen in the study nominated those peers they considered successful, it appears that they picked good students who were also hardworking, well-organized achievers in other areas. This "success" criterion was related to a clearly different pattern of earlier achievements compared with those measures that predicted grades. Furthermore, personal ratings by admissions staff contributed substantially to predicting who would be nominated by peers but not who would make the dean's list. We saw special significance in this finding and wondered whether the faculty's nominations in the senior year would show a similar pattern of relationships.

AN OVERVIEW OF THE PHASE II REPORT

Chapter 2 describes some prototype studies that give different research perspectives on success in college. For example, there is a substantial research literature on outcomes of education in which different types of student development are emphasized. Such work tends to have more implications for improving the educational process than for validating admissions measures. There have been many validity studies of admissions measures, of course, though they are largely based on first-year grades as the measure of success. Chapter 2 describes some studies that have gone beyond first-year grades. It also cites some critical references on related topics. A principal conclusion of that chapter is that colleges have given surprisingly little attention to how the grading system operates, or other ways in which success might be evaluated.

Chapter 3 describes this study and examines the question of how to measure success in college. For the purposes of the study, we concluded that the best representation of success is the student's *accumulated record* of achievement over four years. This accumulated record included yearly grade averages and several measures of attainment but focused especially on 10 marks of success in three broad categories: scholarship (college and departmental honors), leadership (elected offices and appointed positions), and significant accomplishments (scientific, artistic, communications, physical, organizing, and other independent achievements). In addition, a representative committee of faculty and staff on each campus selected those students who were judged to be most successful overall.

Chapter 4 gives an accounting of the accumulated record of the class. Of the 4,814 entering freshmen, 3,676 (76 percent) were still enrolled in the fourth year. Among these seniors, 30 percent earned either departmental honors or a grade average high enough to graduate with college honors. More than a third of the senior class (35 percent) held an important position of leadership—elected or appointed. About one senior in four was recognized for one or more of six types of significant accomplishment. Women graduated cum laude more often than did men, though some of that difference was due to stronger qualifications at entry.

In nominating their most successful students, the colleges placed at least some weight on a number of different specific types of success. As a group, these nine institutions put very nearly equal emphasis on scholarship, leadership, and accomplishment when they picked the students they regarded as most successful overall. There was only a moderate degree of overlap among these three success groups.

Chapter 5 addresses this key question: What preadmissions measures were most useful in predicting success in college? The two traditional academic predictors, high school rank and admissions tests scores, were by far the best in forecasting scholastic types of achievement. Comparing the two, we found that school rank was a somewhat better predictor of college honors (cumulative grade average), while the Scholastic Aptitude Test (SAT) was a somewhat better predictor of departmental honors (based on independent scholarship). While supplementary evidence in the school record was not very helpful in predicting scholastic achievement, such evidence was frequently better than school rank and test scores in predicting different types of leadership and accomplishment.

A central issue in this study was whether there is supplemental information over and above school rank and test scores that can be helpful in identifying applicants likely to be most successful in the institution's eyes. The answer was clearly yes. Of a large number of measures examined, the best additions were high school honors, successful follow-through in extracurricular activities, a well-written personal statement, and a strong reference from the secondary school. These four measures improved prediction of which students would be most successful by 25 percent over school rank and test scores alone. They improved prediction of leadership by 65 percent, accomplishment by 42 percent, but scholarship by only 7 percent.

Follow-through was the strongest addition. This new measure reflects productivity in out-of-class activities in secondary school. The rating was based on a pattern of persistent effort and successful achievement, preferably in more than one area of activity. Among all measures examined, it had the largest weight in predicting leadership and accomplishment and the second-largest weight in forecasting which students were likely to be most successful overall in college. Students who did well on follow-through were overrepresented by 20 to 30 percent in each of these success categories, even after school rank and test scores were taken into account.

Several analyses in this study indicated that the admissions officers did a good job in identifying the most promising students. Their evaluation of the applicant folder was a useful complement to the objective academic measures. Their rating of applicant interviews was not. Earlier analyses indicated that in several colleges students who had outstanding interviews received substantial preference in admissions decisions. Four years later we found no evidence that these students had achieved beyond expectation on any measure of success.

In general, the students' background was not a useful basis for forecasting success. Although some groups of students varied considerably in their typical qualifications at entry (e.g., students from different types of secondary schools), the college achievement of these groups was accurately indicated by their previous track record.

Persistence within individual colleges was not much related to academic qualifications or, in most cases, to college grades. Among students who withdrew, evidently few were in academic jeopardy at the time. On the other hand, admission to advanced study (medical, law, or Ph.D. programs) was mostly associated with academic qualifications plus the earlier intention to pursue such study.

Chapter 6 examines the prediction of yearly grade averages. School rank and test scores predicted the cumulative college grade average as well after four years as after the first year. Individual yearly averages, however, became less predictable from all preadmissions measures. The most likely explanation appeared to be deterioration in the quality of the grade average from freshman to senior year. For example, it was found that grades in departments with weaker students tended to climb substantially from the freshmen to the senior year while grades in other departments remained steady. Furthermore, weaker students tended to migrate into departments where grades climbed. As a result, upper-division grades appeared to be a poorer representation of academic performance than were lower-division grades. That assumption was borne out by the fact that upper-division grades were *less* closely associated than lower-division grades with "most successful" nominations and with admission to advanced study.

Chapter 7 examines the student's view of success. In rating the importance of educational goals, seniors put 12 goals in almost the same rank order as they had when they were freshmen. The only large shift was less emphasis on the importance of grades. Typically, four out of five seniors indicated satisfaction with what they had accomplished in areas that were important to them. Career exploration was an exception. "Sense of direction" seemed to be a persistent problem.

Five out of six seniors felt that their college career had been "mostly successful." When students rated their peers, they put much the same emphasis on objective evidence of scholarship, leadership, and accomplishment as did the faculty. Their ratings of their own success were much less objectively based and more developmentally oriented—"How have I changed for the better?"

Given the fact that it is possible to improve on the identification of successful students if one goes beyond school rank and test scores, Chapter 8 examines the practical implications. What is the best way to take advantage of that finding and how much difference is it likely to make? An analysis of applicants illustrated that it is only the more selective college that can have much noticeable effect on its incoming group by modifying its selection strategy. This is partly because the "best" strategy usually identifies much the same applicants as would the acceptable alternative strategies, and partly because in the less selective college most applicants will be selected in any event. In such colleges the additional indicators of promising students are mainly useful in recruiting.

It was shown that colleges could aid recruitment by looking for students who demonstrated productive follow-through in extracurricular activities. Productivity was generally a poor substitute for academic qualification. It was clearly favorable as an additional qualification when choosing between two students of equal academic ability. Depending on an institution's enrollment situation, productive follow-through can be a useful complementary qualification, i.e., a useful trade-off for a somewhat higher rank or test score.

This study demonstrates the rich diversity in the college experience and the numerous ways in which students form commitments, direct their energies, and achieve success. It documents the impressive accomplishments of many students and the significant educational progress of most. Concerning recruitment/selection policy, the main issue motivating the study, there were several principal conclusions.

The traditional academic measures, school rank and test scores, were by far the best predictors of scholarship, whether after one year or four years, but these colleges viewed success quite broadly. They put substantial emphasis on leadership and accomplishment as well as scholarship in singling out their most successful students. The study demonstrates that the most successful students cannot be identified most effectively on the basis of school rank and test scores alone. The additional useful information is largely concrete evidence of achievement in the student's track record. Subjective appraisal of students based on brief encounters is shown to be particularly suspect.

Chapter 9 suggests a workable recruitment strategy: Look for students who have demonstrated productive follow-through—academic or extracurricular—in their secondary school years. The essential conditions of reliability, validity, and fairness can be met if productivity is defined as a significant accomplishment that is publicly recognized.

Finally, it is noted in Chapter 9 that this is a period when most colleges are giving primary attention to maintaining enrollment. Although these results are useful in showing that the pool of promising students can be broadened, there are several other equally important implications for admissions policy. The marginal effects of a modified admissions policy can be substantial. Even a limited number of very productive students in a particular area of interest can make a difference because of the leadership they provide. From a broader perspective, it is socially effective to encourage diverse talents and to encourage striving and accomplishment. In recognizing young people who have been productive in significant ways, colleges serve broader goals in keeping with their vital social role.

2

Selected Studies of Special Interest

Several types of literature are related in one way or another to "success in college." Great gulfs separate them. There have been thousands of prediction studies with a heavy statistical orientation and mostly concerned with first-year grades. There is also an extensive literature of studies on achievement in college motivated by a variety of research interests—learning theory, instructional methods, the role of personality in achievement, etc. There is a substantial literature, much of it nonempirical, on the nature of the educational experience and how it does and does not foster success and satisfaction and the personal development of the individual.

In this study success in college has a particular frame of reference; namely, if an institution wishes to identify which of its students have been successful after four years so that its admissions staff can be better informed as to where to look for more such students, how is success best defined for that purpose? When success has been defined, how are preadmissions measures of applicant potential related to such measures of eventual success in college? Surprisingly limited research has attacked this broad but straightforward question. There are, however, some studies of special interest on which this work builds.

The purpose of this chapter is threefold: to describe several prototype studies concerned with long-term success in college, to identify some useful selected references on several related topics, and to comment briefly on several implications of these studies and the status of research in this area generally.

But first a word about the selection of items. The work of Anastasi and her colleagues was trailblazing. It established that preadmissions measures other than academic achievement were related to an institution's view of college success. The rating studies by Davis explored the institution's view of what constitutes a successful student. Later work by Taber and Hackman at Yale considerably extended that kind of analysis both with respect to methodology and the types of achievement represented. Their work resulted in different dimensions and categories of successful college students (athletes, artists, grinds, etc.). A related line of research is represented in the study by Richards, Holland, and Lutz, which demonstrated that different types of achievement in college are best predicted by the corresponding types of achievement in high school. Their work had its roots in a series of important earlier studies that refined the technique of assessing different types of achievement through the use of student questionnaires about earlier activities and accomplishments.

The study by Astin and Panos also involved the use of student questionnaires but for a rather different purpose. Their study of student development focused more on the educational process and the effects of different environments on educational outcomes, particularly regarding students' career decisions. Whitla's study at Harvard is an example of the use of standard tests to assess intellectual and moral development.

Humphreys's studies of long-term grade prediction represent one of the few efforts to analyze systematically the one measure of success in college that is commonly used by thousands of institutions. While the grade point average may be a limited conception of talent and achievement, it is the measure of performance that is systematically accumulated and preserved in the student's official transcript. Willingham's longitudinal analysis of academic performance is closely related. It examined the intricate relationship between faculty grading and institutional policies governing academic standing and how these two in concert define who succeeds and who doesn't.

In the descriptions of the following eight studies we have tried mainly to indicate the purpose and general character of each and enough of the results to give a sense of the study's import. Following these eight studies we briefly cite seven additional topics that bear an important relationship to subsequent chapters in this report. In discussing these several topics, our objective is only to identify a few representative references in each that can serve as useful leads for further inquiry.

EIGHT STUDIES

Anastasi, Meade, and Schneiders (1960)

In *The Validation of a Biographical Inventory as a Predictor of College Success*, a pioneering study conducted at Fordham University, Anne Anastasi and her colleagues addressed two closely related problems in institutional research: the definition of success in college and the prediction of that success from preadmissions data. In addressing the first question—the definition of college success—Anastasi et al. attempted to refine rather than replace the traditional measures of college success. They suggested that evidence of superior academic performance alone is not sufficient.

The general design of the study was to define three groups of students—positive, average, and negative—and to identify students in the sample who typified these groups. Then, using biographical information from preadmissions data, a scoring key was developed that best predicted membership in each of the groups.

The authors began by obtaining an official statement of Fordham's objectives. They defined the three groups of students as follows: positive—a student who fulfills the institution's objectives, has not been on academic probation, and shows no signs of maladjustment; average—a student who shows no signs of academic or personal superiority or inferiority and shows no signs of maladjustment; and negative—a student who does not fulfill the objectives of the institution, has not made the dean's list during the period under investigation (freshman to junior year), and has shown signs of maladjustment.

Using these group definitions, the investigators identified 268 possible candidates from the class of 1958 and 291 candidates from the class of 1959. A committee of three (all of whom had taught at Fordham for a number of years) was then asked to review each case and to identify the 50 students who most closely resembled each group definition. The committee was given the official statement of objectives, the group definitions, and nine sources of information on each student to aid them in making their decision: (1) faculty ratings, (2) faculty adviser reports, (3) reserve officer training corps records, (4) honors program, (5) extracurricular honor society, (6) student government records, (7) office of psychological services records, (8) dean of men records, (9) academic records.

The relationship between group membership and preadmissions data was then examined. These data were available from a biographical inventory that had been developed at Fordham and administered to both classes upon entrance. The questionnaire yielded information on each student's socioeconomic background, educational experiences and interests, career goals, social life, anticipated problems at college, and long-term plans. Items on this questionnaire that distinguished among groups were retained for use in the biographical scoring keys. It was the intention of the authors to develop two keys, a positive and a negative key, that would be used sequentially for prediction of positive and negative group membership.

Only the positive key was found to be effective in distinguishing among groups. When the key was applied to the 1959 cross-validation class, the significant relationship between the selected biographical items and success at Fordham was indicated by the number of students in each criterion group who scored high, medium, or low on the original positive key (Table 2.1).

A revised key was developed on the basis of the total sample from both years. Membership in the positive group rather than the negative group correlated .58 with scores on the revised key. The authors point out that the biographical key differentiates among the criterion groups better than does either the SAT-verbal or SAT-mathematical alone. It was not clear, however, how much the selected inventory items added to SAT and high school record (HSR), taken together.

The means for the three criterion groups on aptitude, achievement, interest, and personality tests lined up in the direction expected by the authors. The positive group scored highest on measures of aptitude and achievement and obtained scores indicating greatest emotional stability on the personality tests. The main difference between the average and the negative groups was in the level of personal adjustment. The typical member of the positive group received high school awards for scholarship, participated in extracurricular activities in high school, anticipated similar participation in college, and was interested in literature and languages. The favorite high school subject was Latin, and the least preferred was social studies. The student anticipated few problems in college, either social or academic.

Table 2.1 Results of the Fordham Study

Score on the 1958 Positive Key	N in the 1959 Criterion Groups		
	Positive	Average	Negative
Highest 50	30	16	4
Middle 50	11	17	22
Lowest 50	9	17	24

In their assessment of these findings, the authors did not advocate use of the scoring key in admissions decisions. They did, however, see a potential use for it in student counseling, noting that members of the negative group were not lacking in talent but were, rather, in need of assistance in adjusting to college. Aware that the key developed in this study was not context-free, they encouraged similar research at other institutions.

Davis (1965a)

Davis published the results of a series of studies based on data collected from eight institutions in 1962 (Davis 1964a, 1964b, 1964c, 1964d, 1965b, 1966), most which are summarized in "What College Teachers Value in Students." The purpose of the data collection and the analyses was to identify and describe those characteristics and traits that faculty value in students. In collecting the data, Davis used an 80-item, 5-point rating scale, which had been developed from analysis of free-response descriptions of students by faculty. This questionnaire covered the areas of performance and the personal attributes noted by the faculty in their free-response descriptions. In addition to this 80-item questionnaire, information was also available on each student's SAT scores, high school rank, and freshman grade point average (FGPA). Some items on the questionnaire dealt with the rater's perception of the student's academic ability. The last item, which was used as a measure of overall desirability, rated the student along the continuum "the kind of student this institution should/should not admit."

At each institution a random sample of approximately 50 upper classmen was selected. An attempt was made to obtain two raters for each student. Each rater was selected at random from among the students' instructors for the last term of the academic year 1961–62. The data were collected at the end of the term. In all, 696 ratings of 398 students were obtained from 407 faculty members. In a second data collection faculty members were provided with a list of participating students. They were then asked to nominate any students known to them who deserved to be included in one or more of six "success" categories. The first category identified students who would make a substantial contribution to society after college. The last category identified students who, though not notable, had certain characteristics that made them desirable students for the institution. The other four categories dealt with epitomizing ideals of the college, intellectual growth, personal growth, and suitability for graduate school.

In a study of the data from the questionnaires, "the kind of student this institution should/should not admit" was treated as a measure of desirability. Sixteen factors were extracted from the rating scales. Davis (1965a) described these factors as making up four clusters—intellectual qualities, characteristic approach to work, traits of character, and relationships with peers. It was found that desirability was strongly influenced by the rater's perception of the student's ability and performance. Aside from this perceived performance, desirability was positively influenced by factors such as altruism, open-mindedness, ethicality, and likableness. Actual performance, as measured by FGPA, had a weaker relationship to desirability than did perceived performance. Faculty perception of student performance was based not only on actual performance but on factors such as dependability, motivation, and maturity.

The SAT scores contributed positively to desirability insofar as they were associated with high academic performance. However, there was some variance associated with SAT scores, unrelated to academic performance, which actually had a negative relationship to desirability. Davis suggested that in a selective college, having high SAT scores is not particularly distinctive. He also suggested that the faculty may value students who appear to do better than expected.

Analysis of the second set of data—nomination of the students to laudatory categories—showed that nearly all students (99 percent) were known to at least one faculty member and that most (96 percent) were nominated to some laudatory category. A significant positive correlation between acquaintance and FGPA suggested that visibility may depend to a very large extent on academic performance. As in the rating scale analyses, academic performance was found to be the most important factor in assessing a student's desirability, and the criterion upon which there was most consensus. Students nominated most frequently to the top three categories had higher FGPAs than did the rest of the sample.

Davis concluded that while college grades appear to be the most important criterion for faculty in their assessment of the desirability of a student, some less able students were viewed in a positive light if they were considered to be ethical, mature, or altruistic. He noted that almost every student is seen in a positive light by at least one faculty member. He suggested the need for further analysis that might isolate a visibility factor apart from a desirability factor.

Taber and Hackman (1976) and Hackman and Taber (1979)

In "Dimensions of Undergraduate College Performance," their first report on a major criterion study at Yale University, Taber and Hackman addressed the problem of the objective measurement of both academic and nonacademic aspects of college performance. According to these researchers, the problem with the use of the traditional academic criteria alone to assess student performance is that these criteria focus on only one aspect of performance, while success or failure, as judged by the academic community to which the student belongs, depends also on other, nonacademic accomplishments.

To define success and failure within the particular context of Yale College, Taber and Hackman began by identifying those students whom the academic community considered successful or unsuccessful. Those interviewed were not given any information or guidelines to aid them in making their nominations, as in Anastasi's study. Instead, they were asked to nominate students as successful or unsuccessful, and then to give their reasons for these particular choices. A sample of 136 was chosen in such a way as to be representative of the entire academic community: students, faculty, and staff. These interviewees were asked to name four students from the classes of 1971 to 1975, two of whom they considered to be most successful and two of whom they considered to be least successful. They were then asked to given concrete examples of the nominees' behavior that supported their selection. These behaviors were used to develop a questionnaire made up of 67 five-point rating scales anchored with behavioral examples from the interviews.

This questionnaire was then administered to 376 members of Yale College, again selected to represent the entire college community. As in the original interviews, respondents were asked to identify two successful and two unsuccessful students, whom they rated on each item.

Factor analysis of these data resulted in the retention of 14 common factors for the most successful nominees and 11 for the least successful nominees. Taber and Hackman interpreted both sets of factors as representing two domains, academic and nonacademic. A benefit of this study emphasized by the investigators was that previously acknowledged dimensions of student behavior such as academic effort, in the academic domain, or personal responsiveness, in the nonacademic domain, were shown to be amenable to objective description and measurement.

In the second study, "Patterns of Undergraduate Performance Related to Success in College," the same data were analyzed to identify twelve patterns of behavior, seven for successful students and five for unsuccessful students. The seven success types were Leaders, Scholars, Careerists, Grinds, Artists, Athletes, and Socializers. The five unsuccessful types were Disliked, Extreme Grinds, Alienated, Unqualified, and Directionless. Certain resemblances were found between the successful and the unsuccessful types. For example, the Directionless were like the Socializers in that they ranked high on interpersonal sociability. However, they were much lower on all other dimensions, were found to be incongruent with the college, and showed very little personal or intellectual growth during their college years. Extreme Grinds were similar to Grinds but were rated lower on all dimensions. They did not successfully combine the academic and nonacademic aspects of college life. Athletes ranked lower on the academic dimensions than did the other six success types. They were very high on athletic ability and moderately high on personal growth and ethical behavior.

Distributions of these types across class years showed that there was a fairly even distribution of the unsuccessful types. Among successful types, however, Socializers were mainly from the freshman and sophomore classes, while Leaders, Scholars, and Careerists were nominated mainly from the three older classes. Grinds and Athletes were nominated fairly evenly.

Women were overrepresented among the Leaders, while men were overrepresented among the Athletes and Careerists. Other types did not show any disproportionate representation of either sex. Analysis of the distribution of the types across racial groups showed that successful black nominees had relatively fewer Grinds and Leaders and more Socializers than did the other racial groups. For the other four types of success the distribution was approximately even. Extreme Grinds and Disliked students were overrepresented among the white unsuccessful nominees, while the Unqualified were underrepresented among the white nominees and overrepresented among the black unsuccessful nominees.

Student types differed in performance at college. With the exception of the Socializers, who had a mean GPA lower than that of the Disliked or the Extreme Grind, all of the successful types performed at a higher level, academically, than the unsuccessful types. Average grades also varied within typologies as did the predictability of group membership from preadmissions measures, but these data are difficult to interpret because of the small N's involved.

Richards, Holland, and Lutz (1967)

This important study, "Prediction of Student Accomplishment in College," follows in the tradition of earlier work at the National Merit Scholarship Corporation. It was one of a series of studies concerned with the assessment of different types of achievement in high school and their association with similar types of achievement in college.

The sample for this study was made up of two samples from a previous study. The first sample included 7,208 students at 22 institutions who had completed a survey questionnaire and taken the ACT tests in the year 1962–63 as part of their application for admission to college. Information on college achievements was obtained from these students in the spring of 1965, at the end of their sophomore year.

The second sample was made up of 2,483 students at six institutions who had also taken the ACT tests and entered college in the fall of 1964. These students also filled out a college achievement questionnaire in 1965, at the end of their freshman year.

The predictors were scores on the ACT battery, high school grades, and measures of extracurricular achievement in six areas, obtained from the earlier survey. These last measures were simply the number of achievements checked by the student in each area on a questionnaire. The areas were art, music, literature, drama, leadership, and science.

The college criteria were college grades, as reported by the student, nonclassroom achievement in 12 areas, and public recognition for academic achievement (such as winning an award or a scholarship). Six of the areas in nonclassroom achievement were similar to the high school extracurricular achievements, and the remaining six had no analogous high school measure; they were social participation, social service, business, humanities, religious service, and social science. College achievement was assessed in the same manner as high school achievement— the student indicated on a checklist which achievements were attained in each of the 12 areas. The items on the high school and college questionnaires ranged from rare, such as "had a scientific paper published," to relatively common, such as "participated in a demonstration."

By regression analysis, each of the criteria was predicted from the high school measures of achievement for both student groups. Moderate correlations were found between high school measures of academic performance and college measures of academic performance. Similar correlations were found between measures of nonclassroom achievement in high school and measures of similar achievements in college. However, low correlations were found between nonacademic measures of achievement and academic measures, and between measures of dissimilar nonacademic achievement. The most efficient predictors of academic accomplishment in college were found to be high school grades and test scores. The best predictor of nonacademic achievement was a measure of similar achievement in high school. The measures for which no analogous high school achievements existed were best predicted by high school measures that most closely resembled them. For example, the best predictor of social participation was leadership.

Several aspects of the findings were stressed by the authors. Non-academic accomplishments could not be predicted from academic measures of achievement. They could, however, be predicted moderately well from nonacademic measures of achievement. The median correlation between grades in high school and grades in college was found to be .38, while the median correlation between nonacademic acomplishment in high school and accomplishment in the same area in college was .39. The prediction of college grades was improved, of course, by using the ACT tests as well as high school grades as predictors. The results related to the six areas of college accomplishment for which no direct analogues existed pointed up the importance of the specific content in the predictor and criterion.

The authors urged the development of nonacademic measures of achievement and their use in admissions procedures. They suggested that such measures were valid in their own right, not merely as weak supplementary measures to conventional aptitude and achievement tests. These results replicated earlier work on highly talented students at the National Merit Scholarship Corporation, particularly studies by Nichols and Holland (1963) and Holland and Nichols (1964).

Astin and Panos (1969)

The Educational and Vocational Development of College Students is based on data gathered between 1961 and 1965 from a large national sample. The purpose of this study by Astin and Panos was to assess the effect of different college environments on the educational aspirations and the vocational development of the student. Previous research in this area had focused almost exclusively on the number of students from a given college who pursue a Ph.D., as a measure of the institution's productiveness, and had not taken into consideration input differences such as academic ability, vocational and educational plans, and family background. Three types of data were identified by Astin and Panos: student input data, student output data, and environmental data. Student output data were first predicted from student input data. The residual student output, with input measures controlled, was then compared with environmental data, and systematic relationships between the two were identified.

The initial sample consisted of 127,212 entering freshmen, in 1961, at 246 accredited four-year institutions countrywide. These students completed a brief questionnaire upon college entry, giving information about their academic record in high school, particular extracurricular achievements, career plans, highest degree planned, probable college major, and father's education and occupation. The student body at each institution was described in terms of six factors: intellectualism, aestheticism, leadership, pragmatism (high interest in technical fields), status (interest in enterprising careers, socioeconomic status), and masculinity (high percentage of male students and students planning professional careers). A subsample of 36,000 students completed a questionnaire in 1965, which yielded the student output data. The data from these questionnaires gave information on 28 output measures, which dealt with attrition, attainment of the B.A., highest level of degree planned, career plans, and college major. A dropout was defined as a student who had not completed four years of coursework in the four years since matriculation, regardless of enrollment status in 1965.

The environmental data were obtained from published sources, and a questionnaire was administered in 1962. In this questionnaire the students indicated whether or not certain events had occurred during their time at college—such as voting in a student election. There were 250 such items. They also responded to 75 subjective "image" statements, such as "there's a lot of school spirit here." Two categories of environmental measures were defined: measures that remain the same for all students at a given institution, such as size, control, and image, and measures that differ for students within the institution. An example of the latter would be the housing selected by the student—dorm, home, or private off-campus housing.

The most systematic finding was the student's tendency to conform to the dominant career and major choices of peers. Choice of major and career choice were very unstable over the four-year period, with only one-quarter of the sample choosing the same career in 1965 as they had chosen in 1961. Students attending technical institutes were more likely to persist in their interest in pursuing a career in engineering than if they had attended any other type of institution. Similarly, students attending teachers' colleges were more likely to pursue a career in teaching than if they had attended a university or liberal arts college. Astin and Panos interpret this as being due to the influence of peer choice on the student and also to the fact that a student wishing to change majors or career goals in these relatively homogeneous institutions would probably have to consider changing to a different school as well as to a different curriculum.

More than one-third of the overall sample did not complete four years of college during the four-year period under investigation. Factors associated with attrition were attendance at large universities, lack of cohesion in the student body (as defined by the number of students listed as close friends by students in the survey), and attendance at coeducational schools. Students who were supported by their parents financially or who attended college on a scholarship were less likely to drop out than was the average student. Students who were married when they began college or who married during their undergraduate years were more likely to drop out.

Selective institutions (as measured by the quality of the academic credentials of the incoming students) had a positive association with persistence and the student's desire to attend graduate school and obtain a Ph.D. However, student achievement (as measured by performance on the Graduate Record Examination (GRE) for a small subsample of the group—600 students approximately) was found to depend not on the quality of the institution, in terms of selectivity or funding, but on the student's own ability as measured prior to college entry.

Astin and Panos' major conclusion from these findings relates to institutional policy. They discouraged attempts to convert technical institutes into universities or colleges with broader curriculums, as this would result in the loss of trained manpower in technical fields. Likewise, they discouraged the trend on the part of teachers' colleges to become liberal arts colleges, as this would result in decreases in the number of trained teachers in the work force. Whatever advantages the conversion of single-sex schools to coeducational schools may have both for the institution and for the student socially, they saw this trend as resulting in larger dropout rates and lower levels of academic competitiveness. History indicates that these recommendations on institutional mission were running against the tide. As most of the environmental effects noted by Astin and Panos related to elements in the peer environment, they suggested the need for further research into the nature of undergraduate peer groups and the impact that these groups have on the individual student.

Whitla (1981)

In "Value Added and Other Related Matters," an invitational paper for the national Commission on Excellence in Education, Whitla gave a preliminary report on a research project then nearing completion at Harvard University's Office of Instructional Research and Evaluation. The purpose of the project was to measure the effect of college on students' moral, affective, and intellectual development over and above that due to maturation.

Eight objectives of a liberal arts education were identified and measures of these qualities agreed upon. A detailed description of the eight objectives and the tests used to measure development in these areas is contained in a technical report published by Whitla in 1977. Freshmen and seniors (second-year students in the case of a junior college) at six institutions were assessed by these measures. The results were compared across colleges and for particular groups, such as athletes within colleges.

The learning objectives identified were (1) the ability to communicate in writing with clarity and style; (2) the capacity to analyze problems; (3) a sensitivity to ethical considerations; (4) an ability to master new concepts; (5) a critical appreciation of the ways in which we gain an understanding of the universe, society, and ourselves; (6) a sensitivity to interpersonal relationships; (7) a viewing of life experiences in a wide context; (8) a broadening of intellectual and aesthetic interests.

Writing samples were coded for grammatical and spelling errors, and also for quality of argument, as a measure of the first objective. Kohlberg's test of moral development was used as a measure of growth in the third objective. Although no control group of noncollege students was included to test the hypothesis that growth along these dimensions could be attributed to maturation alone, it was hoped that the inclusion of differing institutions and the examination of groups differing in their involvement with college life would resolve this difficulty.

It was found that in general seniors performed at a higher level on measures of the objectives than did freshmen, with the exception of speed of learning. While there was no overall improvement in ability to learn, it was found that ability to master concepts in one's field of specialization did improve. There were differences among colleges in the average growth shown by the students at each college. In measures of writing ability, students at Boston State showed greater improvement in grammar than did students at any of the other institutions, while students at Harvard showed the greatest improvement in a measure of analytical ability.

Within the universities, it was found that students who were highly involved academically and in extracurricular activities showed the greatest growth on all dimensions. Academic involvement characterized the second-highest growth group. Athletes were the next. The poorest group was made up of students who were neither involved academically nor participants in extracurricular activities.

The conclusions drawn from this study were that colleges can and do have an impact on the students' growth. This growth is not purely maturational. As involvement in college life is characteristic of those groups that show the greatest gain on the growth measures, involvement on the part of the student is indicated.

As a genre, this study represents one approach to assessing success in college—developing or selecting tests to measure important outcomes in a standard manner. Dressel and Mayhew (1957) reported an early classic effort of this type. Forrest and Steele (1982) describe a battery of tests developed at ACT in recent years. Pace (1979) provides a recent review of tests used to assess outcomes of undergraduate education.

Humphreys (1968)

The grade point average is, of course, the most commonly used measure of success in college. There has been only limited research on measures traditionally used in the admissions process as predictors of the student's performance in successive terms beyond the freshman year. The main questions addressed by this particular study, "The Fleeting Nature of the Prediction of College Academic Success," were whether validity holds up over time and whether it is adequate to validate selection measures on freshman data alone.

Humphreys's sample consisted of the freshman classes of 1962 and 1963 at the University of Illinois—over 8,000 students in all. Independent semester GPAs were computed for each class (six for the class of 1967, eight for the class of 1966). Data on high school rank, and separate and composite scores on the ACT tests, were also available. Intercorrelations among the preadmissions scores and the college GPAs were computed. These correlations were adjusted for restriction in range due to possible differences in ability between earlier and later student groups in the sample. The adequacy of this adjustment was tested by computing correlations based on graduating seniors for the class of 1966 rather than entering freshmen (approximate $N = 1,600$). The same pattern emerged when both techniques were used.

Humphreys found that while the correlations showed the expected strong relationship between the predictors and the criterion—college performance—for the freshman semesters, this relationship became progressively weaker in the later semester. The highest correlation for the final semester was .22—the correlation between high school rank and semester GPA for the group of graduating seniors. The common variance between high school rank and college grades dropped from 26 percent in the first semester to 8 percent in the final semester.

Accepting GPA as a suitable criterion measure, Humphreys concluded that the traditional predictors were not adequate. However, as no more reliable predictors were available, he saw implications for admissions research and probation policies rather than any immediate implications for admissions procedures. He suggested the use of a residual freshman-senior measure of performance as a possible criterion for prediction on the basis of nonintellective predictors, the idea being to enhance prediction of academic performance by identifying the non-common variance between senior performance and freshman grades. Humphreys's recommendation for probation regulations was that the student be given enough time to change the level of performance. He recommended that students making minimal progress toward an acceptable graduation average be kept in college. This recommendation was based on the fact that his data show the instability of academic performance during the undergraduate years. Freshman performance was not an adequate predictor of senior performance. He argued that this probation method would not necessarily result in maintaining weaker students, as excellence in the freshman year was not a reliable indicator of excellence in the senior year.

This landmark study provoked considerable response because it brought important issues into focus. It was not the first study of its kind. Humphreys anticipated some aspects in 1960. Willingham published similar results in longitudinal studies at the Georgia Institute of Technology in 1962 (see below). His recommendations with regard to preferred probation procedures were quite similar to Humphreys's later conclusions. (Both conclusions now appear oversimplified in light of the results of the data reported here.) Juola (1966) published data showing the declining predictability of successive term grades, though not on the large sample or in the same detail as Humphreys's study.

Other important work has been done on this topic by Humphreys and associates (Humphreys and Taber 1973; Lin and Humphreys 1977). As a result, the problem took on significant new dimensions and changed character in important respects. Wilson has recently (1983) published a thorough review of the literature on this subject (see also the discussion of Chapter 6, to which this work is closely related).

Willingham (1962)

Much attention is devoted to the fairness and effectiveness of the measures and the process through which students are admitted to selective institutions. If one thinks of admissions as the primary screening that determines who will face the challenge and enjoy the benefits of higher learning, there is also a process of secondary screening that determines who graduates. The system of academic standing is at once a selection process for deciding who will succeed and a criterion of who has succeeded. The rules of academic standing are sometimes complex and their actual effect no doubt varies considerably from campus to campus, but the process goes largely unexamined. *Longitudinal Analysis of Aca-*

demic Performance, a four-year study of a class of 1,059 students at Georgia Institute of Technology, is possibly the only detailed analysis ever undertaken of the relation of grading to academic standing and how they jointly determine success in college.

The study traced the movement of students on and off academic probation, in and out of the institution, and from department to department. It demonstrated two main points. One was that academic standards varied substantially among departments so that success at Georgia Tech had to be qualified as success in what field—physical science, engineering, industrial management?

The second point was that the probability of a student's graduating was best predicted at any particular point almost exclusively by the cumulative point average at that time. Preadmissions measures, trends in grades, patterns of course grades—none of these made any difference. The extant system of academic standing, on the other hand, emphasized quarter-to-quarter grade averages and was demonstrably inferior as a basis for deciding who should be allowed to stay in the institution. The study illustrates one more reason why success in college is more complicated than meets the eye. Institutional policies regarding major changes, academic standing, and readmission can have much influence in defining "success" and the extent to which the educational process is fair and efficient.

RELATED TOPICS OF INTEREST

Freshman grade prediction

Freshman grade prediction has occupied center stage in admissions research for many years. While no one would argue that the freshman grade average is not an important measure of college achievement, it has, for a number of practical and theoretical reasons, been the criterion of choice to the neglect of other possible measures of success (Schrader 1971). Typically the measures used to predict freshman average are also intellective. The most commonly used are admissions test scores and grade average or rank in high school class. However, there has also been considerable research into the predictability of the freshman grade from nonintellective predictors. Fishman and Pasanella (1960), in a review and summary of college admission and selection studies conducted between 1949 and 1959, reported that 23 percent of the studies reviewed by them used nonintellective measures, alone or in conjunction with intellective measures, to predict intellective criteria. The typical criterion was the freshman grade average. Lenning, Munday, Johnson, Well, and

Brue (1974a) published an interesting bibliography of research literature issued between 1963 and 1969 that was concerned with nonintellective correlates of college grades. Some of the studies were described briefly, but most were simply listed. Literature before 1963 is covered by previous reviews cited by Lenning et al.

Schrader's report on the validity of the SAT (1971) contains a very useful description of the design of the typical validity study and a discussion of use of the freshman grade average as a criterion. Schrader also reviewed and summarized the results of validity studies conducted during the first two years of the Validity Study Service, a service provided by the College Board to aid colleges in designing and conducting their own validity studies. This service was initiated in 1964 and has done much to increase the volume of validity studies conducted countrywide.

Ramist (in press) has recently summarized a considerable portion of this work. He focused on studies that use SAT-verbal, SAT-mathematical, and the high school record to predict freshman GPA for all freshmen. Ramist presents information on the validity of these admissions measures for various subsamples in the population of all college freshmen, and gives the reader a clear idea of the range of validities associated with these measures. The report contains an interesting discussion of the effect that restriction in range, due either to student self-selection or college selection, has on the validity of the admissions measures. Table 2.2 gives an overall view of the range of correlations typically found in such validity studies.

Correlation coefficients for various subgroups can vary. For example, Ramist reports mean correlations with FGPA as follows: for women, SAT-V .38, SAT-M .40, HS record .47, and the three together .56. Comparable coefficients for men were .31, .34, .44, and .51. Ramist also provides summary data for minority groups, handicapped students,

Table 2.2 Validity Coefficients Typically Found with Different Combinations of Predictors

| | Correlation with Freshman Grades | | | |
| | | Percentiles | | |
Predictor(s)	Mean	10	50 Median	90
SAT-verbal score	.36	.21	.36	.52
SAT-mathematical score	.35	.20	.35	.50
HS record	.47	.31	.48	.64
SAT-verbal and mathematical scores	.42	.27	.42	.57
SAT-verbal and mathematical scores and HS record	.55	.40	.55	.70

and older examinees. There is a similar compilation of validity data on the ACT tests (ACT 1973).

Admissions policy and practice

Most of the research and descriptive literature on admissions focuses on selective admissions. The main lines of inquiry have been how selective admissions actually works, what measures are used, how they are used, and the fairness and legality of the system. A useful introduction to the subject is Wechsler's *The Qualified Student* (1977), which gives a history of selective admissions and its early use as a tool of exclusion as much as a tool of inclusion. Moll's popularized *Playing the Private College Admissions Game* (1979) gives a different kind of insight into the subject by describing, in a very lively and readable style, the decision-making process at a typical selective college.

In 1977, in the context of the *Bakke* case, Willingham and Breland published an account of admissions processes at five types of institutions—undergraduate, graduate, law schools, medical schools, and graduate management schools. A similar account was published recently by Skager (1982), which looks at the same five types of institutions separately. The College Board–AACRAO national survey (1980) describes current institutional admissions policies and practices, the ways in which test scores are used in the selection process, and the extent of special admissions procedures for certain groups.

Willingham's sourcebook (1973) provided an extensive annotated bibliography of studies relating to various aspects of access to higher education. The introductory chapter examines broad social aspects of access to higher education. Manning's discussion of fairness in admissions (1977) considers the social-legal implications of selective admissions, and specifically, the legitimacy of race as a relevant student characteristic in admissions decisions.

Alternative admissions measures

The use of any measure in the admissions process raises a number of questions. Is it reliable and valid? Is it relevant to the admissions process and to institutional objectives? Does it make a useful contribution to prediction of success, to selecting a class, to ensuring fairness, to encouraging student achievement? While all of these questions apply to the use of high school rank and admissions test scores, they apply with special force to alternative measures that have not been subjected to the same research scrutiny nor developed the same social acceptance over time. Several studies address the question of other measures in admissions.

Bowen (1977) and Wickenden (1979) provide useful descriptions of the institution's rationale and practice in the use of other measures in admissions. Nichols and Holland (1963), Wallach (1976), and Willingham (1980, 1983) also discuss the rationale of using different measures in admissions, but more from the standpoint of the educational system at large. Willingham writes on the variety of measures used and the particular purpose they serve, Wallach on the need for more emphasis on publicly recognized accomplishment, and Nichols and Holland on how to measure accomplishment.

Three reviews provide a number of useful references and discussion of individual measures. Baird (1976) reviewed the use of self-reports, focusing on truthfulness, reliability and validity as predictors, and usefulness in the college setting. Breland (1981) used similar criteria to review a number of different types of measures such as biodata, interviews, references, and personality measures. A comparable review of the literature on measures used in employee selection was prepared by Reilly and Chao (1982).

Alternative selection strategies

Of considerable interest in admissions research is the effect, intended or otherwise, that a given selection strategy will have on the incoming class and hence on the institution as a whole. Webb (1966) and Campbell (1971) have described the side effects of selecting students on the basis of aptitude and ability. Both found that as the ability level of the incoming students increased, other systematic differences in attitudes and interests were also found.

Another approach to this question is exemplified by the work of Baird and Richards (1968) and Wing and Wallach (1971). Baird and Richards, using a sample of over 5,000 students at 35 two- and four-year institutions, compared the effects of selection on the basis of traditional academic measures with selection strategies based on nonacademic accomplishments. They focused their attention on the college achievers (in the freshman year) who would be excluded by each of the strategies. Wing and Wallach, using applicants to Duke University, compared the classes selected on the basis of SAT alone, high school rank alone, SAT and rank, or a selection strategy based on extracurricular accomplishments, with the class actually selected by the university for that year. The basic premise in these studies was that academic and nonacademic accomplishments are relatively independent of each other, and that selecting solely on the basis of one strategy or the other will result in the rejection of very different types of talented students. Werts (1967) questioned this view. He showed that academically low-scoring students were less likely to be high achievers in nonacademic areas than were the academically average students.

Retention

One of the most difficult questions to resolve in any discussion of retention is that of the definition of the term. There are stopouts and dropouts, failures and transfers, those who leave with an exciting alternative, and those who don't know what to do with themselves. Ramist (1981) reports that the dropout rate cited in the research literature is anywhere from 60 to 65 percent to 10 to 35 percent, depending on whether a dropout is defined as a student who does not graduate from the college of entry within four years or as one who does not graduate at all within ten years of beginning college. In his extensive review, Ramist summarizes the findings of previous research on factors affecting retention. He notes a change from a focus on the student in the earlier research to an increased interest in the institution's perspective (i.e., enrollment maintenance).

Tinto (1975) published an interesting theoretical model of dropout (an institutional model rather than a systems model), based on a combination of Durkheim's theory of suicide and a cost-benefit analysis of student decision making. This study is of interest also for its synthesis of research from the sixties and early seventies. It contains an excellent reference list of relevant studies. A major national study was conducted by Astin (1976), using student data from more than 300 colleges. This was a predictive study and presented data on students by race and sex. Students were defined as dropouts, stopouts, or persisters. Astin looked at the effect of factors such as financial aid, residence, employment, and particular student characteristics on the student's probability of persisting to graduation.

Grading standards

One of the problems in predicting student success in college is that the criterion measure, the grade, tends to reflect local standards. Data on average freshman GPA at 27 public colleges in Georgia (Pounds, Brown, and Astin 1970) showed that while the average SAT scores of the freshmen at the various institutions varied considerably, the GPA did not. Aiken (1963) and Wilson (1970) found that while SAT scores and high school ranks of incoming students improved, the FGPA did not show a similar increase. Such studies illustrate the floating nature of the college grade.

Another aspect of the nonequivalence of college grades is the problem of grade inflation since the late sixties. Birnbaum (1977) compared data from two classes, 1968 and 1974, and concluded that students in the later sample were receiving higher grades for equivalent work. The study contains a useful reference list on this aspect of the grading problem. While grade inflation also illustrates the floating nature of grading, it does not necessarily result in less valid prediction. As Bejar and Blew (1981) demonstrated, during the period of greatest grade inflation, the validity of the SAT held steady and the validity of high school grades declined somewhat.

Goldman (with Hewitt 1975; with Slaughter 1976) presents data in support of an "adaptation level" interpretation of the grading level practices of college faculty. Goldman et al. looked primarily at differences in grading standards for different majors and reported that fields of study with higher-ability students tended to have more stringent standards than did fields of study that attract lower-ability students. Goldman and Slaughter found that GPA was more difficult to predict than grades in individual classes, and they presented data to support the hypothesis that college grades in different fields are not equivalent. (See Chapter 6 for further discussion of the effects of grading variations on prediction.)

Student development

Although success in college is typically quantified in terms of GPA or class rank, broader goals of education are certainly acknowledged in the college catalog and in research literature. It has always been assumed and accepted that the emotional and moral development of the individual is of concern to the educator (Bowen 1977), though these types of "success" are not so directly relevant to admissions policy (see discussion in Chapter 3). An excellent reference source for research and writing on this topic is Feldman and Newcomb's *The Impact of College on Students* (1969). This work reviewed the major studies and findings on the subject from the mid-twenties to the mid-sixties. The authors assessed the impact of various aspects of the college experience on the students' attitudes and beliefs.

In *Education and Identity*, a highly regarded work, Chickering (1969) identified positive instances of student development that the institution should encourage and, based on the findings of previous research in the field, discussed ways in which the institution could bring about these developments. Lenning, Munday, Johnson, Well, and Brue (1974b) published a lengthy bibliography of studies on the nonacademic aspects of college success. Lenning, Lee, Micek, and Service (1977) have recently summarized a number of taxonomies of educational outcomes, many of which could be used as an organizational tool or as a point of focus in policymaking at the institutional level. Astin, in *Four Critical Years* (1978), reported the findings of a national study conducted over the course of several years using data from more than one incoming class. This study emphasized students' satisfaction with their education at various types of institutions. Astin found that these patterns of satisfaction were associated with the degree and type of involvement in college life on the part of the student. The Astin and Panos study described earlier in this chapter was a forerunner to this one but placed more emphasis on the effects of institutions and environments.

Several implications of this literature are worth brief comment. Studies of student development will no doubt continue to have some impact on how we think about the educational process and how we try to improve it. Studies in this area have never been much oriented toward, nor had much effect upon, selection and recruitment of freshmen. It is not apparent that they should.

Collegewide tests of general educational outcomes are useful for research purposes and for periodic institutional assessment. As measures of individual student achievement, they have never proved a very effective substitute for faculty grades assigned on the basis of class performance, special assignments, departmental tests, etc. This is possibly a reflection on the diffuse heterogeneity of the undergraduate curriculum in most academic areas. Faculties usually have great difficulty agreeing on the content of an examination that would fairly assess the educational objectives in their respective areas. This problem has proved quite an obstacle to research on the outcomes of education. Ironically, objective tests covering large blocks of work are much more commonly used in graduate and professional schools, where educational outcomes are presumably more complex and difficult to assess in an objective manner.

Another curious fact is that faculty ratings are often considered critical in key decisions on the training and employment of advanced students, but there has been little inclination to use any form of structured faculty ratings to evaluate the performance of undergraduate students on various important educational objectives. As a criterion, ratings appear relegated largely to periodic research studies and some special situations where expert judgment of performance is the only means of assessment available.

Accomplishments in college are a particularly attractive criterion because there are many opportunities for students to show what they can do and gain recognition for doing it. There have been important advances in the development of research measures of accomplishments in college, but they suffer some important shortcomings. Studies described here have typically used student questionnaires administered at the end of the freshman or sophomore year. It is not clear how valid such self-reports are so early in a student's college career. Scores on scales administered at the time may better represent participation than real accomplishment, and therefore reflect interests more than developed abilities.

One critical problem with all these measures is their lack of direct connection with the administrative apparatus of the institution—i.e., admissions policy, policy on academic standing, and formal systems of recognizing achievement, such as the transcript. The grading system is intimately so connected and seems to be a fertile ground for research. Limited research on this topic indicates that the dynamics of grading differ in important ways from department to department and from lower division to upper division. A student's record of achievement in college can be significantly complemented by more formal assessment and recognition of accomplishments not represented in grades, but meanwhile grades are the criterion and there is evidently much to learn about what they mean.

3

A Description of the Study

The Personal Qualities Project has had two major phases. The first phase involved the analysis of admissions decisions of some 25,000 applicants to the nine participating institutions—Bucknell University, Colgate University, Hartwick College, Kalamazoo College, Kenyon College, Occidental College, Ohio Wesleyan University, University of Richmond, and Williams College. Almost half of these students were accepted, and 4,814 actually enrolled. The first phase of the project centered on the question of how personal qualities were related to admissions decisions. In 1982 these results were reported in *Personal Qualities and College Admissions,* by Willingham and Breland (hereafter referred to simply as *Personal Qualities*). A brief summary of the main findings was provided in Chapter 1.

The second major question that concerned us was this: Are personal qualities other than traditional academic predictors useful in recruiting and selecting students who are likely to be viewed as successful overall, taking full account of the educational objectives of these colleges? To get at that question, we believed that it was essential to have information about the experience and accomplishments of these students through four years of undergraduate life. Gathering and analyzing such information was the purpose of Phase II.

How to measure success was a major issue in its own right—an issue complicated by theoretical as well as practical questions. We first take up that issue; namely, what measures of success did we use in this study and on what basis did we decide that? The final section of this chapter describes briefly the organization and procedures of this phase of the project.

MEASURING SUCCESS

What is success in college? In imagining a successful student, most would think first of the student with a good grade record. What is wrong with grade point average as a measure of success? The GPA is certainly widely used by graduate schools, employers, and almost anyone else who wants to get a fix on an individual's capabilities. This remains the case despite a good deal of research that casts some doubt on whether college grades are very closely related to success in life. Hoyt (1966) gave a pessimistic view of that relationship.

It may be that the GPA is widely used partly for the simple reason that it is neatly quantified and available, but that seems too simple an explanation. Most people respect academic honors and other indications of intellectual competence, realizing all the while that there is a lot more to success in a given real life situation. And despite some technical shortcomings (that we get into later), there is no arguing with the fact that the GPA does represent the accumulated judgment of numerous faculty as to how well the student has mastered the coursework. There is no reason to believe that the cumulative grade average is not a reasonably reliable and generally valid criterion of success in college.

So what is the complaint? Mainly there are two problems: what the GPA doesn't cover and what it doesn't reveal. Most would agree that grades earned in courses do not cover all types of success that are relevant to the educational objectives of the college. Also, the GPA reveals little as to *what* the student has learned. It mostly rank orders students as to how good a job the faculty thinks they have done on a quite important aspect of college life. In some respects this is a fine criterion for examining the validity of measures used in recruiting and selecting students. On the other hand, the GPA offers limited help in improving our understanding of different kinds of success or how preadmissions information might be used to better advantage. As we saw in Chapter 2, virtually all validity studies are based exclusively on the GPA, usually the freshman GPA.

In what other ways do people think of success in college? There is quite an array of possibilities (see Baird 1976; Feldman and Newcomb 1969; Lenning, Lee, Micek, and Service 1977; Richards, Holland, and Lutz 1967; Hackman and Taber 1979; Wallach 1976). For example, one could reasonably argue that a successful student is one who has:

- Acquired the particular types of skill and competence necessary to succeed in his or her chosen career.
- Demonstrated considerable intellectual growth since the freshman year.
- Acquired the generalizable intellectual skills that are essential in order to analyze and evaluate new problems.
- Produced creative works of high quality.
- Shown capability for effective leadership.
- Received honors for independent scholarship.
- Been admitted to a very demanding graduate or professional program.
- Acquired an understanding of cultural heritage and its modes of expression through the arts, letters, and technology.
- Graduated on time.
- Gained a sense of social confidence in dealing with different types of people.
- Gained a sense of direction and self-awareness.
- Learned an awareness of social problems and moral issues and the need to balance conflicting values.
- Won public recognition for service to peers, community, or institution.
- Won a competitive award for outstanding performance in an area of personal interest and commitment.
- Been judged by faculty to have demonstrated unusual qualities of scholarship or leadership.

Any one of these measures of success might be extremely important to a particular student, and, needless to say, they vary a great deal. Also, these various instances of success illustrate well how diverse and complex educational objectives really are. And there are very different points of view on what constitute successful outcomes of education. To one social theorist the important thing may be transmitting culture and improving social awareness. A more pragmatic observer may see the value of higher education primarily as laying the groundwork for a highly competent work force. A student, on the other hand, is more likely to view the successful college experience in terms of personal development—that is, broadened horizons, improved self-confidence, getting the act together.

These distinctions illustrate that some measures of success in college are directly relevant to the purposes of this study, others less so. It is useful to distinguish two. First, one can measure success as *beneficial outcome*. The great majority of research and writing on "outcomes of education" is concerned with success measures primarily from the standpoint of understanding and improving the educational process.

This includes particularly such objectives as improving curriculums and methods of instruction, increasing cost-effectiveness of programs, enhancing the educational development of individual students, and enlarging the social benefit of education generally.

With a somewhat different purpose in mind, one can think of a success measure as a *performance criterion*. In this case, as in the present study, the purpose is to identify students who have succeeded in areas important to the institution and to understand how such individuals might better be recruited and selected. Thus, the purpose is to validate and possibly improve admissions procedures and the information used in evaluating potential freshmen. These two interpretations overlap, of course, but they are not the same. In particular, personal improvement is not likely to be seen by most colleges as a useful criterion for validating measures used in admissions. For example, enhanced confidence in social interaction, or an improved sense of career direction, or new ethical insight may be extremely beneficial to particular college seniors, but the institution would seldom view lack of prior progress in these areas as a basis for rejecting an applicant. Few selective colleges have actively recruited students because they have shown little evidence of educational achievement and might therefore have special potential for gain. In the main, students are neither selected nor graded on the basis of improvement.

One other question merits attention. What assessment method is most appropriate? Taber and Hackman (1976) have demonstrated that ratings (faculty, staff, and student) can be used very effectively in a research context. As others have convincingly demonstrated, however, it is difficult to obtain reliable ratings (Reilly 1974; Davis 1965a). Another obvious tactic is to develop tests and other standard means of assessing skills and accumulated knowledge in specific areas of interest (see, for example, Pace 1979; Forrest and Steele 1982). This approach offers objectivity in comparing outcomes across colleges—not a goal of this study. A shortcoming of a standard test is uncertain relevance to local educational objectives. Dressel and Mayhew (1957) give a fascinating account of the frustrating efforts of one group of institutions in trying to agree on the design of tests to measure outcomes of general education.

Student questionnaires represent another common tactic. Student self-reports of experience and achievement are useful but may suffer from lack of objectivity and incomplete data. There is also a substantial body of research, much of it quite shaky, using various attitudinal or other psychological inventories (see Lenning et al. 1974 for an annotated bibliography).

A serious weakness of all these assessment techniques is the lack of much direct connection between the assessment and the educational process. The GPA has that connection. It takes a 2.0 to graduate; make a 3.4 and you get to add cum laude to your résumé. But what does it mean to get a rating of 7 on the faculty rating of scientific achievement? Even less clear is a score of 42 on the altruism inventory from the Institutional Research Office. The point is this: It is a reasonable bet that the less familiar a measure of success is, the less likely its inclusion in a research study will shed much useful light on educational policy and practice.

One important characteristic of the undergraduate college that bears directly on the assessment issue is that, in many respects, college is a testing ground. It offers many opportunities for students to test their wings, to learn adult skills, to produce and perform in many areas of possible interest, to make mistakes and correct them with the help of peers and mentors. In addition to cognitive development, there are many opportunities for effective learning of interpersonal skill, emotional control, and effective leadership. There are also many challenges where students can exercise initiative, develop a capacity for persistent effort, and produce independently a meritorious piece of work.

Many students seize these opportunities and excel. They offer some of the best examples of success as the college likes to think of success. And there are many ways that colleges recognize such success, though typically not in any quantified manner such as a grade average that goes on the permanent record. Nonetheless, there is a trail of evidence behind each student—a record of evidence that can be accumulated. Such evidence is a particularly valuable resource in broadly defining success in college.

From these various considerations, the author and the Personal Qualities Steering Committee adopted the following orientation. For the purposes of this study, success is best represented as the *accumulated record* of recognized achievements of each student. The accumulated record includes not only grades but other marks of success, attainment, and the summative judgment of the institution as to who has done well. We decided that in this study measures of success should be:

- Significant achievements that are clearly noteworthy and imply a great deal more than simply active participation in college life.
- Logically related to admissions policy, i.e., types of success institutions have in mind when they recruit and select freshmen.
- Broadly representative of the educational objectives of the institutions with due attention to unique types of success.

- Generally comparable across institutions, but defined within each so as to be locally relevant and valid.
- Based as much as possible on reliable assessment procedures already in place, i.e., checkable items of record such as evaluations, competitions, appointments, awards.

On the basis of these considerations, we defined and collected data on 27 success criteria, 6 of which are composites of the other 21. Unless otherwise indicated, information was collected on all criteria for the total group of 3,676 students enrolled in the fourth year. For many of these criteria we concluded that the most reliable and practical method of assessment was to identify a success group. In the list following, measures were scored in that manner (yes/no) unless some other scale is indicated. Further specification for some of the measures is provided in Appendix B.

Grade point average
    1. GPA1—Average grade (converted to 4.0 scale where necessary) for all courses taken during the first academic year
    2. GPA2—Same for second year
    3. GPA3—Same for third year
    4. GPA4—Same for fourth year
    5. CGPA—Cumulative four-year average

Marks of success
Ten marks of success were identified that were practical to assess and appeared to cover reasonably well those types of achievement frequently encountered in college. They fell into these categories: scholarship, leadership, and accomplishment. The three overlap and are often mutually dependent, but they can be usefully distinguished. Scholarship represents traditional forms of *cognitive* achievement. Leadership places more emphasis on such *affective* qualities as maturity, personal effectiveness, and the ability to inspire confidence in others. Accomplishment refers to *productive* capability, i.e., examplary instances of independent effort resulting in a meritorious product, project, or developed skill.

    6. Scholarship—All students who received either college honors or departmental honors.
    7. College honors—Those students who earned a cumulative GPA sufficiently high to graduate cum laude (varied by college).
    8. Departmental honors—Students who completed a senior honors project with distinction. The measure was defined in this

manner to differentiate clearly this type of scholarship from GPA. In most institutions the measure was identical to departmental honors as defined by the college.

9. Leadership—All students who held either an appointed position or an elected office (see Appendix B for data collection guidelines).

10. Appointed position—Students selected by the institution for important positions (e.g., dormitory counselors, admissions tour guides, student boards) primarily on the basis of personal qualities and the ability to represent the college or serve as a role model for younger students.

11. Elected office—Students elected by their peers to serve in positions of major responsibility that are taken seriously on the campus.

12. Accomplishment—All students who were identified for significant accomplishment in any of the following six categories (13–18). To qualify as significant, an accomplishment had to involve independent initiative and persistent effort and had to produce a tangible outcome of unusual merit, such as a developed skill, a finished product, or a completed project (see Appendix B for data collection guidelines).

13. Scientific/technical achievement

14. Artistic achievement

15. Communications achievement

16. Physical achievement

17. Organizing achievement

18. Other independent achievement

19. Scholastic achievement (any of 13–15)

20. Overall success—A linear model of the group nominated "most successful," based on 7, 8, 10, 11, 16, 17, 18, 19 above. (See Chapter 4 for discussion.)

Attainment

21. Persistence to the senior year—All students enrolled in the fourth year (1982–83) were classified for the purposes of this study as seniors ($N = 3,676$), which was the base group for collection of all criterion data reported here. This group is almost the same as "graduates" and is so treated in this study.

22. Time to graduation—Classified as early, on time (May 1983), or late.

23. Double major—Those students who fulfilled requirements for graduation in more than one major. Does not include minors or other forms of subsidiary field concentration.

24. Advanced study—Admitted as of late spring 1983 to a medical, law, or Ph.D. program. These were identified by the students' undergraduate advisers or college offices charged with the co-ordination of graduate and professional applications.

Nominations

25. Peer nominees—Students who received at least three nominations for best exemplifying success in college. See question 5 on Senior Questionnaire, Appendix A.
26. Self-rating of overall success—See question 6 on Senior Questionnaire, Appendix A.
27. Most successful—Students identified by the college by whatever definition and procedure each thought best represented the educational objectives of the institution. (See Chapter 4 for discussion of how this was carried out.)

ORGANIZATION AND PROCEDURE

In the summer of 1978, conversations were initiated with a group of some 20 private colleges that used the Common Application form exclusively. These institutions provided a unique context for a cooperative study of personal qualities in admissions because they used an application form that provides (1) a common data base and (2) a wide range of objective as well as narrative information relevant to the study. Nine institutions met the minimum requirements for number of entering freshmen, were interested, and were invited to participate. All accepted and have been actively involved in the project since that time.

Staff and steering committee roles

The analytic work and preparation of the major reports of the project were carried out by ETS staff. Staff and faculty of the nine institutions participated actively in rating the qualifications of applicants, supplying data on academic performance, identifying students with noteworthy accomplishments, etc. The steering committee, composed of representatives of the participating institutions, was responsible for policy direction of the project and approved all work plans and reports. Special care was exercised to protect privacy.

Data collection

The procedures for obtaining and processing data reflected throughout the usual concerns for completeness of records, accuracy of retrieved information, and efficiency of handling. The principal sources of data were:

1. Admissions policy statements prepared by the participating institutions.
2. The Common Application form.
3. Routine admissions data retrieved from institutions but not on the Common Application form.
4. Institutional evaluations of applicants' personal and academic qualities (made especially for the project).
5. A fall 1979 entrance questionnaire and a spring 1980 follow-up questionnaire.
6. Criterion data on freshman performance and persistence.
7. A questionnaire to seniors in 1982–83.
8. Academic records through the senior year.
9. Other institutional records from individual departments and offices throughout the campus.
10. Nominations from faculty and staff.

The first six of these data sources refer to Phase I of the project and are described in *Personal Qualities* with additional information concerning individual measures as well as the background and organization of the project. Except for a listing of measures 1–140 and a few essential technical details, this volume does not repeat scale definitions or data collection and security procedures reported in Chapter 4 and the appendixes of *Personal Qualities*.

The senior questionnaire was distributed with a confidential return envelope addressed to the local project representative on each campus. College staff used multiple follow-ups, personal contacts, and a variety of other techniques to obtain a response rate of 70 percent. Academic records were retrieved in large part on magnetic tape in common format. Records from other campus sources and nominations from faculty and staff were collected by staff on each campus under the supervision of the local representative to the Personal Qualities Steering Committee. This effort was guided by a data collection notebook providing detailed instructions including scheduled steps, guidelines, prototype forms and materials, and illustrative lists of achievements of various types. (See Appendix B, for example.)

Measures

The collected data were classified into the following measures: application, academic achievement, personal achievement, background, college ratings, educational goals, reasons for college choice, education/ career interests, freshman experience and performance, senior criterion measures. The application measures consisted of those variables that tend to categorize applicants—for example, acceptance versus rejection, whether financial aid was offered, whether the applicant came for an interview. Academic achievement included the usual test scores, high school rank, and other academic variables. Personal achievement was represented by 11 research staff ratings from the Common Application form information described previously. Background measures included a variety of items such as age, sex, ethnicity, and socioeconomic level. The college ratings included a number of flags for specific qualities, overall personal and academic ratings, and a rating of the interview if there was one. Educational goals and reasons for college choice came from questionnaire responses at matriculation. The measures describing freshman experience and performance came largely from the spring follow-up questionnaire.

The definition and collection of the four-year criterion measures were described earlier. Other data collected in Phase II came from the senior year questionnaire, which is reproduced in Appendix A. Following is a list of the 140 measures from Phase I of the study. For additional information on these, see Chapter 4 and Appendix B of *Personal Qualities*. Six of the more important preadmissions achievement measures were combined into three composite scores to improve reliability and avoid missing-data problems. "Personal Statement" is the average of the writing and content scores (22 and 23 below). "High School Honors" is a composite score based on a 5-point rating of "Academic Honors" (14 below with valedictorians receiving a score of at least 4). "School Reference" is the average of "Teacher Reference" (25) and "School Report" (24) or either score if one was missing.

Application
1. Accepted (admissions action)
2. Enrolled (student decision)
3. Aid applicant
4. Came for interview (optional in all colleges)
5. Sent work sample (also optional—art, writing, etc.)
6. Aid offered
7. Early-decision applicant
8. Multiple applicant (to two or more of the nine colleges)

Academic achievement
9. High school rank (HSR) (normalized; $\bar{x} = 50$)
10. SAT average (ACT equivalent where SAT not available)

Reasons for college choice (From entering questionnaire; 12 of 33 reasons selected for analysis identified by number.)

83. General academic reputation (1)
84. Campus beauty (27)
85. Social atmosphere (6)
86. Particular academic program (3)
87. Area of country (23)
88. Particular location (24)
89. Teaching emphasis (5)
90. Athletic facilities (30)
91. Favorable staff contact (32)
92. Rejected elsewhere (33)
93. School advice (12)
94. Financial aid offer (17)

Educational/career interests

95. Degree plans
96. Probable major at time of application
97. Probable major at time of matriculation
98. Career interest
99. Statement orientation

Freshman experience and performance

100–111. Spring goals—importance
112–123. Spring goals—progress
124–136. Spring view of reasons for college choice
137. Freshman GPA (converted to 4.0 scale as necessary)
138. Peer nomination
139. Goal progress composite
140. Freshman dropout (not enrolled, fall of sophomore year)

Sampling and analytic procedures

Table 3.1 shows, by college, the number of students in each of several successive data bases: applicants, accepted applicants, enrolled freshmen, Personal Quality Project seniors, senior questionnaire respondents. Phase I of this project was much concerned with institutional behavior (i.e., policy and practice). This phase is mainly concerned with student behavior (i.e., achievement). Correspondingly, there is an important difference in the orientation of this analysis and that reported in *Personal Qualities*. A major emphasis in the earlier work was the analysis of admissions decisions that could and did vary substantially from college to college. Much of that analysis was focused on individual

Table 3.1 Sample Sizes by College

Sample	BUC	COL	HAR	KAL	KEN	OCC	OHI	RIC	WIL
Applicants	5,400	4,944	1,594	991	1,360	1,168	2,070	2,860	4,156
Accepted applicants	2,094	1,738	1,322	901	1,081	896	1,916	1,576	915
Enrolled freshmen	776	644	383	398	382	389	728	656	458
Seniors	692	570	240	260	300	286	450	455	423
Senior questionnaire respondents	416	280	153	160	209	214	307	347	357

Note: Here and occasionally elsewhere the nine colleges are designated by the first three letters of their names.

colleges in order to examine such differences. It was not only of special interest to do so but also possible because of the large samples of applicants available. In predicting performance there is no corresponding expectation of policy differences resulting in large (and interpretable) differences in regression analyses from college to college. Also, the sample sizes here are too small to reveal reliable differences among colleges in most of these analyses. Consequently, the analysis of this phase concentrates much more on the total group of students (pooled within group or averaged across colleges) in order to establish more stable and dependable results. Where indicated, the extent of college differences was examined. Also, more and less selective colleges were compared in some analyses.

For several important analyses it was necessary to break down the sample by graduating major (or major at that time for students who had not graduated). An unexpected complication was that a substantial number of students—about one in six—had double majors. Since there was no good basis for preferring one major over the other, double majors were handled in one of three ways, depending on the nature of the analysis. In some cases samples were based on the first major listed; in other instances double majors were excluded; and sometimes samples of graduates by major were based on all students who fulfilled requirements, resulting in the last case in substantially more graduating majors than graduating students.

A variety of analytic techniques were used. Attention is called particularly to the development of a pooled-within-college correlation matrix corrected for missing data (Chapter 5), a residual analysis similar to that used in *Personal Qualities* (Chapter 5), a within-department analysis (Chapter 6), a weighting procedure to correct for questionnaire nonresponse (Chapter 7), and a linear modeling of overall success in order to examine the effects of different selection strategies (Chapters 4 and 8). These are explained as the results are presented. Those readers interested in more detail will find further specification in the Technical Notes of Appendix C. A study of this type generates a very large amount of tabular material. Only those tables of special interest have been included in the text; additional tables appear in Appendix D.

4

The Accumulated Record

Who succeeds in what ways that are important to the institution? We ask the question from a particular perspective—namely, can a better understanding of success in college contribute to more effective policy and practice in recruiting and selecting a freshman class? To answer that question, we have tried to build upon and take a step beyond what has been done in the past.

Looking back at Chapter 2 for a moment, we noted there that colleges have done a great many validity studies where the success criterion has almost always been freshman grade point average—an important criterion but a limited definition of success, most would admit, considering the time devoted to undergraduate education and the importance of upper-division work. There is another extensive research literature that views success as personal development. It includes studies of particular attitudes or types of achievement, plus other studies that employ more of a clinical or holistic approach (e.g., the case history) in an effort to understand the educational process. The latter body of work is often more interesting than the freshman validity studies, but harder to interpret with much confidence and much less clearly related to admissions policy.

Finally, in Chapter 2 we examined in more detail a few trailblazing studies that demonstrated the possibilities of a broader definition of success in college. A weakness of these important studies is that all have utilized student questionnaires, special research procedures, etc., that provide no way of directly linking admissions strategies with student performance outcomes that are valued and formally recognized by the institution.

Chapter 3 then provided a rationale for defining success broadly, but used measures that come directly from the educational program and activities and can therefore be more readily translated into admissions implications. In short, we have defined success on the basis of the student's *accumulated record* of recognized achievements over four years. In asking the colleges to identify their most successful students, we get a reading on which parts of that record they consider most important. To do justice to the complexity and variety of the record, it was necessary to collect information on 21 different measures plus 6 more composites, as previously described. In this chapter we give an accounting of the accumulated record.

Several questions, or issues, will provide the framework for this discussion. First, it is useful to have a sense of how these students did on conventional measures of academic achievement and attainment. How many students remained enrolled? What sort of grades did they earn year by year? How many graduated on time? How many went on to advanced study, particularly in prestigious graduate and professional programs? One other attainment in which we were originally only incidentally interested is the double major.

This increasingly prevalent practice raises a second issue that needs to be examined in order to give an adequate description of the accumulated record: What is the academic context in which the student is working? As we shall see, there are sharp differences from major to major in the way students of different academic ability choose and change their major. So we devote one section of this chapter to describing the academic program, especially the nature of student migration among majors.

Third, what is the incidence of different types of important achievement? How many students earn the 10 marks of success outlined in Chapter 3? What do faculty think of those different types of success? How do they characterize each? Are there large differences in the occurrence of different types of success for men and women? Students in different majors? Different colleges?

Fourth, what is overall success? How are different types of success related? Are leadership, scholarship, and accomplishment rather similar or quite different? When colleges are asked to select their most outstanding graduates, whom do they choose? How much weight do they give to different types of success?

Grades and attainment

Typically, students are classified as juniors or seniors on the basis of how many credits they have accumulated and when they are expected to graduate. Not so here. For the purposes of this study, date of entry was the key issue because it was necessary to follow the same cohort through four years. Consequently, we defined "seniors" as those students in our original group who were enrolled four years later, regardless of whether the college had them so labeled.

There were 3,676 such students—76 percent of the entering group. Most of these students graduated on time in June 1983. Very few completed requirements before that time (2 percent); about one senior in nine did not make it by June. Virtually all these students had a grade average high enough to meet graduation requirements, or very nearly so, and the colleges assumed that almost all would eventually graduate. A few probably never will, but they will be offset by a few others whom we have classified as dropouts but who will return someday and finish. In any event, for research purposes it is convenient and reasonably accurate to think of these seniors as graduates—of these colleges, that is. Many undoubtedly continued their education elsewhere. We did not follow up the 24 percent who withdrew, because that would have been a substantial study in its own right and was not necessary to meet the objectives of this study.

The overall dropout rate of one in four did not vary a great deal according to sex and other background characteristics, but there were large differences from college to college. In the more selective institutions (BUC, COL, WIL) about one out of ten entering students was not enrolled in the senior year; the less selective institutions (HAR, KAL, OHI) lost a third or more of their freshmen over the four years. In fact, the correlation was .90 between dropout rate and selection rate for these nine colleges. A commonsense explanation might be that the less selective institutions are accepting more marginal students who are later more likely to flunk out. Is it that simple? Not really, as we shall see in the results on predicting persistence in Chapter 5.

Figure 4.1 shows the pattern of grades earned by those students who were enrolled one to four years. The figure illustrates several points. First, it does show that students who dropped out were more likely to have lower grades, but it also shows that grades were generally up at a level (well above 2.0) where most students are not likely to get in academic hot water. This is a common pattern that indicates that these colleges are attracting (through institutional and self-selection) a

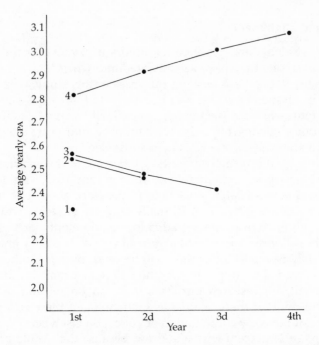

Figure 4.1 Trend in average yearly GPA for students classified by number of years of attendance (i.e., line 4 is based on students who were enrolled for four years).

student body whose academic ability matches reasonably well the academic standard of the college. It may also reflect to some extent the grade inflation that took place some 15 years ago (Bejar and Blew 1981). A second point is that grades tended to drop off before students withdrew. This probably reflects an influence of grades on students' decisions, especially if they are in academic jeopardy. Of course it is seldom clear whether students become discouraged by grades or some other personal matter. In any event, the general pattern shown in Figure 4.1 has been observed previously (Lins and Abell 1965; Wilson 1983).

Finally, what is one to make of the substantial rise in grades of students who remain enrolled for four years? Does it mean that students are learning more, or at least getting better at doing what professors require for a good grade? Probably both, but is it also maybe a special form of grade inflation? When one unbundles the seniors and looks at various groups, it turns out that this line—apparently documenting a smoothly consistent ascent from year one to year four—is actually not consistent at all. The average GPA for students majoring in education progresses from 2.6 to 3.3 over four years while the GPA for chemistry students holds steady at 3.1 Does this show that education students are learning more than chemistry students? Hardly, but it does make clear the need to take account of a student's major in evaluating performance in college.

Another important measure of attainment is admission to a highly selective program of advanced study. As of June in their fourth year, 412 of these seniors had been admitted to a medical or law school or to a Ph.D. program. This is about 9 percent of the entering freshmen and can be compared with 39 percent who held such aspirations at that time. But they do not give up easily. In the fall of the fourth year, one-third of the seniors still indicated plans for such advanced graduate or professional work at some time. Substantially more planned master's level work.

Except for Colgate, which was high, and Hartwick, which was low, there were only small institutional differences in the proportion of seniors admitted to a law, medical, or Ph.D. program. Despite the fact that women had somewhat higher colleges grades, about half again as many men were admitted to such advanced programs. There were more striking differences among academic majors. The proportion of students so admitted ranged from .05 in arts to .27 in biological science (see Table D.5 in Appendix D). This is another indication of the importance of considering the student's academic program in trying to comprehend the various aspects of success in college. We turn to that now.

THE ACADEMIC PROGRAM

Students in different academic majors live in different subcultures to some extent, have different learning experiences, and, one would expect, succeed in different ways. Success in college should make more sense within the familiar context of traditional academic majors. There is, however, a substantial migration of students among majors during their undergraduate years. It is important to have some feel for these migratory patterns because, as will become apparent in Chapter 6, such migration has odd effects on the upper-division grade scale—an important criterion of success in college.

Consequently, in this section we take a slight detour to examine the movement of students from a tentative to a final major. In so doing it is necessary to take account of the fact that many students have two majors—an awkward but interesting complication. All academic programs were classified into 1 of 21 majors within 7 areas as follows:

Arts
     1. Art/Music/Drama

Business
     2. Accounting
     3. Business administration

Biological Science
     4. Biology/Zoology/Botany

Humanities
     5. English
     6. Foreign language
     7. History
     8. Philosophy (and Religion)

Physical Science
     9. Chemistry
     10. Engineering
     11. Geology
     12. Mathematics
     13. Physics

Social Science
     14. Economics
     15. International studies
     16. Political science
     17. Psychology
     18. Sociology (and Anthropology)

Other
     19. Education
     20. Health
     21. Undesignated

For the purposes of this analysis, the final or graduating major(s) is taken to be the student's major during the senior year at the time these data were collected. One might argue that only this final destination is important, though much is to be learned from the way students move from earlier to later academic interests. In many institutions, these included, students are not required to declare a major at entry. In this discussion the freshman major is the student's intended major as indicated on a questionnaire at entry (or on the application blank for students who did not fill out that entry questionnaire). Many students were quite uncertain about an academic major at that time. In fact, about one in five stated no preference.

Double majors

For many years there have always been a few students who completed degree requirements in more than one major (above and beyond the so-called minor), but only recently has the full-fledged double major become a common undergraduate program strategy. Double majors are likely motivated by a variety of considerations, including practical market value as well as intellectual curiosity. Also, now that electives outnumber requirements in most curriculums, it is probably much easier for students to schedule the necessary courses for a double major without extending their undergraduate tenure.

In any event, the double major is certainly no oddity in these colleges. Among the seniors, one in six was so designated. From a somewhat different perspective, if one looks at the roster of seniors in individual departments, more than one student in every four was completing degree requirements in another department. This is a bit disorienting for anyone used to imagining students neatly slotted by major. Worse still, it poses perplexing problems in analyzing data by major field. For example, in comparing students in different majors, what does one do with a student who is just as much an economics major as a mathematics major?

There are three ways of handling this problem, none entirely satisfactory. One approach is to use only those students who have a single major. This is arguably the best way to understand differences among majors. Another approach is to treat each major (rather than each graduate) as a separate case. The effect is to count the double majors twice. This approach seems appropriate if the main interest is to accurately characterize students who obtain degrees in particular academic areas. A third approach is to use, arbitrarily, one of the majors whenever there are two. In the various analyses reported here we have used whichever of these three methods seemed most reasonable for the question at hand—sometimes using two methods to see how the results compare.

On the positive side, the double major phenomenon provides an additional success criterion: Fulfilling degree requirements in two areas is not a trivial accomplishment. It can reasonably be viewed as a measure of attainment, generally similar to persistence or time to graduation. The extent of double majors varies considerably by field. Compared with the average undergraduate, students in natural science were less likely to have a second major (about one in five); students in business, even less so (about one in sixteen). In arts, humanities, and social science, the proportion of double majors was typically more like three in ten. The clear exception was foreign languages, where 62 percent were double majors. Evidently a language major is often seen as a useful adjunct to another discipline.

Choice and migration

It is well known that many college freshmen are quite uncertain about their choice of a major. There is a good deal of sifting and sorting as students try different courses, change their orientation, and finally find their place or withdraw altogether. How to understand this process? What are the important issues and outcomes to look for?

It proved useful to frame the question as follows: What is the best way to describe the changes from freshman to senior year in the constitution of a particular academic group, say students majoring in biological science? There are three things going on in the transition from freshman to senior year that change the constitution of that group. Some students take on a second major, some students shift from one major to another, others drop out of college altogether. We would like to know how many and what types of students are involved in these three types of transition.

There are many ways one could describe these students, but the most interesting question is how they vary with respect to their academic capabilities. Freshman average is used here as an indicator of academic capability because it is the best available representation of that competence that is approximately comparable from one student to another. (As we see later, successive yearly grade averages are untrustworthy for that purpose.) Furthermore, first-year average is the salient academic index that likely influences the freshman's assessment of his or her academic future (and decisions) more than any other single piece of information.

Figure 4.2 brings all these factors together for students in six academic areas (see note 4 for Chapter 4 in Appendix C and Table D.6 in Appendix D for detailed data on individual majors). First, this figure indicates from the size of the circles how many students are doing what. Second, the vertical placement of the circles indicates the first-year grade average (GPA1) for the group. The freshman (far left) circle indicates the number of students who expressed a preference for a major in each of the six areas at matriculation. The senior (far right)

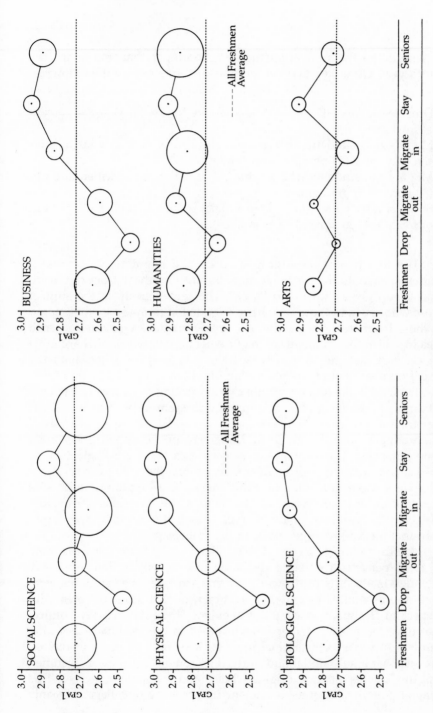

Figure 4.2 Evolution of groups of seniors majoring in six academic areas. (Size of circles is proportional to size of group. See text.)

circle indicates the number of students majoring in that area during the fourth year. Other key parts of the transition process are the following:

- Drop—students who leave college before the senior year (24 percent of freshmen).
- Migrate out—students who remain enrolled but not in a major indicated at entry (49 percent of freshmen).
- Migrate in—students who graduate in a major not specified at entry (80 percent of graduates).
- Stay—students who graduate in a major originally chosen (28 percent of freshmen; 36 percent of graduates).

The first two of these groups—drop and migrate out—represent students "lost" to the academic area. Subtracting those from the freshman group gives those who "stay." The senior group is the sum of those who stay and those who have migrated in from some other major. In these latter two groups, the 586 double majors are counted in each area in which they fulfilled the requirements, i.e., twice. This accounts for the fact that the sum of these two groups is 586 larger than the actual number of students remaining in school.

Figure 4.2 illustrates a number of interesting dynamics in the evolution of the senior groups majoring in different areas. Some of these are striking similarities across academic areas. For example, in all six of the academic areas, some 20 to 25 percent of the entering freshmen drop out before the senior year. In each area these are students who have made noticeably lower freshman grades, more so in natural science, less so in arts. On the other hand, many students with fine academic records dropped out. In each of the nine institutions, the variability of freshman grade average among the dropouts was larger than that for freshmen generally in that college.

Another interesting consistency is that in most academic areas some 35 to 45 percent of entering freshmen migrate out of their originally intended major (arts was lower), and in each case these students were quite representative of entering freshmen in that academic area with respect to freshman grade point average. These data clearly confirm that uncertainty as to major is widespread in the freshman class. Regardless of the area of original interest, it seems that one can rely on the fact that a substantial and fairly representative group of freshmen will think better of their original choice and try something else. This general pattern was quite consistent from college to college, the only exception being a lower rate of changing major at Bucknell and Hart-wick. Finally, the data indicate that those students who stayed in their original major were, in almost all cases, a somewhat more able minority compared with the original group of freshmen in that major. Again, this same result was found in all nine colleges.

The significant corollary is this: Major changes from the freshman to the senior year in the group of students associated with a given major did not come about because of differential dropout or differential shifting out of the major. The significant changes from freshman to senior year are due almost entirely to in-migration—that is, the extent to which the major attracts students in the course of the four years. The number of in-migrants and their average freshman GPA varies quite substantially from one academic area to another.

The arts, humanities, and social sciences all attracted a great many more students than they lost, although the academic capability of those students varied somewhat from one major to another. The foreign languages and international studies were more likely to attract students who had done well in the freshman year. Sociology attracted many students who had not done well. Economics attracted an unusually large number of in-migrants who on the average had freshman grades much like students who started in that field as freshmen.

Physical and biological science, along with business, showed a very different pattern. These areas attracted no more students than they lost—in some cases, fewer—but they were typically strong students. Geology was somewhat of an exception among the physical sciences; it tended to attract students with lower freshman grades. The other majors in physical science attracted students with freshman grades more than half a standard deviation above the average for the class.

Note that there are three ways a major attracts students: students who declared no major at the outset (21 percent of seniors), shifts from other majors (44 percent of seniors), and double majors (16 percent of seniors). On all three counts, business and natural science were less likely to attract students than were the arts, humanities, and social sciences. This pattern suggests that students in business and natural science are more likely to have a more focused and long-term interest in their field of choice.

Coursework and work experience

To get a somewhat better sense of the learning experiences of these students, we asked respondents to the Senior Questionnaire to indicate how many courses they had in particular academic areas and what types of work experience they had during college. With respect to coursework, there were relatively small differences in the proportion of men and women students who had taken at least a year's coursework in various academic areas. As might be expected, somewhat fewer women had taken a heavy dose of physical science; on the other hand, women were somewhat overrepresented in biological science coursework. Differences in the amount of coursework followed rather predictable lines for students in different majors. Physical science majors take a lot of math, business majors take a lot of economics, and so on (see Table D.4 in Appendix D for details).

The most unusual aspect of the data regarding the amount of coursework was the pattern of institutional differences. Table 4.1 shows the percentage of seniors who took a year or more coursework in various areas and the very wide range from college to college. For example, in several institutions (Bucknell, Hartwick, Kenyon, Williams) some 25 to 35 percent of seniors took at least a year in a foreign language, while at Kalamazoo and Richmond the corresponding figure was 80 to 90 percent. Undoubtedly there are inaccuracies in these student-reported data, though they do show some significant curriculum differences among these liberal arts colleges.

As for work experience, one senior in four held a full-time internship during college. One-half reported holding a full-time job that was, in the student's view, valuable experience. One in three had a full-time job that was related to the student's career interest, and one in six held an assistantship at the college. There was very little difference between men and women in these proportions. Differences among curriculum

Table 4.1 Percentage of Seniors with a Year or More Coursework in Selected Academic Areas

	All	Institutional Range	
Academic Area	*Seniors*	*Low*	*High*
Biological science	31%	23%	44%
Computer science, math	61	22	93
Economics, political science	63	45	74
Foreign languages	47	26	91
Literature, history	78	54	95
Music, art	38	16	78
Philosophy, religion	34	11	57
Physical science	41	28	54
Psychology, sociology	55	28	87

areas tended to reflect traditional patterns; i.e., students in natural science were more likely to hold assistantships than internships whereas the opposite was true for arts, humanities, and social sciences (see Table D.3 in Appendix D). There were relatively few important institutional differences in the pattern of work experience.

TEN MARKS OF SUCCESS

For the purposes of this study, 10 overlapping but relatively independent marks of success were identified. As described in Chapter 3, the 10 fell in three broad categories: two types of scholarship, two types of leadership, and six types of significant accomplishment. The faculty in the nine institutions determined whether each of their seniors did or did not meet the qualifications for each of these 10 success groups.

This section gives a brief accounting of how many achieved these various marks of success, how much variation there was among different groups of students, and how the faculty characterized different types of success (see Table D.5 in Appendix D for more detailed data).

Scholarship

At these institutions, about one senior out of four earned a cumulative grade point average high enough to win college honors (i.e., cum laude) at graduation. One senior in nine won departmental honors; 30 percent of the seniors were recognized for one or both of these types of superior scholarship. While the college honors reflected GPA, departmental honors were based on faculty judgment of outstanding independent scholarship on a senior thesis. Some gave glowing testimony.

> Her senior thesis was a monumental piece of work—original, imaginative, and very thorough. I was somewhat awed by the terrible tenacity with which she hung in there against odds that would have induced most students to quit.

Departmental honors were proportionately represented among men and women. But not so college honors; half again more women than men won that distinction. Among two groups receiving special preference in admissions, 27 percent of alumni children and 9 percent of minority students were represented in one of these scholarship honor groups. There were typically not large differences in scholarship honors from one major to another, although this may simply reflect the tendency for faculty in different areas to pass out academic honors in similar proportions. There were substantial differences from college to college in the proportion of students winning scholarship honors— partly because college honors were defined differently by different institutions, but especially because some institutions had much more extensive departmental honors programs than did others.

Leadership

Among the seniors studied, 18 percent were elected by students to a major campus office and 23 percent were appointed by the institution to a responsible position. Overall, more than one out of three held some such position of leadership during their four-year college career. This is a remarkable figure, considering that each of these positions was judged to carry important responsibility and respect on the campus. They ranged from the exceptional:

> Caroline was an unusually effective student body president. She brought students back to an understanding of their role and responsibilities in the governance area.

To the dependable role model:

> John has been a fine student adviser, thoroughly dependable and always helpful to his fellow students.

Men and women were represented equally in elected offices; the college-appointed positions went somewhat more frequently to women. Both minority students and alumni children were slightly overrepresented in the leadership group. There were not large differences among academic areas, although students in the arts were somewhat less likely to be leaders while those in biological science were overrepresented in this success group. Some colleges tended to have more elected offices and others more appointed positions, but overall there were not large differences, college to college, in the number of students designated as successful leaders. All of these colleges appear to provide substantial opportunity for leadership experiences.

Significant accomplishment

The colleges typically used quite demanding standards in nominating 24 percent of their students for one or more of these six types of significant accomplishments: scientific/technical achievement, artistic achievement, communications achievement, physical achievement, organizing achievement, other independent achievement. Only one in twenty was nominated in two areas; one in a hundred was nominated in three areas; only three students managed more than three areas.

Students cited for scientific/technical accomplishment (3 percent) were sometimes characterized as brilliant, but were more often selected for a high level of technical skill (e.g., computer programming, financial analysis, petrology of rocks) and for extensive independent research.

This research project (in biology) has required enormous effort and initiative from Jane over the past year. It is one of the best honors theses in biology, and I expect that she will publish the results.

Artistic accomplishment (4 percent) was typically associated with unusual talent (as a performer or creative artist) and a high degree of self-discipline and productivity. These students frequently had a lot to show for their effort.

Stanley has performed in several roles, produced a number of films, and has independently directed plays both in class and out.

Students cited for communications accomplishment (3 percent) were known for extensive activity and responsibility in writing, editing, or speaking. Most showed a very high level of productivity resulting from much hard work.

Elizabeth has acquired extraordinary fluency in spoken and written Japanese during the past four years. She has acquired a level of skill one can describe as near native, indicating exceptional talent and truly unusual devotion of effort.

In nominating students for physical achievement (5 percent), the emphasis was almost always on skill and achievement in sports competition. The usual reference was to formal recognition through records or awards.

The outstanding feature of Jim's years here is his success at football. He was named an all-league player in his junior year. Twice during that year he was named league player of the week. During his senior year he was voted team captain and named most valuable player.

Unusual entrepreneurial activity (e.g., developing a substantial business, organizing a major campaign, creating a new campus activity) was often cited as evidence of organizing achievement (6 percent). These students were often characterized as a major force in getting things done, as serving the college or community, or as having introduced some commendable innovation.

Robert began as a political volunteer in the governor's office. He rose to be director of all volunteers statewide and a member of the transition staff after election day.

Students cited for other independent accomplishments (10 percent) were often described in exceptional terms and in some detail. They were highly respected and even "sought after" by faculty. These students were often recognized in national competitions or were recipients of major campus "all-around" awards. Many appeared to be students who did not seem to fit clearly in the other accomplishment categories but were undeniably outstanding. Often they were described as leaders as well as scholars; for example,

This student is hard to classify. He's done independent research in two departments, organized a campus chapter, and been a full member of the Academic Policy Committee (he probably understands the campus better than do half the faculty.).

The students cited for significant accomplishment were involved in widely diverse activities. In the faculty's view they were clearly very successful in the activities cited, sometimes remarkably so. They were very able students, and their accomplishments reflect how they opted to spend their time. This method of defining success in college is somewhat like an inkblot test. The college provides a diverse set of opportunities; then students channel their talents and energies as their interests take them.

Is there any commonality or recognizable theme among these types of success? On the surface, perhaps not, but certain characteristics tended to come up repeatedly in faculty and staff descriptions of significant accomplishments of students. Typically, these students were extremely hard workers; they often acquired a high level of developed skill; they were unusually productive.

There were almost no sex differences in the incidence of significant accomplishments. The only exception was more frequent achievement by males in physical activities. Also, significant accomplishments were well spread among students in different majors although the specific type of accomplishment tended to vary somewhat, as one might expect, on the basis of different student interests in, for example, arts versus science (see Table D.5 in Appendix D). The pattern of accomplishments varied somewhat from college to college in two respects. Evidently the academic and extracurricular programs of these institutions offer somewhat different opportunities for achievement in different areas, i.e., artistic versus scientific versus leadership. Also, some institutions evidently chose to interpret the guidelines (described in Chapter 3) more stringently than did others.

WHAT IS OVERALL SUCCESS?

It is evident that college students excel in many different ways. It is also clear from this study and from earlier work (Davis 1965a; Hackman and Taber 1979) that institutions recognize and value different types of excellence. But are not some more important than others? When all is said and done, who *are* the successful students?

This study takes two orientations to the question. One orientation is to reject any single definition of success and, rather, try to understand its multiple dimensions. Thus, scholarship, leadership, and accomplishment are best seen as contrasting forms of success. Then the question becomes: How are these related, one to the other?

The second orientation is to avoid any a priori definition of success as this achievement or that achievement and to let overall success in college be defined in terms of the achievements of those students whom the institution regards as its most successful. Then the questions become: How much weight does the college place on various achievements when it chooses its most successful students? Do the students and faculty have a similar view of undergraduate success? How about graduate and professional school admissions committees?

In this study we have used both approaches. They complement one another, and with each orientation the eventual questions are the same: How is preadmissions information related to different types of success (Chapter 5) and how can the institution be sure it is attracting the students it most wants (Chapter 8)? We first take up the question of how various marks of success are related.

Contrasting types of success

Does the same group of top students tend to account for most instances of outstanding success? Top students were more likely to succeed in other areas than were poor students, but that was certainly not always true. Much depended on what form of success. If one examines different types, it is apparent that a substantial percentage of the students in most of the success categories had cumulative grade averages below the B level; for example, physical accomplishment 64 percent; elected office 43 percent; appointed office 29 percent; other independent accomplishment 20 percent; departmental honors 12 percent; scientific accomplishment 12 percent. From a somewhat different perspective, those students who had a C+ average rarely succeeded in areas related to scholarship, but they were not infrequently in positions of leadership (22 percent). (See Table D.12 in Appendix D for details on the number of students at various grade levels who were successful in different areas.)

The pattern of correlations is another and, in many ways, superior method of understanding the marks of success. Table 4.2 indicates that the correlations ranged from high down to zero, depending upon how different are the various achievements. (See note 1 for Chapter 4 in Appendix C.) What can one make of the pattern of correlations? The pattern for college honors and departmental honors is similar. It is no surprise that these two categories of scholarship are closely related.

The two forms of leadership provide a somewhat different story. An obvious difference in their correlational patterns is that elected leadership is more closely related to physical achievement while appointed leadership is more closely related to scholarship. Evidently

Table 4.2 Correlations among Eight Marks of Success

| | *Schol. Honors* | | *Leadership* | | *Accomplishment* | | | |
	Col.	*Dept.*	*Elect.*	*Appt.*	*Schol.*	*Phys.*	*Organ.*	*Other*
College honors								
Department honors	.70							
Elected leader	.18	.24						
Appointed leader	.41	.38	.27					
Scholastic achievement[a]	.42	.48	.28	.30				
Physical achievement	−.02	−.01	.43	.02	−.11			
Organizing achievement	.28	.28	.40	.45	.38	.00		
Other achievement	.45	.40	.33	.42	.30	.18	.50	

Note: Correlations are tetrachoric. (See note 1 in Appendix C.)
a. Scholastic achievement represents any significant accomplishment in the arts, science, or communications.

when the faculty and staff choose students for positions of responsibility, they lean toward those with high grades, but when students elect their peers, they are influenced to some extent by prowess on the playing field. One is tempted to assume that different values are being expressed here by faculty and students (i.e., whom do you respect?). On the other hand, this pattern of correlations may largely be due to the fact that people pick students whom they know.

That both these measures were moderately well related to organizing achievement and other independent achievement suggests that they do in fact reflect leadership. In Chapter 5 we shall see further confirming evidence of this sort in the similar pattern of preadmissions measures that predict elected and appointed leaders. But why is the correlation between these two only .27? Probably many students engaged in one are less likely to take on the other because of time or other restraints. For example, two of the more common instances of elected and appointed leaders were fraternity presidents and residence hall advisers, respectively. One student is unlikely to hold both positions because of the different living arrangements, if for no other reason.

Among the various accomplishments, scholastic achievement is related more to scholarship, and organizing achievement is related more to leadership, as one would expect. Other independent achievement appears to be related to both, and physical achievement to not much of anything except the elected office connection noted earlier. The pattern of correlations does not suggest that these four accomplishments hang together as a single measurable construct. Again, this may be because students who commit their time and interests to one sphere of activity are, to some extent, less likely to do so in another as well. We have, however, grouped these different accomplishments together partly for descriptive convenience, but also because they do share an important characteristic. In the eyes of the faculty, these students were producers.

Another way of looking at the interrelations is to examine the overlap among the three main categories: scholarship, leadership, and accomplishment. Those three groups were constituted as follows (percentage of all seniors indicated in each case):

Seniors winning these marks of success:	Got credit for:
College honors (26%) Departmental honors (11%)	SCHOLARSHIP (Scholars 30%)
Elected office (18%) Appointed position (23%)	LEADERSHIP (Leaders 35%)

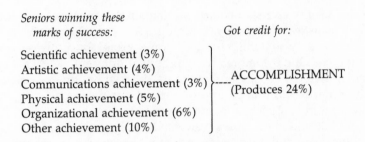

*Seniors winning these
   marks of success:*

Scientific achievement (3%)
Artistic achievement (4%)
Communications achievement (3%) }---- ACCOMPLISHMENT
Physical achievement (5%)   (Produces 24%)
Organizational achievement (6%)
Other achievement (10%)

                                                          Got credit for:

Figure 4.3 shows how the three main groups overlapped (see note 2 in Appendix C). The several segments of the leadership circle totaled 35 percent (14, 7, 8, and 6), which represents the percentage of all seniors who met either of the leadership success criteria. The scholarship circle is somewhat smaller because it represents the 30 percent who won either college or departmental honors. The shaded overlap between the leader and the scholar circles represents that 15 percent (8 plus 7) of the class who were both leaders and scholars.

More than half the seniors (56 percent) were in one or more of these broad success groups. Approximately one student in three achieved one type of success (the white areas combined); one student in six achieved two types of success (the lightly shaded areas); and one in twelve was a triple threat, as football buffs used to say (the darker shaded center). (See note 3.) In comparing any two success groups, typically nearly half the students in one were also in the other.

Women tended to be overrepresented in those areas of Figure 4.3 that involved scholarship. For example, in the white areas of the scholarship circle (scholar only), 58 percent were women while only 47 percent of seniors generally were women.

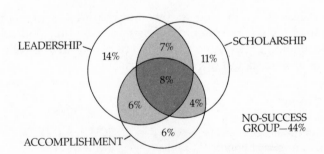

Figure 4.3 Percentage of seniors represented in various combinations of three main success groups—scholarship, leadership, and accomplishment.

How the college viewed success

The second orientation to defining overall success puts the burden on the institution. A key element in our research design was to request from each institution a list of:

> Those students whom the faculty and staff consider overall to be the most successful in having fulfilled the objectives of the college by demonstrating the knowledge, skills, and qualities that the college attempts to foster.

By common agreement among the participating colleges, a committee representative of the faculty and staff was appointed on each campus to determine those forms of success that are relevant to the objectives of the institution, assemble information that indicated such success, solicit informed judgment from faculty and staff as to which students best qualified, and make the final determination on which students should be so designated. The project staff and steering committee purposely avoided giving detailed guidance or suggestions to the institutions so as not to influence the process unduly. The only injunction was that the selection process must be reliable. Suggestions were provided on gathering sufficient information and/or nominations to ensure adequate reliability.

The nine college committees approached this task in various ways. Two committees relied primarily on elaborate selection procedures already in place on the campus to select outstanding students. Another institution developed a definition of what it meant by a most successful student, and then put the actual selection to a vote of all faculty and staff. Two other institutions collected a considerable amount of factual data and then selected students mainly on the basis of decision rules that reflected their own definition of most successful. In the remaining institutions the students were selected by the committees on the basis of accumulated information and nominations.

So what happened? When colleges single out the students of whom they are most proud, are those with top grades routinely included? Do the other types of success cited earlier play much of a role? The striking result was that scholarship, leadership, and accomplishment were correlated to almost exactly the same degree with the "most successful" nomination—.43, .46, and .47, respectively. This outcome certainly reflects the multiple objectives of a liberal education. It is possible, of course, that the fact of going through the process of collecting data on various types of achievement influenced this result.

How did results vary among institutions? The number of students selected varied from 8 percent on one campus to 34 percent on another.

Choices of the most successful students reflected a statistically significant weight on leadership and accomplishment in each of the nine
colleges, though there were variations in emphasis. It is not clear how
much confidence can be placed in such variations. With limited experience and knowledge of results in this type of selection procedure, it
is easy for a committee to put more or less emphasis than intended on
a particular type of achievement. When the institutions were later asked
how much emphasis they believed they were putting on the three main
categories of success in selecting their most successful students, most
indicated roughly equal weights. For purposes of the present analysis,
the pooled group of most successful students selected by nine independent committees likely gives a reasonably accurate view of how institutions such as these view success. With that pooled group we take a
more careful look at how these students were chosen.

The most successful group

Individual students are picked as most successful for various reasons.
It may be very high grades in one case or a specific unusual achievement
in another. But the total group chosen represents an expression of
educational values. One way to understand these values is to examine
a success profile of the group of students chosen as most successful.
Such a profile is shown in Figure 4.4, which gives the percentage of all
seniors and the percentage of the most successful group who won each
of the 10 marks of success.

For example, 60 percent of the most successful group achieved
college honors as compared with 26 percent for the total group of
seniors. The elevation of the profile for the most successful group above
the all-senior line indicates how much the most successful group exceeded the total class on each type of success. Where the incidence of
a given type of success was low (e.g., scientific accomplishment), the
scale is stretched so that the difference between the two profiles is more
accurately represented (see note 5 in Appendix C).

The 10 types are arranged in the figure in the order of that difference from left to right. The fact most obvious in the profile is that the
most successful group exceeded the total group of seniors on all forms
of success. Also, it is clear that while college honors (grades) come first,
this most successful group was also very high on leadership. They were
only slightly above their classmates in arts and athletics.

Another useful way to understand the most successful group is to
develop a model of the nomination process. To construct such a model,
we used the eight marks of success in Table 4.2 to predict which stu-

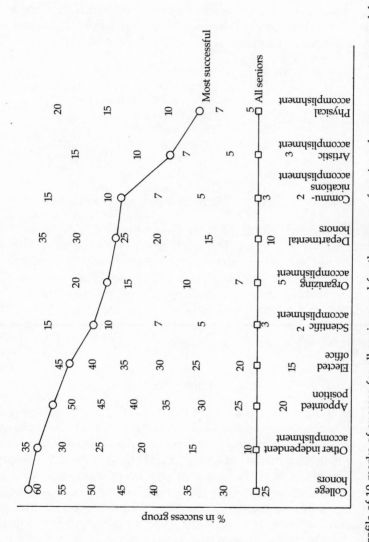

Figure 4.4 Profile of 10 marks of success for all seniors and for the group of seniors chosen as most successful by their college.

dents were nominated as most successful by the faculty (a 0/1 criterion). This procedure serves two purposes. First, it tells us how big a role each of these eight played when the faculty selected the most successful students. Second, it provides a basis for constructing a composite measure of success that may prove to be a criterion that is superior to the nominations themselves. The resulting correlations and standard regression weights were (all significant) as follows:

r	Weight	
.41	.24	College honors
.30	.07	Departmental honors
.36	.19	Appointed leader
.33	.20	Elected leader
.27	.12	Scholastic achievement (artistic, scientific, and communications)
.90	.05	Physical achievement
.25	.08	Organizing achievement
.40	.23	Other independent achievement

These correlations mirror fairly closely the profile of the most successful group in Figure 4.4. The multiple correlation of these measures with the most successful criterion was .63 (equivalent to a biserial correlation of .90). Several other models were tried. When lower-division and upper-division grade point averages were substituted for college honors (which were based on four-year GPA), the multiple correlation and the regression weights for the other predictors remain essentially the same while the GPA regression weights were:

.19	Lower-division GPA
.09	Upper-division GPA

This is a curious result. One would expect that in selecting outstanding students during the senior year, faculty would be more influenced by recent academic achievement in upper-division courses where they are more likely to be personally knowledgeable about the students' work. This result appears to have a significant connection with later discussion of grading patterns. We come back to it in Chapter 6.

Other kinds of success (e.g., completing a double major, being accepted for advanced study) were added to the analysis but did not improve the model. It appears that these eight marks of success account reasonably well for faculty nominations of the most successful students. The heavy weight on college honors is certainly to be expected; the heavy weight on other independent achievement confirmed the content analysis reported earlier. "Other independent achievement" was evidently used often to designate a generally outstanding young man or woman much admired by the faculty and staff of the college—the campus producers often high on scholarship as well as leadership.

That each of these eight measured had a significant weight confirms again that the institutions take a broad view of success. These weights (in raw score form) were used to define a composite measure of "Overall success." There are several potential advantages to such a criterion. It explicitly takes account of various types of achievement for every student. It bases the estimate of overall success upon a number of measures that, taken collectively, likely represent a more reliable measurement than the nomination procedure that simply gives a yes or no for each student. More direct evidence favoring the composite measure over the nomination lies in the fact that the former was somewhat more predictable (i.e., the multiple R based on preadmissions measures was 13 percent higher). (See note 6.)

Another advantage of the overall success composite is that it allows the identification of an equal proportion of successful students at each institution—identified on the basis of objective criteria valued by the institution and possibly less affected by momentary biases that may influence individual committee decisions. Such a success group appears as "top third overall" in Table D.5 in Appendix D. The following groups were at least 5 percent above or below 33 percent representation in this group.

38%	Women
25	Minority students
38	Alumni children
45	Biological science majors
45	Double majors

Contrasting views of success

The model just described is based on the colleges' view of success and, for our purposes here, is a readily defensible way of defining success overall. It is interesting, however, to contrast the colleges' view with that of the students. The most successful students were also selected by peers, who do not necessarily share the views of faculty and staff as to who most deserves to be in that category.

And there is a third way of looking at success overall. Some might argue that the most successful students are those who continue their education in highly selective advanced study (law, medicine, and Ph.D. programs). This is a debatable proposition, since many of the most outstanding undergraduates choose to direct their energies elsewhere.

On the other hand, "Ph.D. productivity" has often been seen as an important measure of the success of an undergraduate college (Astin 1962). In any event, students going on to highly selective advanced study provide an instructive alternative view of success in college.

Purely from a descriptive standpoint, to what extent do these three groups of successful students—college nominees, peer nominees, and those admitted to advanced study—have a similar profile on different achievements in college? We did three regression analyses using scholarship, leadership, and accomplishment as predictors. Table 4.3 shows the results. As previous results in Table 4.2 suggested, the colleges put essentially equal weight on the three. In selecting their peers, students also put substantial weight on all three factors but gave somewhat less emphasis to scholarship, as compared with the faculty. In predicting which students went on to graduate and professional school, scholarship got the heaviest weight.

The size of the multiple correlations in Table 4.3 varies considerably. The college nominations are almost fully determined by the three types of success, the peer nominations less so. This may result mainly from the fact that the college committees had the success data in hand when they did their choosing. Prediction of who goes on to advanced study is less precise because the prediction involves a graduate selection decision as well as a student decision to apply.

Figure 4.5 presents the results in a different way. The object of this display is to show how much difference it actually makes whether a student was or was not in a success group. As in Figure 4.3, the circles represent the three broad success groups: students who were cited for either type of scholarship, either type of leadership, and any of the six types of accomplishment. The shaded areas represent those students who were in more than one of these groups. But in this diagram the

Table 4.3 Weight of Scholarship, Leadership, and Accomplishment in Three Views of Success

View of Success	Standard Scholarship	Regression Leadership	Weights Accomplishment	Multiple R_{bis}
College nominees as most successful	.27	.29	.28	.88
Peer nominees as most successful	.17	.24	.21	.66
Admitted to medical, law, Ph.D. program	.27	.07	.05	.52

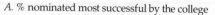

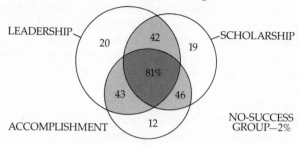

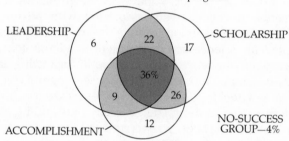

Figure 4.5 Percentage of students with different patterns of success who were— A. nominated as most successful by their college, and B. admitted to a medical, law, or Ph.D. program by spring 1983.

entries represent the percentage of each group who succeeded on a fourth measure—nominated as most successful or accepted for advanced study in a highly selective program. Thus, the diagrams demonstrate graphically the relationship between three independent variables (the three broad types of success) and an overall criterion (e.g., most successful nominees).

Diagram *A* shows that the percentage nominated as most successful increases dramatically with the number of success groups the student was in—2 percent for those in the no-success group to 81 percent for those in all three. Being in two success groups, instead of one, more than doubled a student's chances of being nominated as most successful; being in three almost doubled the odds again. The diagram also shows that the institution's estimate of a student's college career was enhanced by demonstrated competence in one area about as much as another.

Diagram *B* presents a somewhat different picture. Being accepted for advanced study by a highly selective program is a rarer event (11 percent versus 20 percent nominated as most successful), so that entries are generally smaller. More important, the percentages do not increase nearly so rapidly near the center of the diagram, mostly because leadership and accomplishment do little to increase the likelihood that a student will enter such a program. In fact, the single success scholars were about twice as likely to enter one of the selective graduate programs (17 percent) as were those who were cited for both leadership and a significant accomplishment (9 percent). A similar analysis based only on students who intended as freshmen to enter such a program gave a comparable picture—higher percentages but essentially the same pattern.

Diagram B does not tell the whole story, however. Some significant accomplishments in college were associated with advanced study; others were not. Students going into medical or Ph.D. programs were frequently cited for science accomplishment; students going into law were not cited often in science but were cited in organizing accomplishments. Students going into any of the three programs of advanced study were often cited for "other independent accomplishment"—the catchall evidently used to designate generally outstanding students.

In this chapter we have been concerned only with how the students achieved in college, how the different types of success were related to one another, and how those achievements were viewed. A particularly significant finding was that colleges recognize different marks of success in selecting their most successful students. The next question, of course, is how and to what extent success can be predicted and whether colleges can expect to attract the students they want by focusing primarily on academic competence.

5

What Forecasts Success in College?

The nine colleges in the Personal Qualities Project gathered a tremendous amount of information about this class—data about their interests, past accomplishments, personal characteristics (as applicants)—followed by an unusually thorough census of the important achievements of these young people through their college careers. What have we learned? How well can we predict which students are likely to succeed in what ways over four years?

Grades are a principal measure of success. In Chapter 6 we take a careful look at how grades may change as a representation of success year by year. In this chapter we address the central question of this study: What measures forecast different types of success and the most successful student overall?

Careful statistical analysis is a useful way to get at this question, but several caveats come quickly to mind. No matter how structured the schooling, educational experiences and learning outcomes are highly individual. Learning experiences cannot be common because students opt to spend their time in different ways. Learning outcomes cannot be equivalent because what is routine to one student may be life-shaping to another. And certainly for any college student the whole has more meaning than any quantification of the parts.

For all these reasons a statistical analysis of who succeeds is imprecise and often in error in individual cases. There is certainly no expectation that any deterministic model can explain individual student behavior. It is, rather, patterns we are seeking—consistent patterns that may have policy implications as to how institutions might best allocate their resources in trying to attract and select students. It is good to remember also that developing sound admissions strategies is not synonymous with predicting success. Colleges recruit and select students for many reasons that may have little to do with anticipated success—to develop a representative class, to fill particular programs, to maintain institutional ties, etc. (see Willingham 1980, 1983).

Focusing on the more narrow issue of predicting success, there are complications aplenty. It is bad enough that there are scores of possible predictors; they also overlap in various ways. For example, intellectual interests may be related to achieving scholastic honors in college mainly because able students (i.e., those with good previous academic records) are more likely to have intellectual interests. As another example, some measures, like the admissions staff's overall academic rating of an applicant, are based primarily on other information in the candidate's folder. In both examples the critical question is whether the intellectual interests or the high academic rating add unique information to the data already available. So the disarmingly simple question of how much weight different types of evidence deserve in forecasting a particular form of success turns out to be not so simple after all. It depends upon which combination of measures is chosen and how they happen to overlap.

The main predictors

There are two ways of dealing with this complexity. One is to winnow down the preadmissions information into a manageable number of measures. On the basis of preliminary analysis the following measures were selected because they seem the most important and interesting:

A. *Traditional academic predictors*
   High school rank (HSR)
   Admissions test (SAT)

B. *Supplementary achievement measures*
   Objective
   High school honors
   Community achievement
   Athletic achievement
   Leadership
   Creative achievement
   Follow-through
   Work experience

    Narrative
    Personal statement—writing
    Personal statement—content
    School reference

C. *Admissions staff ratings*
    Interview rating
    Flagged for special talent (artistic, athletic, scientific, leadership, or other)
    Flagged for special attribute (maturity, rich experience, cultural background, overcame hardship, work experience, intellectual orientation, unusual references)
    Overall academic rating
    Overall personal rating

D. *Goals and plans*
    Important goal: Career
                   Intellectual
                   Creative
                   Physical
                   Leadership
                   Social
    Uncertain education/career plans
    Educational aspirations

E. *Background characteristics*
    Woman
    Minority student
    Residence
    Socioeconomic status
    Alumni ties
    School type
    School size
    School college-going rate
    Aid applicant
    Early applicant
    Came for interview
    Close-tie school
    College during high school

The main questions

A second way to simplify the problem is to disaggregate it or unpeel it. Toward that end, we have done a number of analyses addressed to various questions at different levels of specificity or that follow a logical sequence related to admissions decisions. For example, the five sets of measures (*A* to *E*) listed above each play a somewhat different role in the admissions process, and they have different implications as potential predictors. We examine these sets of measures in sequence, asking how each contributes to the previous in predicting or otherwise helping to understand different types of success. Thus, the following sections of this chapter are directed to these main questions:

- What preadmissions measures forecast particular marks of success in college? Are some criteria more predictable than others? Does the pattern of predictors vary in important ways?
- When all evidence of achievement in the secondary school track record is considered, what are the best indicators of success in college? How much do the supplemental measures add to the traditional HSR and SAT? How does the pattern vary for scholarship, leadership, and accomplishment?
- Are the ratings of admissions officers good predictors of which applicants are most likely to be successful if admitted? Better than traditional academic predictors? Can admissions staff anticipate different types of success?
- Does an applicant's personal interest or background tell much about his or her likely success in college? Or can apparent relationships between such measures and college success be largely accounted for by the student's track record of achievement in high school?
- To what extent can one predict success when it is defined as persistence or attainment—that is, time to degree, double major, and admission to advanced study?

Notes on analysis

These data posed several problems with respect to statistical analysis. First, the substantial amount of analysis required placed a special premium on devising efficient means of doing so. Second, there was a missing-data problem, which, if handled by any conventional means, would have resulted in the loss of several key variables or an unacceptable reduction in sample size. Third, many of the criteria used here were not continuous scales from high to low, but represented groups of students who achieved particular types of success. Such dichotomous (yes or no) criterion measures are not well suited for linear regression. Finally, despite our efforts to define common standards for different types of success, it was clear that the standard often varied arbitrarily from college to college. This variation confirmed the need to analyze the data within colleges, or an approximation thereof. At the same time it was necessary to pool the results across colleges to identify general trends not confused by small sample fluctuations. Three types of analysis were undertaken to handle these various problems.

First, a number of linear regression analyses were done by college and by means of a specially constructed "senior correlation matrix" of 66 variables, all adjusted for missing data and for college scale differences (see note 1 for Chapter 5 in Appendix C). This matrix permitted the use of several variables where some data were missing, and facilitated far more detailed analysis than would otherwise have been feasible. All linear correlations based on dichotomous criteria are reported here as biserials (see note 2).

Logistic regression was a second method of analysis. With the kind of criterion scores we have here, logistic regression is superior because it gives more accurate predicted scores (which are essential for the following residual analysis) and regression weights that are more comparable from one analysis to another. Figure 5.1 shows why. The curve is a logistic function showing the probability of a student's achieving academic honors at each score level of a preadmissions academic composite based on HSR and SAT. At this institution a student with an academic composite of 50 (point *A*) has a .20 probability of graduating

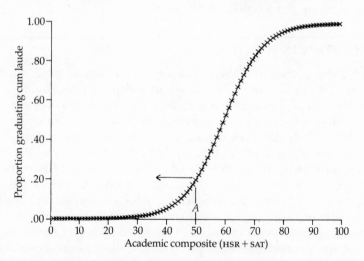

Figure 5.1 Logistic prediction: Number of Kenyon College seniors in different ranges of an academic composite (based on high school rank and test score) and a logistic function showing the proportion in each range who graduated *cum laude*.

cum laude. Thus for any group of students, one can determine the proportion likely to graduate cum laude on the basis of where the individuals fall on the curve. For predicting this two-category criterion (honors–no honors), the logistic function is superior to the usual linear regression model because the logistic function curves to fit the data and stays within the 0 to 1.0 range.

Residual analysis is a third method of investigation that we used extensively. It starts with logistic regression, making use of curves such as that shown in Figure 5.1 to determine for any group of students what proportion are likely to achieve a particular type of success (see note 3 in Appendix C). For example, by this means one can use HSR and SAT to predict how many students with strong references from high school would be expected to win scholastic honors in college. What we are looking for is a residual difference between the predicted and the actual proportion of highly recommended students who earn college honors. If the admissions office considers giving such applicants special preference because of anticipated good performance, the issue is whether the student's residual performance is high. That is, do such students perform better than would be expected on the basis of academic measures normally used in selection? In the following pages this method is used extensively to estimate how much difference, if any, particular characteristics make in forecasting success once other information is taken into account.

WHAT PREDICTS WHAT?

Table 5.1 shows the correlation between various sets of preadmissions measures and eight marks of success in college. College honors and cumulative grade point average (CGPA) give much the same results because these two criteria are essentially the same—the former is based on the latter. Only CGPA is included here. The prediction of yearly GPAs is also an important question that yielded interesting results, but it is a complex topic in its own right. We take it up in detail in Chapter 6.

It is obvious that the two traditional academic predictors, HSR and SAT (lines 1–3 of Table 5.1), were mostly relevant to scholastic types of achievement in college. They even swing a bit negative when it comes to predicting prowess on the playing field (see note 8). Comparing the two, HSR was a somewhat better predictor of college honors (cumulative grade average), while SAT was a better predictor of departmental honors.

Regression weights for the multiple correlations reported in line 4 of Table 5.1 give some indication of how much independent weight each of the achievement measures had in predicting different forms of

Table 5.1 Correlations between Various Sets of Preadmissions Measures and Eight Success Criteria

	No. of Measures		Success Criteria						
		CGPA	Dept. Honor	Elect. Leader	Appt. Leader	Scholas. Accomp.[a]	Phys. Accomp.	Organ. Accomp.	Other Accomp.
1. High school rank (HSR)	1	45	25	12	22	21	-03	11	19
2. Admissions test (SAT)	1	41	32	03	17	22	-22	11	17
3. HSR, SAT	2	53	36	12	25	27	23	14	22
4. HSR, SAT + supplementary measures	12	56	40	24	32	34	51	28	32
5. HSR, SAT + supplementary measure, objective only	9	54	38	23	31	32	50	26	29
6. Admissions ratings	5	51	35	22	26	30	44	22	31
7. Lines 4 and 6	17	58	42	28	33	37	59	32	36
8. HSR, SAT, adm. ratings	7	56	39	23	28	32	46	23	32
9. HSR, SAT, goals and plans	10	55	40	19	28	33	43	23	25
10. All of above	25	59	45	30	34	40	62	35	37

Note: All analyses were based on the senior matrix described in note 1 in Appendix C. Correlations with dichotomous criteria were converted to biserials. $N = 3,442$.
a. See note 8 in Appendix C.

success. These weights are reported in Table D.7 of Appendix D. They must be interpreted with a good deal of caution (see note 6), but several results seem clear.

Corresponding types of accomplishment were clearly linked between high school and college. Physical achievement in high school was by far the best predictor of physical achievement in college. Leadership in school and community were systematically related to those areas of college success that involve leadership. Accomplishment in writing and artistic endeavor (creative talent) was a good indicator of such activity in college (scholastic accomplishment). These results are consistent with those from earlier research (Holland and Nichols 1964; Richards, Holland, and Lutz 1967). They are a good example of an axiom of learning theory: "Past behavior best predicts future behavior." We see other examples of this in Chapter 8.

The pattern of weights also tells us something about the similarities and differences among the success criteria. Recall that college honors were based purely on four-year GPA, but departmental honors depended on successful completion of a substantial piece of scholarly work. The latter would seem to be more characteristic of upper-division, preprofessional work in the discipline. Do the two categories of scholarship call for somewhat different competencies? Not that these measures could reveal. Except for a somewhat heavier weight on the SAT, winning departmental honors seems to depend upon much the same abilities as getting high grades. It is less predictable, however. This is probably because it is less reliable and, like other success criteria included here, a discretionary activity not attempted by all students.

The two leadership types create another point of interest. We observed earlier that different students often tend to hold appointed and elected positions, partly because of the practical difficulties of holding both. Are the two based on similar qualities? Yes, but with interesting differences. Both types of leaders were likely to be better than average students who had been school and community leaders earlier. But those appointed by the college were more likely to be able students who had impressed teachers earlier—they came with good references—while those elected by students often have the benefit of a reputation in sports. This is essentially the same picture we got in Chapter 4, which looked only at the interrelations among different types of success in college.

Four measures do add

We move now to an analysis that gets to the heart of this study—partly because it summarizes critical results and partly because it is a necessary building block for analyses to follow. Given the accumulated college record, we know which students have been cited for outstanding scholarship, leadership, accomplishment. Is the supplemental information helpful in identifying who those students are likely to be? Is a broader view of the high school track record useful in identifying students who are likely to be selected by the college four years later as "most successful" seniors? On both counts the answer is clearly yes. Which information adds most in forecasting success in these three broad areas and overall? The results are shown in Table 5.2.

First, a word on why these particular predictors are included in Table 5.2. An initial task in the analysis was to determine which of the 12 measures in the secondary school track record (categories *A* and *B* in The Main Predictors, the first section of this chapter) were most generally useful in predicting different types of success in college. A number of linear regression analyses against some 20 success criteria indicated several initial conclusions. Work experience made little contribution. The two scores based on the student's personal statement—content and quality of writing—worked better as one combined score, possibly because of improved reliability.

A number of regression analyses against various criteria were carried out to determine how best to represent extracurricular accomplishment in high school (i.e., achievement in community, athletic, leadership, and creative activities, plus follow-through, a special rating of continuous commitment and success in the previous four areas). As would be expected, the best weighted composite of the four types of achievement was always somewhat better than a total rating for the four. Follow-through was typically a better predictor than was the total rating of extracurricular achievement and just as good as a multiple correlation based upon the four types. Also, follow-through consistently added to combinations of these measures. Thus, follow-through appears to be a good way to "score" a student's extracurricular achievement and a good single measure to represent that area of accomplishment (see note 4 in Appendix C).

Now to the results in Table 5.2. The data show that the supplemental indicators of achievement in high school (measures 3–6 in the table) made a substantial contribution to predicting which students are likely to be identified by the college as most successful. Predictions made on the basis of HSR and SAT correlated .36 with this overall measure of success. Adding in the additional four predictors raised the correlation to .45, an increase of 25 percent (or an increase of more than 50 percent in variance accounted for, a yardstick preferred by some). The contribution of the supplementary measures varied considerably, however, depending upon the type of success one is trying to predict.

Table 5.2 Prediction of Four Types of Success: Scholarship, Leadership, Significant Accomplishment, and Those Selected by the College as Most Successful

Preadmissions Measure	Standard Logistic Regression Weights			
	Scholarship	Leadership	Accomplishment	Most Successful
1. High school rank	1.55*	.47*	.52*	1.02*
2. SAT	1.25*	.13	.35*	.58*
3. High school honors	.44*	.20	.20	.41
4. Follow-through	.23	.57*	.60*	.72*
5. Personal statement	.49*	.15	.13	.25
6. School reference	.37	.22*	.32	.52*
R_{bis}[a] (HSR, SAT)	.57	.20	.24	.36
R_{bis} (6 Measures)	.61	.33	.34	.45
Increase in R due to adding measures 3–6	7%	65%	42%	25%

Note: All results are averages for nine colleges (total $N = 3,337$).

a. R_{bis} is a linear correlation between actual criterion scores and scores predicted from logistic regression analyses within each college.

* $P = .01$. (See note 5 in Appendix C.)

The additional information improved the correlation 65 percent for leadership and 42 percent for accomplishment, but only 7 percent for scholarship.

Follow-through was the strongest addition. Among all six measures it had the largest weight in predicting leadership and accomplishment, and the second-largest in forecasting which students were likely to be most successful. The measure high school honors emphasizes academic achievement, so it is not surprising that it mainly contributed to predicting scholarship. But it is not clear why that is true of the personal statement as well. It may be that serious, competitive students are especially prone to take the personal statement seriously, using every device—even correct writing—to gain favorable attention for their candidacy for admission. Interestingly enough, the school reference also made some independent contribution, even though many assume that federal disclosure requirements have robbed references of much of their value.

It is noteworthy that scholarship was much more predictable than the other types of success. This is partly because colleges give far more care and attention to measuring academic competence than other educational outcomes. It also reflects the fact that the other criteria included in Table 5.2 are more heterogeneous than scholarship. Accomplishment, for example, includes several very different types of achievement. Note that physical accomplishment, which is specialized and also usually has clear cut standards for recognizing outstanding achievement, was as predictable as CGPA (line 7, Table 5.1).

The failure of work experience to prove useful as a predictor was disappointing and somewhat unexpected in light of other results found here. Work experience would seem to be an important arena, in addition to school activities, in which students often demonstrate follow-through and achieve significant accomplishments. But neither extent nor level of work experience showed any useful relationship to later success criteria. Why not? It may be that the brief student self-report of work experience available in this study provided a poor indication of work experience. Without the elections and competitions that characterize extracurricular activities, valid measures of work experience may simply require a more systematic description or a more objective third-party assessment.

To sum up, there is information in the student's application other than HSR and SAT that is highly relevant to forecasting who is likely to succeed in college. The important qualification is that the relevance of the information is selective. Supplementary measures of achievement offer limited improvement in predicting scholarship. The importance of such measures in recruiting and selecting students hinges upon what value the college places on leadership and accomplishment as success criteria.

Size of effects

How much do these supplementary measures actually add? More specifically, say an applicant has been a class president or comes with terrific references from the high school. How often do such individuals become scholars, leaders, or producers of significant accomplishments in college? To what extent are they more likely to achieve such success than would be expected on the basis of their high school rank and test scores? Table 5.3 gives some answers.

For each of several high achievements in high school, this table shows the predicted and actual proportion of that group that succeeded in four main areas of success in college: scholarship, leadership, accomplishment, and most successful overall. The predicted figure provides a baseline based only on HSR and SAT. For example, of all students in the study who remained in college through the senior year, 475 had won academic honors in high school. On the basis of their HSR and SAT, half of these would be expected to repeat in college. Actually, 57 percent did. For the first five categories of high school achievement listed here, the high group was defined as all college seniors who had achieved a rating of at least 4 on the preadmissions measure—meaning high recognition in the local community or school. For the remaining four measures, the high group was defined as a rating higher than 4 because the scores tended to run higher.

Table 5.3 illustrates that an applicant can have an outstanding distinction, such as valedictorian or other high honor from secondary school, but that does not necessarily mean that the student will do any better in college than the high expectations based on his or her superior rank and test scores. In this case those with such high school honors were 14 percent overrepresented (.57/.50) in the scholarship success group, but otherwise their college performance was not significantly higher than expected.

One minor note is the apparent similarity between achievement in community activities and school leadership. Achievement in the former is less frequent, though both augur well for success in college. The pattern of predicted and actual success for these two groups is similar.

The results for follow-through are particularly interesting. The sizable group of students who scored at the highest level of this rating (N = 665) were overrepresented by 20 to 30 percent in each of the three main types of college success as well as the most successful category— i.e., even after taking their HSR and SAT scores into account. It seems

Table 5.3 Relationship of High Achievement in Secondary School to Four Types of Success over Four Years in College

Type of High Achievement in High School	N	Percentage Attaining Four Types of College Success							
		Scholarship		Leadership		Accomplishment		Most Successful	
		Pred.	Actual	Pred.	Actual	Pred.	Actual	Pred.	Actual
High school honors	475	.50	.57*	.40	.43	.32	.36	.27	.29
Community activities	231	.32	.36	.35	.44*	.26	.30	.22	.29*
Athletics	1,091	.27	.28	.33	.37*	.25	.29*	.19	.19
Leadership	620	.34	.37	.36	.43*	.28	.34*	.22	.28*
Creative	451	.34	.39*	.36	.40	.28	.36*	.23	.27*
Follow-through	665	.32	.38*	.36	.45*	.28	.35*	.22	.29*
Work experience	284	.29	.29	.34	.40*	.26	.29	.19	.20
Personal statement	1,036	.30	.36*	.34	.39*	.27	.29*	.20	.23*
School reference	430	.34	.38*	.35	.40*	.30	.35*	.21	.27*
All seniors	3,337	.30	.30	.35	.35	.24	.24	.20	.20

* An asterisk on actual figures indicates a significant ($p = .05$) departure from the predicted value for that group. Logistic predictions are based on HSR and SAT. (See notes 3 and 7 in Appendix C.)

reasonable that such a pattern of persistence and cumulative success in secondary school would be related to subsequent leadership and productivity, through it is a bit unexpected that such students should overachieve in scholarship as well. The follow-through rating placed more stress on (and was more highly correlated with) athletic achievement than on the other extracurricular achievements, partly because it was most frequently reported by high school students. But athletic achievement was correlated negatively with every measure of scholastic success in college! Part of the explanation for the apparent contradiction may lie in the fact that a high score on follow-through was possible only if a student showed perseverance and success in two or more different areas—that is, not in sports alone.

We learned earlier in Table 5.2 that the applicant's personal statement and school reference are also useful in forecasting different types of success in college, though not to the extent of follow-through. Table 5.3 shows how much. This raises an interesting practical question. The first seven measures listed in Table 5.3 are reasonably objective in the sense that they are largely visible in the student's record and are, in theory anyway, subject to verification. The student's personal statement and the school reference are another matter. These narrative documents are much less objective. Individual references may be subject to bias, and personal statements can easily be manipulated. Many colleges are experienced and willing to work with such materials. Others are less so. How much of the useful information in the supplementary achievement measures can one realize by sticking only to the more objective information? The answer is quite a bit. As line 5 of Table 5.1 indicates, much of the improvement (over HSR and SAT) in forecasting different types of college success comes from the more objective measures.

But in any institution that actively recruits or practices selective admissions on anything other than a mechanical set of decision rules, there is an inevitable degree of subjectivity. In most colleges the admissions staff has to interpret institutional policy and make judgments as to how much effort to exert in seeking to enroll what types of students. In addition to other institutional objectives that an admissions officer must take into account, that assessment usually involves some estimate of the likelihood that an applicant will do well in some area important to the college. We now get to the question of how effective those judgments are.

ADMISSIONS RATINGS

All of the foregoing results were based on 12 preadmissions achievement measures that reflect the information in each applicant's folder as objectively as possible. These measures either came originally in quantified form (HSR and SAT) or were based on ratings by trained research assistants. Since the ratings were assigned on carefully prescribed standards (see *Personal Qualities*) and without knowledge of other facts about the applicant, these measures are reasonably independent one from the other and comparable from college to college.

We also wanted to get from each college its views on its applicants—views based on the total folder and reflecting the institution's orientation to admissions. Admissions staff at the participating colleges provided three types of ratings on their applicants. First, the interview protocol was rated in all instances where an applicant came to the campus and talked with a staff member. Second, applicants were flagged for any of several special talents or attributes that were judged sufficiently noteworthy to influence positively an admissions decision (these are listed in The Main Predictors early in this chapter). Thus, each flag generated a group of individuals marked by that particular qualification. Many of these groups were quite small, even nonexistent at some colleges. For correlational analysis it was necessary to collapse the flags into two categorical measures: any talent and any attribute. Third, each applicant was assigned an overall academic and personal rating (5-point scale) that took into account all information in the folder.

For our research purposes, these five measures—the interview rating, two flag measures, and two overall ratings—represent the admissions staff's assessment of the applicant. How well does this assessment predict different types of success? How does it compare with the analyses just described?

Going back to Table 5.1, we see that line 6 shows multiple correlations between the admissions ratings and various marks of success. The correlations are typically as high as or higher than those for HSR and SAT (compare line 6 and line 3). It is evident, however, that the admissions ratings are largely dependent upon what the staff sees in the folder. Both HSR and SAT are salient parts of that record because, as we confirmed in *Personal Qualities,* these are the best predictors of who will be admitted and who will make good grades in the freshman year. The better question is how admissions ratings go beyond HSR and SAT in forecasting success.

Table 5.4 helps to get at that question by showing predicted and actual success rates of various groups of students rated high by admissions staff for different reasons. One interesting result comes right at the top of this table. We found in *Personal Qualities* that applicants who had an outstanding interview were much more likely to be admitted than their HSR and SAT scores would indicate. Four years later we find no evidence at all that this group has performed any better than their

Table 5.4 Relationship of High Ratings by Admissions Staff to Four Types of Success over Four Years in College

		Percentage Attaining Four Types of Success							
		Scholarship		Leadership		Accomplishment		Most Successful	
College Rating	N	Pred.	Actual	Pred.	Actual	Pred.	Actual	Pred.	Actual
Outstanding interview	384	.34	.35	.37	.39	.25	.26	.23	.22
Talent flag:									
Artistic	307	.36	.40	.37	.39	.30	.41*	.21	.26*
Leadership	227	.34	.41*	.34	.48*	.32	.42*	.21	.31*
Athletics	491	.24	.22	.33	.37*	.26	.34*	.17	.19
Any talent	971	.30	.32	.34	.39*	.28	.36*	.19	.24*
Attribute flag:									
Maturity	246	.46	.52*	.40	.45	.33	.41*	.28	.36*
Outstanding references	226	.36	.41	.35	.45*	.31	.40*	.21	.30*
Intellectual orientation	124	.52	.66*	.37	.37	.34	.44*	.24	.24
Rich experience	316	.29	.30	.34	.40*	.27	.30	.19	.22
Culture background	156	.22	.15*	.31	.35	.30	.34	.15	.17
Any attribute	922	.34	.36	.35	.39*	.30	.33*	.21	.24*
High overall rating									
Academic (5)	351	.53	.60*	.48	.53*	.29	.36*	.33	.38*
Personal (5)	333	.32	.36	.41	.47*	.23	.32*	.26	.33*
All seniors	3,337	.30	.30	.35	.35	.24	.24	.20	.20

* An asterisk on actual figures indicates a significant ($p = .05$) departure from the predicted value for that group. Logistic predictions are based on HSR and SAT. (See notes 3 and 7 in Appendix C.)

rank and test scores alone would lead one to expect. This and related analyses revealed no basis for expecting that the admissions interview can be useful in identifying successful students—its influence on admissions decisions notwithstanding!

Students flagged for evidence of unusual talents or attributes, however, did frequently exceed expectations. As the table shows, some flags were not valid contributors beyond HSR and SAT, through in many instances the flagged group was overrepresented in the success category by 20 to 30 percent—in one case even 50 percent. Where there is a direct comparison, the pattern of such differences is quite similar to that observed earlier with the supplementary achievement measures. Artistic (creative) talent, leadership, athletics, and references can be so compared with the results in Table 5.1. The groups identified by flags are more frequently successful, but that would be expected because these are all more select groups. If one compares the two methods of identification by correlating the talent with the most relevant later success, it appears that the two procedures (research staff ratings versus admissions staff ratings) are equally predictive. Outstanding references may be a minor exception—possibly because admissions officers sometimes obtain more candid information on the telephone than appears in writing.

The overall academic and personal ratings presumably take account of these special talents and attributes to some degree. Results here also confirm a general conclusion: The admissions staff assessment of applicants clearly adds to HSR and SAT. The next question is whether the admissions staff ratings add to the carefully constructed full record of HSR, SAT, and 10 supplementary achievement measures. Line 7 of Table 5.1 suggests that the answer is a qualified yes. The multiple correlation in line 7 is always larger than the corresponding one in line 4, but not by much. One useful way of thinking about these data is to consider the more holistic admissions rating (line 6) and the more objective supplementary measures (line 4) as complementary. Each adds something to the other. The objective measures add more because the validity coefficients in line 4 are consistently higher than those in line 6.

How evidence complements

What does each add? What does the admissions officer see that is not clear in the record? What is in the record that the admissions officer does not see—or at least does not give sufficient heed to? We used partial correlation techniques to detect where the admissions ratings were significantly related to the success criteria even after taking account of all 12 of the achievement measures. There appear to be three main areas where admissions staff consistently add a small but significant bit of forecasting.

The academic rating reflects some intelligence not found anywhere else in the record as to who is likely to earn good grades (partial r = .17). Whether it is knowledge of the secondary school (a persistent idea negated by several studies—see Lindquist 1963; Linn 1966; Willingham 1963c), keen assaying of the high school courses on the transcript, or whatever, is not clear. Second, the academic and the personal ratings reflect to a small degree a sense of who is likely to be most successful in the college—that is, a hunch that adds some .04 to the multiple correlation beyond the objective record. Finally, the admissions staff has some unique information as to who is likely to succeed in the physical area. Here it is no mystery whence the insight springs. Students were often flagged for athletic ability because they were on the coach's recruiting list—often based on a sophisticated and painstaking assessment.

What aspects of the student's track record are useful in forecasting success above and beyond the judgments reflected in the ratings assigned by admissions staff? There are three areas where the admissions ratings do not appear to take full or accurate account of the record. The most obvious is predicting scholastic success. All three of the main academic predictors—HSR, SAT, high school honors—have a significant correlation with the four-year grade average after the admissions ratings are partialled out (.21, .15, and .14, respectively). Which is to say, these measures are useful in identifying the better academic achievers in college, even among applicants who receive identical academic ratings from the admissions staff.

Particular extracurricular achievements, notably creative and athletic, were more useful in predicting parallel accomplishment in college than is reflected in admissions ratings (partial correlations of .15 and .34, respectively). Similarly, follow-through had useful prognostic information about college leadership that was not fully recognized in the admissions ratings (r_p = .14). Finally, in predicting which students would end up most successful overall, follow-through made more of a contribution to admissions ratings than did any other aspect of the student's track record (r_p = .13).

BACKGROUND CHARACTERISTICS AND PLANS

The preadmissions measures discussed up to now all reflect previous student achievement in one way or another. All were either direct measures of talent or accomplishment or ratings of different types of achievement. It is reasonable to think of such measures as potential predictors of success in college and to evaluate them on that basis. But what about all the other student characteristics that may play a role in recruitment and selection of students? In carrying out its job, the admissions staff must often take into account sex, ethnicity, alumni ties, secondary school origin, intended major, and so on. What role do such background characteristics and student interests play in enrolling students who are likely to succeed?

It is important to recognize again that a college has various objectives in mind when it works to attract and enroll a freshman class. Some students may get preference because they help to balance the class. Others may get preference in the interest of maintaining effective institutional ties. Unusual prospects for a successful college career may not be an important consideration in either group. Nevertheless, it is useful to know how various groups of students perform so that all sides of an admissions policy can be better informed and weighed.

Also, there are endless hunches and versions of delivered wisdom about how different students perform, who tends to overachieve, etc. There is research literature on some student characteristics, and we have cited examples. Here too, the great majority of research on predicting success in college is restricted to the freshman year. Studies that go beyond the freshman year are concerned almost exclusively with GPA. Exceptions include parts of the retention literature and a few studies described in Chapter 2. But in large part, the results in Table 5.5 provide a new view of how different types of students succeed in college. Take note that the predicted values in this table are based on six predictors: HSR, SAT, high school honors, follow-through, the personal statement, and the school reference. The question here is whether students with particular background characteristics are more or less likely to do well in college than their full secondary school track record would indicate.

Personal characteristics

The women in this study were more likely to graduate with academic honors than were the men (36 percent versus 25 percent). About half of that difference was due to the fact that the women were somewhat more able (mostly due to higher HSR). But to a small degree the women did achieve honors more often then predicted. This result is consistent with Clark and Grandy's (in press) recent review of sex differences in academic achievement. They suggest that half of the apparent female advantage in overachievement may be due to sex differences in choice of major. That possibility is reflected here in a somewhat larger pro-

Table 5.5 Relationship of Background Characteristics to Four Types of Success over Four Years in College

| | | Percentage Attaining Four Types of College Success | | | | | | | |
| Background Characteristics | N | Scholarship | | Leadership | | Accomplishment | | Most Successful | |
		Pred.	Actual	Pred.	Actual	Pred.	Actual	Pred.	Actual
Women	1,559	.33	.36*	.37	.37	.25	.25	.24	.24
Minority	113	.16	.09*	.30	.37	.24	.29	.16	.21
Local resident	353	.32	.32	.37	.36	.22	.21	.25	.25
400+ mile resident	871	.27	.28	.35	.36	.25	.25	.21	.19
Socioeconomic status									
High	539	.31	.32	.35	.36	.25	.26	.20	.23
Low	400	.29	.24*	.35	.35	.24	.24	.22	.18*
Parent alumni	310	.26	.25	.34	.40*	.25	.22	.20	.24*
Sibling alumni	272	.28	.31	.36	.35	.23	.22	.21	.23
School type									
Small public	137	.32	.38	.35	.42	.25	.27	.24	.26
Large public	661	.32	.34	.36	.38	.24	.27	.22	.22
Private (67% to col.)	505	.21	.23	.30	.28	.22	.21	.14	.12
Public (67% to col.)	405	.28	.31	.34	.39*	.23	.27*	.19	.22
Public (33% to col.)	405	.37	.36	.39	.40	.26	.26	.29	.27
Aid applicant									
Aided	849	.35	.35	.37	.42*	.28	.32*	.25	.28*
Not Aided	455	.32	.28*	.38	.36	.26	.25	.24	.23
Early applicant	697	.32	.34	.36	.39	.26	.26	.21	.22
Came for interview	1,610	.30	.30	.36	.37	.25	.25	.22	.21
Close-tie school	871	.24	.24	.32	.33	.22	.23	.17	.17
College during h.s.	201	.37	.37	.36	.39	.30	.26	.25	.22

* An asterisk on actual figures indicates a significant ($p = .05$) departure from the predicted value for that group. Logistic predictions are based on the six preadmissions measures listed in Table 5.2. (See note 3 and 7 in Appendix C.)

portion of men than women majoring in natural science where, as we see in Chapter 6, the grading standard appears to be tougher than in other areas.

Because of the small number of minority students available in this study, the underrepresented minorities (black, Hispanic, and American Indian) were analyzed as a group. As Table 5.5 indicates, this group was academically less qualified at entry than the average student at these colleges, and was less likely to graduate with honors than would be predicted on the basis of their previous record of achievement. This group was somewhat more likely to achieve success in leadership and accomplishment, but the differences were not significantly higher than predicted values. In examining black and Hispanic students separately, we found that black students alone were significantly overrepresented in the leadership and accomplishment success groups (more than a third over the number predicted), while the two groups showed a similar, though separately insignificant, pattern of lower academic achievement than predicted (see note 10 in Appendix C).

Students from families with a low socioeconomic (SES) level, who were mostly majority students, also tended to achieve academic honors less frequently than expected. This result was not mirrored at the other end of the SES scale; high SES students succeeded at about the levels expected. The several significant residuals associated with aided or nonaided groups probably reflect a tendency of the colleges to aid the more promising aid applicants when all requests cannot be met.

What about students who have some apparent tie to the college? Local residents frequently have such a tie. Applicants who come to the campus for an interview or, even more, those who apply as early applicants may arguably have a bit more affinity to the college. The same may be true of students from close-tie schools from which the college has recruited many students. Certainly such ties are present when a sibling or a parent has attended the college. It is not unreasonable to hypothesize that such students might more readily adjust to college and do well there. Do they? Of these various groups the only one that was overrepresented in a success group in Table 5.5 were the legacies—students with alumni parents. This group was successful beyond expectations, mainly in the area of leadership.

Otherwise these data provide little evidence for assuming that students with some tie to the college are more or less likely to do well than their qualifications would indicate. Justification for giving such students preference in admissions (which they tended to receive) is properly based on other institutional objectives. The prior record speaks for itself.

School background

The question of whether a particular type of secondary school provides a better education has always been a matter of intense interest and debate among educators and the public. It was not a purpose of this study to evaluate educational outcomes of different types of schools, nor do we have the data necessary to do so. What we do have is some information on one particular question: Is there evidence that students from different types of schools are likely to be more or less successful in college than a careful evaluation of their secondary record would indicate?

As to type of control, these data give very little indication that graduates of either private (independent) or public schools are likely to succeed beyond expectations in any of the areas examined. (Parochial schools were unreliably identified in our data so their graduates could not be analyzed.) Also, there were no differences among small, medium, and large public high schools as to predicted versus actual success in any areas. (See note 9 in Appendix C for a definition of these groups and the proportion of the students in each.)

Our data file included one measure that many assume is related to the quality of the secondary school—the proportion of seniors going on to college. To compare students from public and private schools that are similar in that respect, we identified all students from schools that report sending at least two-thirds of their graduates to college. Similarly for comparison, we identified graduates of public schools that reported sending no more than one graduate in three on to college. The most obvious and interesting difference among these three groups is their qualifications at entry. As Table 5.5 indicates, the proportion of these groups predicted to win college honors was .21, .28, and .37, respectively. The proportions of the three groups expected to be designated most successful vary even more. The main reason for those different predictions is their high school rank. In these three groups 18 percent, 38 percent, and 67 percent had been in the top decile of their high school class. Once we take account of these substantial differences at entry, the actual success rates tend to follow expectations fairly closely. The exception occurs among students from public schools that send many students to college. In this group there were somewhat more leaders and somewhat more were cited for significant accomplishments than predicted.

Goals and plans

Up to now we have considered three kinds of preadmissions information: the track record of achievement, the admissions staff's evaluation of the applicant, and the student's background. But young people come to college with their own intention and purpose. Does knowledge of an individual student's goals and plans offer any improvement in predicting success? Or, from another angle, students come to college with different interests and competencies manifest in their achievements. Is there any evidence that the freshman who *declares* a particular interest or commitment is any more likely to achieve in that area than her or his particular track record would indicate?

Going back to Table 5.1, we see the extent to which eight measures of goals and plans (listed as D in The Main Predictors early in this chapter) add useful information in predicting different criteria. The student's goals and plans do add consistently to HSR and SAT in predicting success in college (compare lines 9 and 3), but not so much as do the supplementary achievement measures (line 4).

To see whether goals and plans made any significant contribution to the track record, a number of residual analyses were undertaken using the same six predictors upon which Table 5.5 was based. In general, students who indicated that a particular educational goal was very important (e.g., developing intellectual skills or social competence) were not more likely to end up in a success group than would be expected on the basis of their track record. The same was true of groups of students who gave particular reasons for having chosen the college they did. There were a few exceptions. Students expressing a strong interest in extracurricular and physical activity were overrepresented in the leadership and accomplishment success groups. There were two other interesting patterns. One small group (10 percent of the class) who had expressed strong interest in community and social problems were more often college leaders than predicted (.42 versus .35). Another small group who were much concerned with ethical, moral, and religious issues were more likely than expected to be identified by their college as most successful (.31 versus .25).

For the most part, knowing a student's career plan (or whether he or she had one) offered little help in forecasting success in college. Premedical and prelaw students were exceptions. Both groups were somewhat overrepresented in the most successful group—because of leadership achievement, not scholarship! Of course the much smaller groups who actually gained admission to medical or law school immediately after graduation were highly successful on all counts. An interesting small group ($N = 95$) were those who, as freshmen, planned an artistic career. They were overrepresented in scholarship and accomplishment by one-third and were five times as likely to be cited for significant artistic accomplishment as was the typical freshman. On the other hand, this group was one-third less likely to be leaders. The number identified as most successful overall was at about the level predicted.

Going back to the initial question, does knowledge of the student's goals and plans help in forecasting who is likely to be successful in college? The bottom line of Table 5.1 suggests a summative answer. Line 10 shows multiple correlations based on all 25 measures combined—the full track record, the admissions staff ratings, and the goals and plans reported by the student. Information about the student's goals and plans clearly adds to the track record (compare line 10 and line 4); it also adds to the judgment of the admissions staff (compare line 10 and line 6). But notice that line 10 adds very little to line 7. Evidently, whatever useful predictive information there is in the student's report on goals and plans is already taken into account by the achievement measures and the admissions officer's appraisal.

ATTAINMENT

All the college success measures considered up to now have been concerned with the level of accomplishment. That is, which students achieve at a high level in the eyes of faculty and staff. As we have seen—and as one would expect—preadmissions measures of competence give a reasonably good indication of which students are likely to achieve such success. There is another way of looking at success— namely, how the student progresses through the educational system. Measures of progress are sometimes referred to as attainment. Indicators included here are persistence to the senior year, time to degree, double major, and admission to advanced study. Such measures of attainment depend partly upon the student's competence, but also reflect students' personal decisions based on their experiences during college. Trying to unravel those decisions would have been a major project in its own right, and that was not our purpose. We do address in the following paragraphs the same question that parallels the previous discussion: To what extent can one forecast measures of attainment from preadmissions information?

Persistence

As we have seen, scholarship is reasonably well predicted by evidence of academic competence. So if a college wishes to have more scholars in the student body, it can accomplish that goal to some degree by attracting more students with high test scores and high rank. Does the same logic hold for retaining students? Are more academically able students more likely to persist?

When all the students were pooled into one analysis, there was a positive relationship ($R_{bis} = .29$) between persistence and the preadmissions measures of academic competence (HSR plus SAT). But that relationship was much lower within individual colleges. In fact, the correlation was not even significant in six of the nine colleges. This apparent inconsistency is due to the fact that there was a very high relationship ($r = .79$) between the average academic composite (HSR + SAT) for a freshman class and its persistence rate. The correlation between college selection rate and college dropout rate was even higher ($r = .90$).

The college attended evidently plays a dominant role here. This is demonstrated by the fact that the student-based multiple R_{bis} between HSR and SAT with persistence increased from .29 to .39 when the college attended was taken into account—i.e., when college dummy variables were added to the regression analysis. The correlation was .37 using only the dummy variables! In other words, once you know the college attended, HSR and SAT added little useful information in forecasting who would persist to the senior year.

Table 5.6 shows how much persistence rates varied for students with very high and low HSR and SAT scores in a college with a hypothetically average selection rate. These estimates are based on logistic regression analysis including HSR, SAT, and college selection rate as predictors. The illustrative SAT points are arbitrary extremes near the top and bottom of the overall freshman distribution; the HSR points represent a comparable spread (about three and a half standard deviations). The point of the table is unambiguous. Within these individual institutions, even quite large differences in high school rank and test scores are associated with differences in persistence rates of only some .10 to .15. A glance at Figure 5.1 shows, on the other hand, that such extreme HSR and SAT scores are associated with quite large differences in the probability of a student's earning academic honors.

Table 5.6 Proportions of Students at Extreme High School Rank and SAT Scores Who Persisted to the Senior Year (at a Medium Selective College)

Standardized High School Rank	SAT Score	
	350	650
67	.69	.82
32	.58	.73

Note: Entries are predictions based on logistic regression of persistence on HSR, SAT, and college selection rate. In this example, the last was set at .51, the average selection rate for these colleges.

Why is there such a modest relationship here between preadmissions measures of academic ability and persistence in individual colleges? The revealing line of evidence is the relationship between the student's current GPA and probability of not returning the following year. We reported in *Personal Qualities* that for those freshmen who had less than a C average, the lower the GPA, the higher the probability of dropping out. That fits the conventional wisdom. But the significant fact was that for the great majority of freshmen who had a C or better average (88 percent), withdrawal was quite unrelated to grade average. That is, C− students, B− students, and A− students were about equally likely to return.

We repeated this analysis at the end of the second year and got essentially the same results. Among those sophomores with an overall GPA in the range of 1.5 to 2.0, one in four did not return the next year. Among those with GPAs less than 1.5, about three in five called it quits. In this low grade range, the lower the GPA, the less likely the student was to return. But altogether these students with grade averages below 2.0 constituted only 8 percent of all sophomores. For the great majority above 2.0, there was little association between cumulative average and withdrawal rate (11 percent withdrawal in the 2.0–2.5 GPA range, 7 percent in the 3.5–4.0 GPA range).

Surely a student's decision to drop out of college is complicated by many considerations that may interact with a personal impression of progress—academic or otherwise. Despite the stable persistence rate of students with GPAs ranging all the way from 2.0 to 4.0, grades may well influence retention—discouraging some weak students and inciting some strong students to seek challenges elsewhere. It does appear, however, that the GPA has a direct bearing on withdrawal (forced or voluntary) mainly when the student is in academic jeopardy. This gives a different perspective on the problem and poses a different question; namely, how many dropped out while in academic jeopardy?

It would be useful to know whether students who withdrew were on academic probation at the time, but the study did not collect that information and it is not possible to reproduce probation status exactly from GPA records because of the complex manner in which academic standards are defined in some individual colleges. The probation standard is usually about C− and typically goes up a bit each year. So, for research purposes, academic jeopardy seems reasonably approximated as follows: a freshman cumulative GPA below 1.7, sophomore below 1.8, and junior below 1.9.

With this definition, approximately one dropout in five was in academic jeopardy at the time he or she withdrew. This means that about one entering student out of twenty eventually dropped out while in academic jeopardy. How is this related to the observation that the three less selective colleges in this group had substantially higher withdrawal rates than the three most selective? It is true that the less selective colleges admitted a larger proportion of students who later withdrew in academic jeopardy (8 percent versus 2 percent). It is also true that in the less selective colleges a larger proportion of students withdrew who were not in academic jeopardy (28 percent versus 6 percent). In these nine institutions anyway, it looks as though there is a very heavy nonacademic element in the question of who persists to a degree.

These results illustrate (and also require appreciation of) an important fact about "dropout." It is, in some respects, a basket term that covers different types of students and circumstances: the able student who switches to a special program of interest at another college, the man who gets bored, the woman who has a job opportunity that cannot be refused, the academic failure, students who lose their personal bearings, and so on. Individual cases may be good, bad, or indifferent, depending on the point of view. From the standpoint of maintaining stable enrollment, however, a student lost is a student lost whether it is because of personal or academic considerations.

All of this suggests that through self-selection and institutional selection, most applicants who are not likely to pass are screened out early and that most dropouts occur for other, personal reasons. Why there is such a strong relationship between college selectivity (or average HSR and SAT) and retention rate is no clearer now than when we reported it in *Personal Qualities*, but that relationship is consistent with the finding reported elsewhere (Peng and Fetters 1978) that more selective colleges tend to have lower dropout rates. Possibly more selective colleges attract more students with stronger academic commitments.

If the decision to leave a particular college is often due to personal factors, is it possible to find other preadmissions indicators of persistence? In general, the supplementary achievement measures from secondary school were of little help in anticipating dropouts. Followthrough was an exception. Among the freshmen who scored high (5) on follow-through; 16 percent dropped out before the senior year; among those scoring low (1 or 2), 32 percent failed to persist. Half of that difference, however, was associated with the fact that students with high follow-through scores were likely to go to colleges that have characteristically low dropout rates.

Several background characteristics of these students showed some relationship to persistence. A number of studies have identified various characteristics that are often associated with persistence (see Ramist

1981 for a recent overview). Such data are difficult to interpret because background characteristics and retention rates vary, sometimes markedly, from one institution to another. The following figures compare actual dropout rates with an expected dropout rate that takes into account which college the students attended:

	Dropout Rate	
Background Characteristic	*Expected*	*Actual*
Age under 17	.20	.28
Minority student	.21	.37
Mother, no college	.24	.28
Father, no college	.25	.32
Public school, 67% college attendance	.23	.18
Came for interview	.22	.20
Early applicant	.21	.18
Close-tie school	.24	.20

Two trends are suggested in these results. One is that persistence has some connection with a lower socioeconomic level—though financial aid applicants were not more likely to drop out. There is considerable information in the retention research literature suggesting that SES is associated with persistence. Another suggestion in the data above is that students who have some affinity for the college may be more likely to persist—though surprisingly, students with alumni ties were not more likely to stay in the family alma mater. In general, these relationships with background characteristics were small and provide a poor basis for improving retention through selective recruitment and enrollment. For predicting dropouts, we also found very little useful information in admissions staff ratings, student goals, reasons for attending their chosen college, or career plans.

The analysis of persistence through four years gives much the same picture as persistence through one year as reported in *Personal Qualities*. The best way to predict the likelihood of dropping out was to know where the student enrolled. In the type of institution represented here, improving retention through more careful admission does not appear at all promising. Becoming more selective would likely improve the retention rate, but over the next decade that is an unlikely prospect for most colleges.

Degree attainment

We assumed here that persisting to the senior year is, for all practical purposes, essentially the same as graduating. There are, however, two other measures having to do with degree attainment that might be viewed as success criteria. One is the amount of time to attain a degree, which we coded simply as early, on-time, or late. Another is the number of degrees attained or, more accurately stated, whether or not the student exerted the extra effort to complete degree requirements in two majors. It is debatable how important either of these measures is as a success criterion. But graduating on time is preferable to being late, other things being equal. The same is true of completing a double major, if that serves the student's educational purposes. Rather than place a value on these outcomes, we address a narrow question: To what extent are these two aspects of degree attainment characteristic of particular types of students or otherwise predictable from preadmissions information?

The quick answer is that neither of these measures was much related to anything. It is true that the more able students are somewhat more likely to graduate on time and do more frequently major in two areas. In both cases, however, the multiple correlation with HSR and SAT was on the order of .15, and that figure was not raised appreciably by including other achievement measures from secondary school. Nor were admissions staff ratings related to these criteria.

As for goals and plans, students planning graduate or professional education were a bit more likely to graduate on time. Students with either a track record of achievement or expressed interest in physical activities were less likely than most students to work on two majors. The opposite was true of creative talent; these students with strong interests or achievement were more likely to double-major. One curious result did emerge. The nine colleges include a substantial number of students who declare prelaw or premed as a likely curriculum interest. The prelaw students were academically average freshmen; 24 percent were double majors. The premed students were clearly above average freshmen (half had SAT scores above 600); only 12 percent were double majors.

Advanced study

For some students undergraduate education is a way station to graduate or professional school. Success in college for these students is much associated with gaining admission to postgraduate training, which may be seen as the site of real action in the unfolding life plan. Furthermore, which students are admitted to selective programs of advanced study represents, in part, the view of graduate and professional schools as to who has succeeded at the previous level.

To some degree, college faculty and administrators are also inclined to see confirmation of college success when one of their students is accepted by a highly selective and prestigious program of advanced study. There was, in fact, a flurry of research in the 1960s based on the narrow, but then fashionable, view that the proportion of college graduates later attaining a Ph.D. is a useful measure of institutional "productivity."

For the purposes of this study, the success criterion "admitted to advanced study" was defined as having been accepted to a medical, law, or Ph.D. program as of late spring in the fourth undergraduate year. This restrictive definition (which only 11 percent of seniors met) was adopted to ensure that the criterion was clearly selective but also available and accurate at the time final data were collected on the class. The participating colleges felt that they did have largely correct information in late spring on all students likely to be accepted by any such program for the following fall. This measure is useful for research purposes, but is clearly incomplete in not taking account of students who later elect to pursue these programs of study.

Let us say an institution is interested in increasing the proportion of its alumni in graduate and professional schools. Is it possible to predict before college entry who is likely to pursue successfully such advanced study? To what extent and on what basis? As it turns out, prediction of this success criterion is the simplest of all to describe. The principal findings were these:

- HSR and SAT predicted advanced study equally well ($r_{bis} = .25$); the multiple R_{bis} was .32.
- Neither supplementary achievement measures nor admissions ratings improved that prediction.
- The entering freshman's stated intention to go to graduate or professional school did add substantially to HSR and SAT in predicting which students actually did ($R_{bis} = .42$). In fact, the regression weight for this stated intention was slightly larger than for HSR or SAT (.14, .09, and .11, respectively).
- The student's career goal (especially professional versus business) did provide some additional indication of who would enter advanced study immediately after college, though no other educational goals or background characteristics were related to this success criterion to any significant degree.

It is important to recognize that we are not here predicting selection decisions of graduate and professional schools. This success criterion results rather from the joint effect of students' decisions to apply and

6

Predicting Grades through Four Years

To most students there is not much ambiguity in the question, "How are you doing in college?" If it is anything more than a rhetorical question or social gambit, the student on the receiving end of that query will likely assume that it means, "What sort of grades are you getting?" Without doubt, the grade point average is the main available indicator of a student's performance in college. It is the carefully accumulated index, course by course, term by term, that determines academic standing, follows a student for years, and tells how she or he responded to the academic challenge. Considering the importance of that grade record, it is unaccountable that colleges and researchers have undertaken so little systematic analysis of grades through the undergraduate years. For the purposes of this study, the important issue is whether prediction of upper-division grades indicates that academic success at that level is any different from success in the lower division.

As noted earlier, the great bulk of prediction research has focused exclusively on the freshman year. Examining the relationship between preadmissions measures and grades beyond the freshman year can shed light on several important questions. How well do the traditional academic measures predict success over the full period of undergraduate study? Is there any systematic change through the four years? What can the pattern of best predictors in the early and later years tell us about the nature of academic performance in the lower and upper division? In validating admissions measures against college grades, is it safe to rely primarily on the freshman year? In this chapter we address such questions by examining grade prediction year by year.

There are two ways of evaluating how well preadmissions measures predict grade point averages year by year. One is to use the cumulative grade point average based on all coursework completed up to the end of each successive year. Another is to use grade point averages based only on coursework taken during each of the four years. Figure 6.1 shows the multiple correlations of high school rank (HSR) and SAT score with each of these GPAs, computed as indicated.

The results are obviously quite different. When the full grade record is the criterion, HSR and SAT predicted academic standing essentially as well after the fourth year as the first. There was little variation from college to college; in eight of the nine institutions the validity of the cumulative average was within .04 of validity for the first year. In other words, the principal measures used to assess academic potential did hold up over four years in forecasting the rank order of students. This result is typical of previous findings that have supported the argument that first-year GPA is a satisfactory surrogate for the cumulative GPA for the full four years.

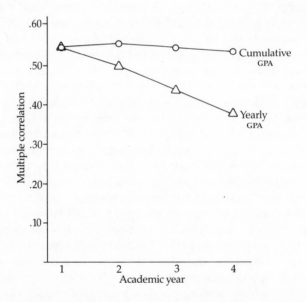

Figure 6.1 Prediction of cumulative and yearly grade point average from high school rank and SAT score (based upon senior correlation matrix; $N = 3,442$).

Averages for the individual years, however, became successively less predictable. The average drop was .17, and all colleges showed the same progressive decline (.10 or greater in each). Now it is not unreasonable to view the cumulative average as more important than the yearly average. It is the cumulative average, after all, that represents the full record upon which students are judged to decide who graduates and who deserves honors. But what is the significance of that consistent decline in the predictability of the yearly average? (See note 7 for Chapter 6 in Appendix C.)

Does the decline in the predictability of yearly GPAs suggest that there is something different about the academic demands of the upper division? Have the preadmissions measures therefore become less relevant in some way, or perhaps outdated in the passage of time? If that were so, it might be that other measures from the secondary level would give a better indication of academic achievement in the third and fourth years, and depending upon how much importance a college attaches to work in the upper division, it might find reason to modify its selection strategy.

Thus, one should not necessarily relax because the cumulative GPA is as predictable after four years as after one year. Whether these two criteria are "statistically interchangeable" from a practical admissions standpoint, as Wilson (1983) has argued, is really a question of whether they are best predicted by the same preadmissions measures. If they are, then the same applicants will be identified as academically promising by use of one criterion or the other, regardless of whether the four-year validity is higher or lower. But if a somewhat different set of measures best predicts the two criteria, then somewhat different applicants will be identified as promising students, depending upon which criterion is used and regardless of whether the validity is the same or different. For that reason, it is important to understand the nature of academic performance in individual years and why it appears to be differentially predictable.

One can speculate about a number of possible reasons why yearly GPAs might become progressively less predictable. They can be considered under three general hypotheses. First, it is possible that students change. If that is so, preadmissions measures of competence and potential could become progressively less dependable through time. Second, the academic task may change. If so, different skills would likely be required and measures that were best suited for predicting freshman grades would become less relevant in the upper division. Third, the assessment of performance may change. If grades were progressively distorted for whatever reason, the GPA could become inherently less predictable. These three hypotheses are discussed in turn in the following section.

LOWER PREDICTION IN THE UPPER DIVISION—THREE HYPOTHESES

In order to examine the nature of prediction through the four years, it is useful to look first at some additional basic information. Table 6.1 shows means, standard deviations, and intercorrelations for the yearly grade point averages. As these data indicate, grades crept up about one-tenth of of a letter grade each year, but there was just as much spread in the grade scale in the fourth year as in the first. The grade creep is not simply a reflection of selective retention of the better students, since each of these GPAs was computed on the same group of seniors. The correlational pattern shows that the farther apart in time two GPAs were earned, the lower their relationship. There is relatively little data of this type in the research literature, but none of these results appear atypical. In fact, Wilson (1983) cites Rogers's estimate in 1925 that independently computed yearly GPAs were correlated about .70— precisely the figure found here!

Figure 6.2 shows how various academic measures were correlated with yearly GPA—i.e., grade averages independently computed on the basis of coursework completed in each year. The striking thing about this figure is the consistency of the downward trend. There appears to be something pervasive about the declining predictability of academic performance, not some quirk that affects one or two measures. There is, however, some difference among the measures. First-year GPA shows

Table 6.1 Means, Standard Deviations, and Intercorrelations for Yearly Grade Averages

	Yearly Average			
	GPA1	GPA2	GPA3	GPA4
Intercorrelations				
GPA2	.70			
GPA3	.63	.71		
GPA4	.55	.62	.70	
Means	2.82	2.91	3.00	3.09
Standard Deviations	.53	.53	.52	.54

Note: All entries are averages across nine colleges; total $N = 3,407$ seniors.

the greatest absolute decline in the correlation with later academic performance; SAT-M showed the largest proportional decline.

Again, these findings are generally consistent with other available data. Wilson (1983) recently reviewed this topic and reported in some detail all the data he could locate on predicting college GPA beyond the freshman year. Earlier data confirm the constant predictability of cumulative GPA year by year, the declining predictability of yearly GPA, the declining correlation of freshman grades with subsequent grades, the declining correlation of high school rank and admissions test scores with yearly GPAS, and a somewhat larger decline in SAT-M than in SAT-V. One inconsistency is that other available data indicate approximately the same decline for HSR and SAT, while in these data HSR declined less. With this background, we consider now the three hypotheses.

Do students change?

In a provocative and informative series of articles, Humphreys (1960, 1968; with Taber in 1973; with Lin in 1977) focused attention on the fact

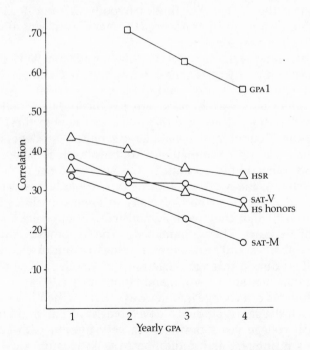

Figure 6.2 Correlation of different academic measures with independently computed yearly grade point averages (averaged across nine colleges; $N = 3,197$).

that academic prediction diminishes from freshman to senior year. Humphreys has been much interested in the so-called simplex correlational pattern. The pattern shows in Table 6.1, where the correlations are highest in the diagonal and diminish with increasing distance from the diagonal. In this case, coefficients farther away from the diagonal represent relationships between measures that are more separated in time. In studies of human development this pattern has often been explained in terms of increasing task complexity (which we consider in the following section) or changing patterns of aptitude over time. Changing aptitudes might explain why an admissions test that predicts freshman grades is less predictive of senior grades and possibly account for the simplex pattern in GPA intercorrelations as well. Humphreys leaned initially toward this "people-are-changing" hypothesis.

One problem with the people-are-changing hypothesis was that most data on human development indicate that important academic aptitudes do not change a great deal by the time of young adulthood. Wilson (1983) accumulated various sets of data confirming the stability of admissions test scores over several years. But the most telling evidence against the changing-aptitudes hypothesis came from a small study by Lunneborg and Lunneborg (1970) and from Humphreys and Taber (1973) in a later article.

The reasoning went as follows. If the correlation between an admissions test and yearly GPAs goes down because of changing aptitudes, then a test administered at the end of the undergraduate years should show the opposite pattern of backward postdiction; i.e., it should correlate lowest with GPA1 because that is the GPA now farthest from the time of testing. Examining data for a large sample of students who took the Graduate Record Examinations Aptitude Test as seniors, Humphreys and Taber found essentially the same pattern as before! As Figure 6.3 shows, the ACT tests and the GRE Aptitude Test were correlated with yearly GPAs at the University of Illinois in almost identical fashion, even though they were administered at opposite ends of the undergraduate years. They commented, "The hypothesis that reduced predictive validities and instability of grades is due to change in the broad abilities during this age range must be rejected." The result was confirmed in a later study by Lin and Humphreys (1977).

But students can change in other ways. Even if their basic aptitudes remain much the same, students' development of skill and knowledge during their college years can follow a very uneven path because of fluctuations in interest and dedication to task. It is obvious that academic motivation varies widely among students, and in any individual there are ups and downs from term to term. But if there were a sub-

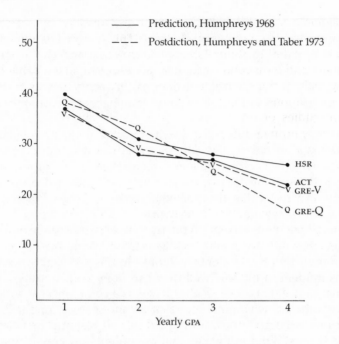

Figure 6.3 Yearly grades predicted by preadmissions measures and postdicted by tests administered in the senior year (University of Illinois).

stantial number of students who got fired up (or cooled down) and earned progressively better and better (or poorer and poorer) grades through the four years compared with other students, decreasing predictability could result.

That possibility was examined in two ways. One was to look for pockets of the legendary "late bloomers" (or their counterpart, late relaxers). We looked for signs of late blooming or late relaxing in more than 100 groups of students defined by various background characteristics, preadmissions achievements, admissions staff ratings, etc. Freshman GPA was compared with four-year GPA for signs of any change different from the class as a whole (which improved about one-eighth of a letter grade). The analysis turned up nothing of consequence. Only a few groups departed from the class norm, and the differences were minor. Several such instances appeared to represent regression to the mean; e.g., students with high school honors or outstanding references did not gain in GPA through the college years quite so much as students generally (statistically significant but only .04 letter grade less).

Another possibility is that successive yearly GPAs are about equally predictable for most students, but there are some groups of students who simply become very unpredictable. This hypothesis was checked by computing multiple correlations between HSR and SAT and each of the yearly GPAs for a number of groups of students (see Table D.10 in Appendix D). The principal outcome of this analysis was to confirm that every group examined showed the same general pattern of declining predictability.

The only sizable difference was that group of senior questionnaire respondents who did *not* indicate that faculty and student contact had a constructive effect on their college careers. Predictability for that group dropped .19 over the four years as compared with a drop of .11 for students who did value the personal contacts. Why? Possibly some students who answered the questionnaire in that way had become a bit alienated and had done more poorly than expected while others who had overachieved saw themselves as self-sufficient. An equally good explanation is that the students' response to the personal contact question was influenced by how well they had done academically.

What to make of these results? It seems a commonsense verity that people do change with time, and that as time passes, one is less able to anticipate accurately how an individual will respond to a new situation. It is possible, if not likely, that as students progress through the undergraduate years, some become quite dedicated to the academic task while others, unaccountably, drift to distracting interests. Such changes among students through time could produce a declining pattern of correlations. But in this analysis of the year-to-year performance and predictability of many different types of students, we have learned very little about who it is that is doing the changing. And when an aptitude test administered in the senior year correlates more highly with freshman than senior grades, it seems very hard to make that fit with an explanation that students' abilities change. Without a verifiable theory or model of the causes or correlates, "people are changing" remains a not very useful explanation of why yearly GPAs become less predictable. We come to the other side of the equation—the learning task.

Does the task change?

Increasing task complexity is one way in which a declining simplex pattern of correlations in successive learning stages has been explained. Increasingly complex skills and higher order competencies are required in learning some tasks. The result is that basic abilities have a higher correlation with performance early in learning and lower correlations in later stages. This is not only plausible but clearly demonstrable if the learning is some novel and highly integrated skill like flight training or complex motor performance (Fleishman and Hempel 1955).

The college curriculum, on the other hand, is complex at the outset, usually not very well integrated, and certainly not unusual for most students. Grades in college seem better characterized as performance on a familiar task than learning something novel. It does seem intuitively true, however, that work in the upper division becomes more intellectually demanding. What changes in the academic task from lower to upper division could account for the declining correlations through time? Does work in the upper division call for a somewhat different pattern of personal qualities, developed abilities, and skills? We have in this study a number of measures with which to test that hypothesis.

One possibility is that the more specialized courses of study in the upper division place different stress on different basic aptitudes. Verbal and mathematical aptitudes are clearly different skills. Perhaps one reason the correlation of SAT with yearly GPA declines is that, compared with the lower division, advanced work in some areas like history calls for increased weight on verbal ability, while in an area like physics advanced work places increased weight on quantitative ability. Giving the same weight to SAT-V and SAT-M for all students could be less effective in the upper division.

That possibility was examined by comparing the relative weight on SAT-M and SAT-V in predicting yearly GPAs by academic field. In natural science SAT-M and SAT-V received approximately equal weight, and that was true in each of the four years. In the social sciences and the humanities, the mathematics score received about one-quarter of the weight, and the proportion varied little from year to year. These results probably underestimate somewhat the relative importance of mathematics because the effect of student choice of major was to restrict the range of mathematics scores more than verbal scores within individual majors. But the result of primary interest here remains undisturbed; within individual majors, upper-division coursework was evidently no more differentiated with respect to verbal and mathematical ability than was true at the lower division (see note 1 for Chapter 6 in Appendix C).

Another possibility is that a subtle form of personalism may be more prevalent in the upper division than in the lower. When classes are smaller and students and faculty have developed closer working relationships, intangibles particularly valued by faculty may play more of a role in grade assignment (e.g., intellectual curiosity, probity, likeableness; see Davis 1965a, b). If that is true, what preadmissions measures might reflect such elements of personal desirability? Three might because they involve a subjective appraisal of personal characteristics: the school reference, the admissions interview rating, and the overall personal rating of each applicant. If there is anything to the hypothesis of more personalism in the upper division, one might expect these measures to be a bit more highly correlated with upper-division GPA than with lower. It did not happen. Correlations with the lower- and upper-division GPA, respectively, were:

.14	.13	School reference
.14	.13	Interview rating
.17	.12	Personal rating

Perhaps upper-division grades are less predictable because they depend more on scholarly productivity and independent work. If so, a measure like high school honors might be more highly related to upper-division grades. This measure includes prizes for scientific and literary achievement, top student awards in particular subjects, etc. It is a reasonable hypothesis, but not sustained by the data. As already indicated by Figure 6.2, lower-division grades were actually more related to whether a student had won high school honors ($r = .37$ versus .29).

Are there other competencies—leadership, creative achievement—that show a closer relationship to upper-division grades? An examination of the correlations for all predictors revealed no measure that had a significantly higher relationship with upper-division GPA (with the possible exception of athletic achievement, which was correlated .08 and .12 with lower- and upper-division GPA—but both negative). In other words, even with the numerous types of information available about these students, there was little evidence of other promising measures to turn to that might do a better job of forecasting academic achievement in the upper division.

Table 6.2 shows multiple regression analyses for the upper- and lower-division GPAs with the same six predictors used in a number of analyses in Chapter 5. In both upper and lower divisions the addition of the four supplementary measures increased the multiple correlation only .03 over HSR and SAT alone. The hypothesis that other promising measures might improve forecasting of upper-division grades was not borne out. On the other hand, the regression weights for the academic measures did tend to be relatively lower.

The sum of the last three measures—follow-through, personal statement, and school reference—was used as a personal achievement composite in some previous analyses in order to compare the predictive

Table 6.2 Validity Coefficients and Beta Weights for Six Predictors of Lower- and Upper-Division Grade Point Average

Predictor	Lower Division		Upper Division	
	r	β	r	β
High school rank	.46	.33	.38	.28
SAT	.43	.29	.31	.19
High school honors	.37	.09	.29	.07
Follow-through	.10	.04	.07	.01
Personal statement	.12	.10	.11	.10
School reference	.14	.08	.13	.08
Multiple correlation	.58		.46	

Note: $N = 3,442$.

effectiveness of these measures with an academic composite consisting of HSR and SAT. Is it possible that such measures of personal achievement play a greater role in accounting for upper-division success in some academic fields and not others? That possibility was examined by predicting yearly GPAs in individual majors, using as predictors the two composites—academic and personal. The results indicated little consistent difference from one academic field to another. There did appear to be a somewhat heavier weight on the personal achievement composite in the natural sciences compared with other disciplines. The more interesting result was that the relative weight on the two measures was almost exactly the same in each year—about one-fifth personal and four-fifths academic.

Contrary to Table 6.2, this result indicates that the relative weight on HSR and SAT does not decrease year to year when the analysis is carried out within departments. Why the different result? Is there something different about the grading among departments? This leads us to the third hypothesis.

Does the grading change?

Anyone who is very familiar with college grading practices and notes the pattern of declining correlations in Figure 6.2 is likely to question the criterion. Perhaps there is not much differentiation in upper-division grades because too many people get A's and B's, or not much spread in upper-division grades because of selective retention of the better students. In general, if the reliability of the single-term GPA goes down for whatever reason, those less reliable GPAs will necessarily be less predictable.

Table 6.1 provides data on these issues; the results are similar to those reported elsewhere. The GPAs did tend to go up year by year, but it was not because of attrition of lower ability students. All yearly GPA statistics presented here are based on the same group of seniors. Also, the standard deviation or spread in the grade averages remained essentially constant from year to year. Finally, the frequently observed constant correlation between GPAs in adjacent years has typically been interpreted to mean that grade averages in successive years are equally reliable (Humphreys 1968; Werts, Linn, and Jöreskog 1978; Wilson 1983). Such data have possibly diverted researchers from giving the quality of the criterion measure the attention it deserves as a source of declining predictability.

The issue is not so much whether the GPA remains reliable but whether its intrinsic validity remains intact. That is, does its essential meaning and comparability from student to student remain the same? The intrinsic validity of the grade scale would deteriorate if the upper-division grades of some students tended to be spuriously increased for any reason unrelated to their academic performance, while grades of other students were spuriously decreased. Any such distortions that work across more than one term (in measurement language, correlated error) could have the effect of increasing (or maintaining) reliability while simultaneously decreasing predictability.

There are several possibilities for such distortions. It is convenient to think of them as working at the level of students, instructors, courses, and departments. With individual students the potential distortion is often referred to as "halo," or the tendency for some individuals to be viewed as strong or weak students and graded accordingly, even if the specific performance observed is not entirely consistent with the predisposition of the grader.

With instructors the potential distortion is arbitrary grading habits. No doubt most campuses have their share of easy and hard graders. Similarly, particular courses garner such reputations. Not every geology department has a course that the students have labeled "Rocks for Jocks," but students are keenly aware that it is much tougher to get a B in some courses than in others. The same is often true of departments. None of these examples is meant to suggest that all differences in grading among instructors, courses, etc., is to be viewed as distortion. We refer here only to any differences that appear arbitrary and out of keeping with the demonstrated competence of the students.

Why would the effect of grading distortions be likely to increase from lower to upper division? If there is grading halo, it would increase as students become better known to faculty. It is not unreasonable to assume that students vary in their tendency to select easy as opposed to challenging or interesting courses and instructors. Freshmen often have a limited choice of instructors and courses; seniors have more choice and far more accumulated savvy on how to exercise their penchant. Departmental grading variations would have a similar effect on junior and senior GPAs but would have less effect in the lower division, when students are taking a larger proportion of their courses in other departments. Also, departmental grading variations may occur mainly in the upper division (see note 2 in Appendix C).

The data available in this study permitted evaluation of only one of these possible sources of criterion distortion—variation in departmental grading practices. The first question put to the data was whether correlations between preadmissions measures (HSR and SAT) and yearly GPAs look any different if they are computed within individual departments instead of within colleges. For this analysis all seniors were selected who had a single major, complete data, and came from a department with at least five seniors. This yielded 2,739 seniors from 128 departments. (Not all 21 majors were represented in each of the nine colleges.) All scores were standardized within each department to expedite computation of pooled correlations unaffected by grading variations across departments. The results are shown in Table 6.3.

The upper portion of this table shows results similar to those of Figure 6.2, but here the sample is smaller because all data are based on students with only one major in order to avoid the problem of deciding in which department to place the student (see note 3). The correlations in the lower portion of the table are lower than they otherwise might

Table 6.3 Average Validities of High School Rank and SAT, Computed within Colleges and within Departments

Predictor	Yearly Grade Point Average				Decline	Cumulative
	GPA1	GPA2	GPA3	GPA4	1 to 4	GPA
Within colleges						
SAT-V	.360	.301	.300	.248	.112	.360
SAT-M	.322	.280	.208	.157	.165	.292
HSR	.413	.393	.352	.330	.083	.432
HSR, SAT	.519	.470	.416	.368	.151	.521
Within departments						
SAT-V	.341	.311	.300	.254	.087	.357
SAT-M	.244	.233	.208	.175	.069	.258
HSR	.374	.360	.345	.324	.050	.402
HSR, SAT	.465	.444	.419	.376	.089	.496

Note: $N = 2,739$ seniors with a single major.

be because of restriction in the range of talent in the departmental groups. That restriction is constant across years but varied among measures; compared with within-college variance, within-department variance was lower by 9 percent for SAT-V, 19 percent for SAT-M, 11 percent for HSR, and 14 percent for GPA1 (see note 4). The principal result in this table is the smaller rate of decline in the yearly validity coefficients when they are computed within departments rather than within colleges. For both SAT and HSR the decline in predictability from freshman to senior year was some 40 percent smaller within departments than within colleges (i.e., for HSR .050/.083 = 60%). When the SAT was broken down into its verbal and mathematical components, it was clear that SAT-M, which had shown the greatest decline originally, now demonstrated the greatest recovery when analyzed within departments (see note 8).

These results support the hypothesis that the yearly GPA criterion is increasingly distorted by grading variations. With the data available it is not possible to determine how much of the decline in predictability might be attributable to other types of grading variations, but the effect of departmental variations alone appears considerable. But it is still not clear how this comes about. It would be useful to see some more direct evidence of grading variations across departments and how those differences might distort the grade scale in the upper division. Answers to those questions become clearer in the following section.

GRADING PATTERNS AND STUDENT MIGRATION

What are the trends in average GPAs, year by year, for students majoring in different areas? Are there consistent differences in the grading patterns? If so, how are such departmental grading patterns related to academic achievement? For answers to these questions, we examined the means of preadmissions measures and yearly GPAs for all seniors in 21 majors (double majors excluded). The detailed data are found in Table D.11 of Appendix D. Some of the relationships are illustrated in Figure 6.4.

There were substantial differences in the average freshman grade for seniors in the 21 majors—the GPA1 means spread more than a standard deviation. Those freshman grade means were highly related to the ability of each group as indicated by their average HSR and SAT. In fact, the mean academic composite (HSR plus SAT) for each group correlated .80 with mean GPA1 (N = 21 majors). The interesting trends got under way after the freshman year.

In some departments, especially for the several business and phys-

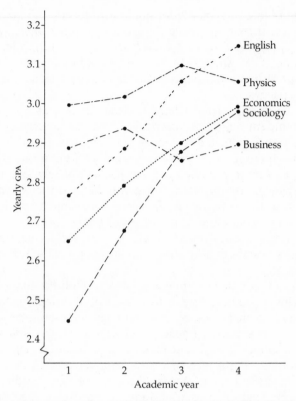

Figure 6.4 Yearly grade point averages for seniors in selected majors (all colleges, excluding double majors).

ical science majors, the yearly GPA mean held fairly steady from freshman to senior year. In others it climbed, sometimes dramatically. Those means that started low tended to climb the most ($r = -.80$ between GPA1 mean and amount of increase). For example, in Figure 6.4 seniors in physics and sociology started college with markedly different freshman averages, but their average for the senior year was very nearly the same. Most of the GPA4 means by major tended to cluster in the range of 2.90 to 3.05. As a result of these trends, the correlation between the mean academic composite and mean yearly GPA for the 21 groups dropped from .80 in the freshman year to .03 in the senior year. In other words, in the freshman year major-to-major differences in average grade closely reflected average ability level (as indicated by HSR and SAT); in the senior year no such relationship obtained.

The average freshman to senior year gains for students in the various majors (e.g., .06 of a letter grade for physics, .55 for sociology) were fairly consistent (see note 5). As an example of the degree of stability in the grading patterns found here, the gain from freshman to senior year GPA was one-fourth of a letter grade larger (one-half standard deviation) in social science than in physical science for eight of these nine colleges.

It will be recalled from Chapter 4 that there was a considerable amount of student migration, particularly into social science. Could it be that the trends depicted in Figure 6.4 represent real differences in achievement—perhaps due to many students "finding themselves" after shifting to a more suitable major? It seems unlikely, but as a check the GPA gains were recomputed, using only those students who started and finished in the same major. The group was much smaller but the results were essentially the same: physical science students gained an eighth of a letter grade. Those in social science and humanities gained a third, and students in education and sociology gained over a half a letter grade.

These grading patterns appear consistent with the foregoing analysis of declining predictability. If faculties in those departments where students tend to make lower freshman grades assign progressively higher grades in successive years, it stands to reason that this noise added to the senior GPA would make it somewhat less predictable. If one "discounted" the senior GPA (i.e., subtracted out the rise characteristic of the student's major), would it then be more predictable? The answer is yes. That analysis was done, using the average GPA4–GPA1 gain by major for the nine colleges as a whole. This is a bit crude, since grading patterns of departments in individual colleges did not necessarily follow the all-college trend (see note 6). Nonetheless, the results came out in the expected direction. In the prediction of GPA4 the validity of HSR was .03 higher for the discounted version, the validity of SAT-M was .07 higher, and SAT-V showed no difference.

In Chapter 4 there were substantial differences in the pattern of student migration from major to major. For example, students moving into physical science tended to have above average freshman grades, while those moving into social science tended to have below average freshman grades. And in this chapter it is apparent that the typical grade assigned in social science increases year by year much more than is true in physical science. Does this not indicate an interaction between faculty grading patterns and student migratory patterns?

In order to examine this further, all seniors who had indicated a major preference at entry were sorted by freshman GPA level. Then the group at each freshman grade level was examined to determine how many students had changed major and, if so, whether they had changed to a major with more strict or more lenient grading in the upper division. For the purposes of this analysis, lenient-grading departments were defined as those in which the average GPA4 was more than one-third of a letter grade higher than the average GPA1. The strict-grading departments were those where the difference was less than one-third of a letter grade (as indicated in Table D.11 of Appendix D). The results are shown in Figure 6.5

First, students with low freshman grades were more likely to change major; i.e., the lower the freshman GPA, the smaller the white area indicating no change. Second, among those who did change major, freshmen with a high GPA were more likely to change to a strict-grading department, while those who had a low freshman GPA were more likely to change to a lenient-grading department. As a joint result, the academically less able freshmen were much more likely to migrate into a department with more lenient grading (60 percent) than was true for the academically more able freshmen (18 percent).

The next step was to determine which preadmissions measures were related to the student's decision to migrate into a major with lenient grading in the upper division. These are the measures whose validity one would expect to decline because of departmental grading variations and whose declining validity would be most correctable by computing validity coefficients within departments. SAT-M, HSR, and SAT-V were all correlated in that order (negatively, as expected) with moving into a major with lenient grading. In the multiple prediction of

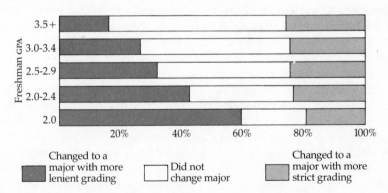

Figure 6.5 Relationship between freshman grade point average and the tendency to change into a major with more strict or more lenient grading in the upper division ($N = 2,920$ seniors who indicated a major preference as freshmen).

that move (R_{bis} = .33), SAT-M had the heaviest weight and SAT-V made no independent contribution. These results help to explain the results of Table 6.3, which they mirror quite closely. The measures most related to a student's moving into a major with lenient grading were the measures most affected by departmental grading variations.

SUMMING UP

Three hypotheses have been examined that might shed light on the declining patterns of validity coefficients one finds in predicting yearly grade point averages. The evidence for changing academic abilities as an explanation seems weak and contraindicated—especially by the results of postdiction studies. While there is no direct evidence, it still seems likely that motivational drift and changing student interests might account for some of the difficulty in predicting upper-division grades. If so, that would suggest that those grades do not well represent what many students are capable of doing.

The data presented here provided little support for the hypothesis that the task changes from freshman to senior year, even though several avenues appeared promising before the fact. There may be other abilities that are more relevant to upper-division work, but none were revealed here. As a corollary, these results do not indicate that any reweighting of information in admissions would yield more students who make good grades in the senior year. Speculating beyond these data, it seems likely that other skills become important as students move through college. It remains entirely possible that better performance measures would show such changes. To some extent these changes may involve learning how to work the system and discovering what is necessary to get a good grade. It is not clear whether that would imply that grades in successive years become more or less valid representations of academic performance.

The results here do provide direct evidence regarding the effects of grading practices. In some departments grades went up in later years, in other departments they did not. Grades climbed the most in departments with the weaker students. Student migration enhanced that effect. Students with poor freshman grades were more likely to change majors and more likely to change to a department with more lenient grading in the upper division. A substantial portion of the decline in predictability of senior grades appears to be due to these patterns. It seems quite plausible that other grading biases that could not be evaluated here would work in the same way, or at least have a similar effect on the predictability of grades.

All of this seems to add up to the conclusion that upper-division GPA is fraught with problems as a criterion—not a very good representation of how good a student a person really is. One further check would be to determine how much weight other parties give lower- and upper-division GPA when they choose successful students. There are a number of reasons why one would assume that the upper-division record would get more weight. It is more recent and presumably a better indication of what the student can now do. Being more recent, it is more likely to be remembered and attended to by persons doing the choosing. More important, the upper-division GPA represents academic performance in advanced work in the student's discipline—arguably, the culmination of the undergraduate career.

Lower- and upper-division GPAs were used to predict membership in three success groups: those nominated most successful by the college, those nominated most successful by their peers, and those accepted for advanced study in law, medicine, or a Ph.D. program. In each the lower-division GPA was more highly correlated with membership in the success group! The differences in the correlations were not large, but consistently favored the lower-division GPA: .434 versus .397 for college nominees, .330 versus .284 for peer nominees, and .280 versus .258 for advanced study. Whatever the selection process was that created these three success groups, it was more closely associated with the students' standing in the lower division than in the upper division. This result casts more doubt on upper-division grades. The weight of the evidence suggests that the criterion is a major problem, if not the main explanation, of declining predictability of yearly grade averages.

7

The Student's View

Because the purpose of this study was to examine success in college from the standpoint of admissions policy, naturally it focuses on success as the college defines success. The objective is to identify more students who will succeed in a similar fashion. Undergraduate faculty and graduate admissions committees may place somewhat different values on different achievements in making judgments about who the most successful students are. But these represent external judgments on who has done best. What about the student's view?

Individual students' assessment of their college experience is relevant for two reasons. First, the college would certainly prefer to enroll students who are likely to feel good about their undergraduate career. The positive effects on institutional morale and alumni loyalty seem obvious. Second, the student's view of success has validity in its own right. After all, the purpose of the enterprise is to further the educational development of the recipients. Their sense of how it is going may suggest useful ways of modifying the institution's view of success in college.

This chapter explores the student's view. The analysis was guided by several questions: How do students think about success? What types of achievement seem to them most significant? How do they evaluate their progress? In what ways is the sense of overall success in college dependent upon a feeling of progress in particular areas? When students judge how successful they have been in college, do they put equal weight on scholarship, leadership, and accomplishment as do college faculty in picking the most successful students? What about peers making judgments about which *other* students are most successful? Can one anticipate before admission which students are likely to view themselves as successful?

To get at such questions, the colleges administered a four-page questionnaire (see Appendix A) to the class during the period of November to January of their fourth year. A few students were off campus, but of the questionnaires delivered, a return rate of 70 percent was achieved through an exceptional effort by staff at the colleges. Since a great deal of prior information was available for the total group, it was possible to develop a weighting procedure to correct for possible bias due to nonresponse, though the resulting corrections turned out to be quite small (see note 1 for Chapter 7 in Appendix C). Summary questionnaire data in Table D.1 through D.4 in Appendix D are weighted; correlational analyses are not. This chapter is based on the questionnaire data, but we start with students' comments about their achievements in college rather than their answers to specific questions.

WHAT ACHIEVEMENTS WERE MOST SIGNIFICANT?

How do students think about success in college? One useful approach to that question is simply to ask them. We did so, but tried to provide at least some framework that would be helpful in thinking about the matter. Educational goals provided such a framework. The group had been asked in this questionnaire and in two previous ones about a series of 12 goals. They are listed in Table 7.1. In reference to these goal statements, students were asked:

> In which area would you say you have made your most significant achievement or accomplished something for which you are especially proud? Could you please describe the achievement and indicate why you think it was significant?

Most respondents accepted the invitation and offered their thoughts on the question. Most were also willing to have their replies used here. Students seemed to take the question seriously. There were few flip responses, though many were brief. Many were similar, following a few basic themes. Some were perceptive and revealing—obviously written after thoughtful consideration.

Making sense out of free-response material of this sort is always somewhat of a puzzle. The 12-goal framework was helpful in sorting out which areas students tended to focus on. As Table 7.1 shows, the percentage of students choosing the various areas to cite their most significant achievement tended to correspond with the perceived importance of the educational goal (from another question in the questionnaire). What was most often cited by these students as especially

Table 7.1 Important Areas of Development and Achievement in the Eyes of Seniors

	% of Seniors Marking		
Educational Goal Area	*Very Imp. Goal*	*Satisfied with Progress*	*Most Signif. Achievement*
Intellectual			
Liberal education (I see college as my great opportunity to read a lot, exchange ideas, learn about the significant cultures of the world, and generally to become an aware and more sophisticated person.)	45%	76%	19%
Intellectual skills (I don't want to just learn a lot of facts in college; to me its very important to learn how to deal with those facts. For example, learning how to reason, evaluate information, and construct a defensible argument are high priorities for me.)	57	74	18
Moral values (I am especially concerned about ethical, moral, and religious issues. In the next year or so I would like to get a better sense of my own values in this area.)	14	54	03
Social awareness (I am very interested in community and social problems and would like to learn more about what's going on in the world. The opportunity to get personally involved in some sort of significant community service activity or environmental project would be important to me.)	11	38	02
Creative talents (I like to express myself creatively. I already have some talent in an area of interest to me [for example, theater, music, painting, crafts, writing] and want to develop it further in college.)	16	40	05

(Continued)

Table 7.1 Important Areas of Development and Achievement in the Eyes of Seniors *(Continued)*

	% of Seniors Marking		
Educational Goal Area	*Very Imp. Goal*	*Satisfied with Progress*	*Most Signif. Achievement*
Personal			
Physical development (I'm an active person. I like sports and other outdoor activities. Developing my talents and interests in this area is important to me.)	19	63	03
Leadership training (Extracurricular activities appeal to me because they are a good way to get a lot out of your education; especially learning how to organize resources, work with others, and take the lead in achieving an objective. I hope to participate fully in this aspect of college life.)	33	64	12
Personal relations (I would very much like to develop a meaningful relationship with another person while I'm in college. If it's lasting, good; if it's not, that's OK too.)	17	60	01
Social competence (In the next few years I would like particularly to develop more skill and confidence in dealing with different kinds of people. I think the social side of college is very important.)	48	79	16
Career			
Professional training (My main goal in college will be to get training for the work I want to do, or make the grades I need to get into a good school after I finish here.)	23	61	11
Practical skills (I view college as a place where a person can learn practical skills valuable through a lifetime. I am especially interested in developing specific skills such as foreign language competency, computer programming, reading and math skills, good work habits, etc.)	16	60	05
Career exploration (I am not at all sure what I want to do for a career. To me it seems important that I get a better sense of direction and I hope to do that in college.)	27	55	05
Total	—	—	100%

significant? Almost half cited an intellectual achievement. The outcome of a liberal education was chosen by 19 percent, and 18 percent chose a closely related area—the development of intellectual skills. Students often characterized such achievements as broadened horizons.

> I came to college with no Russian at all and in the course of my time here I've gathered enough knowledge and developed enough interest to read Russian poetry and prose. This is important because I feel that it is in cultural and artistic achievements that we participate in the best we have shown ourselves to be. (Colgate language major)

> The most important aspect of college is to learn about the world around us and to begin to decide where or how we fit in. I have made many important decisions about my beliefs and I feel that this will help me when I begin a life on my own. (Richmond English major)

Many students talked about developed skills that they judged likely to be of lasting significance.

> My most significant academic achievement has been the realization that education and learning extend beyond mere assemblage of facts to an ability to reason, evaluate, understand a wide variety of problems. (honor graduate)

> This course was most valuable because I learned how to deal with material, how to analyze, present, and debate it. (campus leader from Kenyon)

Some students took a more philosophical, long-term view.

> It's more important that we learn how to think, rather than what to think. Given the complexity of the issues we face and the probability that we will approach rather than reach solutions, methodology is more valuable than a fact or thesis which may well fall apart in the postgraduate world. (Williams student outstanding on several success criteria)

And some students do, in fact, get caught up in the joy of learning.

> My most significant achievement, I think, has been learning how to go to the library to research a given subject solely for my own personal pleasure.

This took some time to arrive at but now that I know I *like* ferreting out information and knowledge, this has become fun. (all-around successful student from Kalamazoo)

One-third of the respondents described significant achievements in areas connected with personal goals. Very often these concerned extra-curricular activities (12 percent) and the development of social competence (16 percent). The two seemed to be frequently linked.

The real learning has been for me outside the classroom, living with others and working with others toward agreed-upon goals. (Occidental woman with a straight-A average)

Not only has becoming an all-American been a boyhood dream but in the same quarter I made the dean's list for the first time. Finally I have proved to myself that I can do well both on the court as well as in the classroom. (political science major)

Extracurricular activities have been especially rewarding for me because they have helped me to discover personal interests that have guided me toward a particular career. They have strengthened my values about myself and my community and enabled me to make some lifelong friends. (accounting major from Bucknell)

The more personal side of the learning experience comes through clearly in some comments.

I considered myself pretty shy and quiet when I came here, not as outgoing as I really wanted to be. Now I have learned how to get along with almost anyone and have gained a lot of social confidence. (engineer)

Coming to a college that has a diversified student body has been a helpful experience for me, as I came from a small rural town. (history major)

The rest of the respondents cited achievements that were more career-related, especially making good grades in order to get into graduate or professional school. Many discussed the topic matter-of-factly, without apology.

My future basically depended upon my performance here, reaching my academic goal. (straight-A senior at Ohio Wesleyan)

The intense competition for entry into American medical schools forces students considering a medical career to be very goal-oriented and grade conscious, willingly or not. Many academicians are unjustly antagonistic to this career-oriented approach. (another straight-A senior)

Many do not put as much emphasis on their studies as I do, but then again many do not realize how lucky they are to be here. I intend to use this education to get more education and earn a better living than anyone in my family's history. (business major, outstanding in and outside the classroom)

Students often referred to their future careers, though the career decision itself was not one of the more frequently cited accomplishments. When it was, it was often with some feeling.

Choosing a major and a career is not something that hasn't been done by hundreds of thousands of other college students. But it is something that has to be done by each and every student, and finding a direction is a fantastic achievement. (top student at Hartwick)

In an effort to understand better what the students were saying, we did a content analysis of about a thousand replies. This analysis focused on two questions: why students felt that the accomplishment was significant and what enabling factors may have been helpful. This exercise was not so useful as hoped. Often the students' replies touched upon several areas or did not address these particular questions clearly. But there were some interesting patterns in their responses.

The college itself (by name) was the factor most frequently cited as a contributing factor to the student's success. Many recognized that "just being here" in this type of environment, with stimulating peers and faculty, with well-structured learning experiences and diverse challenges, was very important in itself. Aside from the college generally, three factors were specifically mentioned with about equal frequency (one student in five): academic work, extracurricular activities, and interpersonal relations—especially with other students. Field experience, particularly foreign study, was mentioned fairly often.

Why did students feel that the accomplishment they cited was particularly significant? Our reading for that question yielded two interesting findings. One was that students cited their own development as an individual far more frequently than other considerations. The five most frequent replies were:

54% My educational development
48   My personal development
26   Achievement will be useful later
15   I received public recognition
7   I attained a goal

Another finding revealed by these percentages was that personal development was cited about as often as was educational development. When students wrote about personal development, one theme came up repeatedly—maturation and enhanced self-confidence through exposure to new ideas and people.

> College has exposed me to a variety of people, ideas, and activities. This has enabled me to develop a greater sense of awareness and tolerance for differing opinions.

> I come from a small city in the Midwest. Even meeting ""preppies" was a culture shock for me. By exposing me to the world, my college career has put me more at ease in it.

> I have gained confidence that I will be successful as a person. That is something I have always doubted.

> The thing that really hits me is how much I have grown up.

HOW STUDENTS EVALUATED THEIR PROGRESS

In the spring of their freshman year the students in this study were asked two questions about the educational goal statements in Table 7.1: how they rated the importance of each goal (on a 5-point scale from not important to very important) and whether they were satisfied with their progress in that area (satisfied, uncertain, or dissatisfied). To find out whether and how the seniors may have changed their evaluations, the students were presented the same goals three years later and asked, "Given your experience in college, how do you view them now?"

The first two columns of Table 7.1 summarize the answers of the class to those questions. Tables D.1 and D.2 in Appendix D give more detailed breakdowns for several groups, including sex and major. In general, men and women tended to hold similar views regarding the relative importance of these goals. But women did attach a bit more importance to liberal education and, somewhat paradoxically, career exploration. Minority students attributed more importance to moral values and social awareness.

There were some substantial differences from major to major—mostly along predictable lines. Students in the humanities were quite strong on liberal education, those in natural science and business much less so. Students in the arts were 10 times as likely as those in business to rate the development of creative talents as very important. And students in the arts and humanities were far less likely than those in biology and business to see professional training as a very important educational goal.

It is evident from Table 7.1 that the majority of these students were satisfied with their progress in most of these goal areas. There was remarkably little difference between men and women, though the women did express more satisfaction in the area of morals, ethics, and religion. Minority students were somewhat less satisfied in the personal area, especially regarding physical and social development. This group was also much less likely than the typical student to see themselves as having had a very successful college career overall. The differences from major to major followed a generally similar pattern as was just described for ratings of the importance of these various goals.

In one respect Table 7.1 underestimates the extent of student satisfaction with their progress. These figures do not take account of the fact that not all goals were significant to all students. The percentage of students satisfied with their progress was always higher among students who considered the goal to be very important. The typical difference was about 10 percent for such general educational goals as obtaining a liberal education and developing intellectual skills or social competence. There is probably an element of circularity in rating importance and progress. But that seems an insufficient explanation for some of the more specific goals (e.g., developing moral values, social awareness, leadership abilities, creative or physical talents). In these areas the level of satisfaction was some 25 to 30 percentage points higher among students who attached special importance to such objectives.

Figure 7.1 presents the data in this manner for students who answered the same questions as freshmen and as seniors. In this figure the length of the bar indicates how many students believed that the goal was very important; the shaded area indicates how many of those were satisfied with their progress at the time they completed the questionnaire.

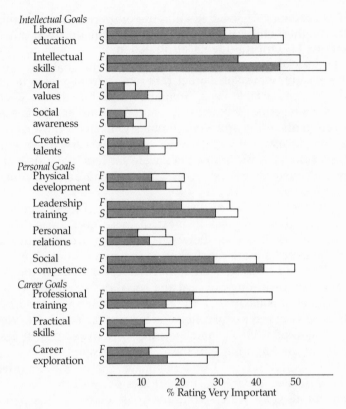

Figure 7.1 Freshman(F) and senior (S) perception of important goals and their satisfaction with progress (gray area). Based on 2,023 students who returned both questionnaires.

In what respects did students change their views, over three years, as to what objectives should be most important in undergraduate education? Overall the seniors put these 12 goals in very nearly the same rank order as they did as freshmen. Liberal education and development of intellectual skills—one might say the heart of the liberal arts curriculum—did take on somewhat more importance. Developing social competence also got more "very important" votes—possibly because at an older age more students were willing to admit it. All three of these goals received a great deal of attention in the comments volunteered by students.

By far the largest shift was in the way students viewed professional training. About twice as many freshmen as seniors thought it was very important to "make the grades I need in order to get into a good school when I finish here." At matriculation the proportion holding that view was even higher. One likes to think that shift in attitude resulted from a broadened view of the educational process.

But note also that the seniors who marked the goal very important were far more likely to be satisfied with their progress than was the case with freshmen. And seniors in the top third of their class on GPA were about half again as likely to endorse this goal and express satisfaction with their progress as were students in the bottom third. Thus it seems likely that, at least in part, the shift in attitude about the importance of professional training resulted from some rationalization by students who failed to make the high grades they had hoped for.

To some extent a higher level of satisfaction in the senior year than the freshman year was true of all goals. In Figure 7.1 the shaded area representing satisfactory progress invariably constitutes a larger proportion of the bar for seniors than for freshmen. In practically all areas the seniors seemed to have more positive glow and confidence—and perhaps more justification for feeling good about their education. This interpretation gets support from the fact that the development of practical skills (like computer programming or a foreign language) was the goal that showed the largest increase in the percentage of students satisfied. This is an educational objective where concrete progress should be readily apparent to students.

The general picture, then, seems positive with respect to the seniors' assessment of their progress. Typically, four out of five seniors indicated satisfaction with what they had accomplished in areas that were important to them. In almost all areas there was also a decline from freshman to senior year in the number of students who were dissatisfied (as opposed to satisfied or uncertain) with their progress toward a goal they felt was very important. The exception was career exploration. There remained in the senior year a fairly substantial number of students dissatisfied in this area (one-fifth of those who thought the matter was very important). Other information in the senior questionnaire sheds some light on this point.

Progress on next steps

"What's next?" is a problem much on the minds of many college seniors. Planning the transition from college to work, or perhaps further education, is an important aspect of a successful undergraduate career—probably more critical for many seniors than they then imagine. Our data on career planning were collected some three to six months before the class was due to graduate. The information is quite limited but tends to confirm that this is a period of considerable uncertainty for many students. A brief summary follows; more detail is found in Table D.2 in Appendix D.

When asked about their plans for the following fall, fewer than half these students (44 percent) anticipated that they would be working at a career-related job. Three in ten anticipated that they would be in school. About one senior in four was uncertain or figured on taking a break while deciding what direction was preferred. Among those students planning to be in school the next fall, the great majority were referring to graduate or professional school. At this point there was a clear sex difference in educational aspirations. More men than women expected to be in advanced training immediately after college (31 percent versus 23 percent); also, more men aspired to doctoral level work at some later date (38 percent versus 30 percent).

Across majors the biggest difference was, expectedly, between business and natural science majors; the former were much more likely to plan direct entry into career-related work, the latter more inclined to graduate study. In these colleges biology was a particular hotbed for predoctoral training; almost two in three had plans for a degree beyond the master's.

A surprisingly large number of students appeared to have given limited thought to the types of jobs that might be available in the fields of most interest to them. When asked whether they had sought such information, more than half the seniors said, "not much yet" or "some, but not in a systematic way." Most were willing to pick a probable long-term career area, but 13 percent were uncertain.

Overall, how confident were these seniors that they were on top of the career-planning matter? We asked, "Do you feel that you have carefully chosen a career and made specific plans to enter it?" Half of these students, in the middle of their senior year, said yes to that question. There were no sex differences in the responses, but the majors tended to line up along predictable lines. In humanities two students in five thought that they had a career plan; in natural science it was three in five, in business a bit higher.

What do these results mean? Surely most students would be better off if they had some career alternatives in mind by the time they approach the end of their undergraduate program. The middle of the senior year is too late to exercise many options as to course selection, much less major. But does the lack of a career plan affect a student's assessment of his or her undergraduate years? This gets us to the question of how students evaluate the overall success of their college careers and what factors influence that judgment.

THE STUDENT'S JUDGMENT ON SUCCESS OVERALL

Well into the senior questionnaire, after the respondents had answered a number of questions about their goals and progress, they were asked, "Objectively, how successful do you think your college career has been, overall?" They marked one of four responses as follows:

32%	Very successful
52	Mostly successful
15	Mixed
1	Not particularly successful

It looks as though some five out of six of these seniors believed their college career had been basically a success. Now, psychologists have a theory of "cognitive dissonance," which suggests that people are not likely to agree with an unacceptable proposition—in this case, that they have invested four years of their lives without a favorable outcome. So 84 percent successful could be on the optimistic side. On the other hand, many other student responses indicated a willingness to admit some disappointment in specific areas, so it is probably not incorrect to assume that the great majority of these seniors did have reason to feel good about themselves and their experience overall.

For the purposes of this analysis we used the more stringent "very successful" response as a criterion so that this success group would correspond more closely in size to other groups with which it will be compared. The interesting finding was that there were typically minor differences in the proportion judging themselves to be very successful (see Table D.2 in Appendix D). The proportion of minority students with a very successful self-rating was low, but in most other groups it was consistently in the range of 30 to 33 percent. The percentage did not vary significantly by sex, by major, or from college to college. Given this consistency, one wonders whether the self-rating is reliable at all. One approach to that question is to see how other measures may be systematically related to it. For example, are there positive and negative aspects of the college experience that are associated with students' self-rating of success overall?

What contributes and what detracts?

In the senior questionnaire students were invited to indicate whether any of nine factors "significantly contributed to or detracted from a successful and satisfying college career overall." The results are shown in Table 7.2. Each of these factors was worded so that it could be interpreted as a positive or a negative influence. The students viewed each as largely positive. As students had indicated in their written comments, personal contacts were an exceptionally important part of their learning experience—especially their contacts with fellow students. Outside interests and work experience were also viewed positively. Financial problems and sense of direction were the biggest problem areas.

Sense of direction was the contributing factor that varied the most from college to college (from 35 to 70 percent). Evidently the differences were associated with the career orientation of the student body. Sense of direction was much more frequently seen to be a positive factor in the colleges with a larger proportion of occupationally oriented pro-

Table 7.2 Factors that Significantly Contributed to or Detracted from a Successful and Satisfying College Career

Factors	% of Students Who Said the Factor:		Weight in Predicting Self-Rating of Success	
	Contributed	Detracted	Men	Women
Ability to organize tasks and use my time effectively	73	18	.17*	.12*
Availability of financial resources	52	28	.00	.01
Health, attitude, eating and drinking habits, other personal factors	63	19	.12*	.07*
Personal contacts with faculty and staff	78	08	.15*	.14*
Personal contacts with students	89	04	.08*	.02
Sense of direction, knowing why I am in college and what career I would like to work toward	56	23	.16*	.21*
Social life on campus	62	23	.05	.14*
Time I have spent on special interests and activities out of class	76	09	.13*	.11*
Work experience during college or in the summer	72	10	.02	.01
R	—	—	.44	.41

Note: $N = 2,379$.
* $P < .05$.

grams like business and engineering (i.e., BUC, HAR, RIC, OHI). The response of students in different majors to the sense-of-direction item showed a similar pattern. The only other large discrepancy noted was the reaction of minority students to "social life on campus." It was a detraction for 46 percent compared with 23 percent overall.

Table 7.2 also indicates the extent to which attitudes about these same factors can account for students' self-ratings of their success in college. There was a moderate relationship, and the factors that appeared to have the largest influence on the self-ratings were about the same for men and women: sense of direction, ability to organize, faculty and staff contacts, and activities out of class.

From another perspective one would certainly expect that the student's sense of progress toward educational goals would influence the sense of success overall. Table 7.3 indicates that satisfaction with progress toward goals does account moderately well for the overall self-rating (R about .53). There was evidently some sex difference in the amount of weight attached to progress on different goals. In assessing

Table 7.3 Relationship of Self-Ratings of Progress toward Educational Goals to Self-Rating of Success in College Overall

Goal	Weight in Predicting Self-Rating of Success	
	Men	Women
Intellectual goals		
Liberal education	.07*	.14*
Intellectual skills	.12*	.08*
Moral values	.06*	−.01
Social awareness	.00	.03
Creative talents	−.03	.01
Personal goals		
Physical development	.08*	.00
Leadership training	.14*	.14*
Personal relations	.09*	.04
Social competence	.08*	.16*
Career goals		
Professional training	.33*	.29*
Practical skills	.07*	.07*
Career exploration	.04	.12*
R	.54	.52

Note: N = 2,371.
* $p < .05$.

their success, women appeared to put somewhat more weight on liberal education, career exploration, and development of social competence.

In general the analysis reported in Table 7.3 gave similar results from college to college, but social competence was an exception. In accounting for a student's self-rating of success in college, the weight on the student's sense of progress in that area varied systematically from the most (.26) to the least (.01) selective college. There seems little doubt that this finding is real. Each of the weights in the five more selective colleges was larger than each of the weights in the four less selective colleges. What it means is less clear. Perhaps students in the more selective colleges are more self-confident academically and perceive a larger challenge in developing their ability to work with others. If so, it would seem more perception than fact. The more able students were more often campus leaders.

But the striking result in Table 7.3 is the weight on progress toward the "professional training" goal. One suspects that the real meaning here is that many students rate their overall success according to how satisfied they are with their GPA (i.e., whether, as the goal states, I "make the grades I need.") This gets us to the question of how the student's self-evaluation is related to the actual record.

The student's view versus the record

Back in Chapter 4 the following question was posed: To what extent is the institution's choice of its most successful students influenced by their success in scholarship, leadership, or other significant accomplishments? Membership in those three success groups got about equal weight in largely accounting for the most successful nominations (R = .88 as reported in Table 4.3). A comparable analysis of the very successful group according to self-ratings gave a very different picture. First, the multiple correlation was only .38. Second, the weights on the three differed considerably: scholarship .19, leadership .13, and accomplishment .06, compared with about equal weights in the faculty staff nominations.

Does this mean that students have a view of higher education very different from that of the faculty and staff of the college? A view much less dependent on objective evidence, but where influenced by evidence, leaning heavily to scholarship? Again, the answer appears to be yes and no. Much depends on whether students are judging their own success or that of others. As Table 4.3 shows, peer nominations were much more predictable from actual success than were self-ratings (.66

versus .38), and the peer nominations reflect more attention to different types of success. Figure 7.2 (diagrams *A* and *B*) illustrates these effects.

These diagrams are similar to those described in Chapter 4. The three circles represent membership in the three college success groups. Entries represent the percentage of students with each success combination who (diagram *A*) rated themselves very successful or (diagram *B*) were nominated as very successful by their peers. The two diagrams reveal two important differences.

First, the self-nominations are much less sharply dependent upon the actual record of success. In both diagrams about 60 percent of the triple-threat students in the heavily shaded center were nominated as very successful. In diagram *B* the percentage so nominated drops off rapidly in the outlying areas where students have fewer marks of success (multiple R_{bis} with the three marks was .66). In diagram *A* the drop is much less rapid (corresponding R_{bis} = .38; see note 2 for Chapter 7

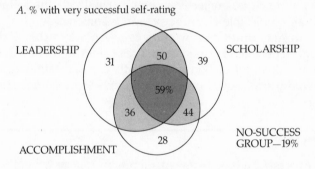

A. % with very successful self-rating

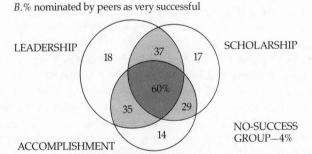

B. % nominated by peers as very successful

Figure 7.2 Percentage of students with different patterns of success who were— *A.* very successful by their own rating and *B.* nominated as very successful by their peers.

in Appendix C). Even among students who were not high in scholarship, leadership, or accomplishment, about one in five rated themselves very successful.

Second, the diagrams illustrate that students put about equal weight on scholarship, leadership, and accomplishment when they judge the college careers of their peers, but not when they judge themselves. For example, 39 percent of students in the scholar-only segment rated *themselves* very successful, about the same percentage (36 percent) as in the group who had been recognized for both leadership and accomplishment. In the eyes of *peers*, on the other hand, there were twice as many very successful students in the latter segment (35 percent) than in the former (17 percent). In other words, in the peer nominations two types of success counted for much more than one.

These results indicate that the student's view of success is much like that of the faculty—when it is someone else's success that is being viewed. The self-rating is relatively more sensitive to grade performance but generally much less objectively based. Finally, is the self-rating of success at all predictable from the preadmissions measures of achievement? The results up to now would suggest no, and that is the case. The six high school achievement measures used extensively in Chapter 5 gave a multiple correlation of .14 with the self-rating of success. Ratings of admissions staff had an even lower correlation with senior self-ratings.

SUMMING UP

Students expressed a broad view of success in college when they wrote about what they had accomplished. They often stressed personal development—their intellectual growth and their improving social maturity. But when asked to quantify their success overall, they tended to face the GPA music—at least to the extent that their self-ratings were influenced by the public record of achievement. It may be that students feel somewhat constrained to rate themselves consistent with the most visible measure of success promulgated by the college—or they may simply recognize that it is the GPA that really counts in future competition for choice educational programs and jobs.

It is evident, however, that from the students' point of view the grade point average leaves much to be desired as a measure of success over four years. The question of career planning, for example, is an issue thoroughly intertwined in the students' minds with how they have done in college. "Sense of direction" was evidently a button-pushing phrase for many students—capturing their anxiety about the future but also dramatizing the feeling that success has meaning as work toward something.

It is no surprise at all that self-ratings are largely unpredictable before admissions. As a criterion, the self-rating is highly subjective and often depends as much on how students perceive themselves and their college experiences as on the objective facts of competence and achievement. In fact, the goal progress ratings predicted the overall self-rating much better than did actual success measures (.53 versus .30). No doubt many rated their success partly on whether they did as well as they thought they should in relation to their level of achievement at entry. It is a developmental view of success that is self-referenced and future-oriented: How have I changed for the better?

Measures of achievement and signs of formal recognition typically used by colleges (and in this report) express more of a summative view of success. Who has excelled? How many have reached the highest level? It is not a matter of one view being right and the other wrong— though the issue is certainly not without controversy. The two views serve different purposes.

A developmental view of success starts with the fact that all students face the tasks of growing up, acquiring skills and understanding, developing competence as well as humanity, taking charge of their lives. It is through the educational program that colleges try to facilitate those objectives. The developmental view of success is particularly relevant to the institutions' efforts to improve the educational program. A summative view of success is more concerned with defining educational standards, recognizing achievement, and deciding who is ready for advanced work. The summative view is particularly relevant to setting admissions policy in a selective institution that does not elect to educate all students. Evidently when students judge the success of other students, they lean toward the summative view; when they rate themselves, the developmental view receives more emphasis.

8

Implications for Admissions

The prediction analyses in Chapter 5 led to one main conclusion. If colleges like those included in this study want to identify and attract students who are likely to be successful in ways the college values, they cannot do that most effectively by looking only at traditional academic measures. These results confirm again that the high school academic record and admissions test scores are the major predictors (of scholarship especially), but they alone are not optimal in forecasting other types of success or students whom the colleges regard as most successful overall. Four other measures made substantial contributions: high school academic honors, follow-through in extracurricular achievement, quality of the personal statement, and quality of the school references.

What are the implications for admissions policy and practice? Say a college shifts from a practice of selecting the best and brightest on HSR and SAT to a practice of selecting students who have the best balance of all six of these achievement measures. How many different people would be accepted? What would be the trade-offs with respect to their characteristics at entry and their pattern of success in college? The purpose of this chapter is to shed some light on those questions.

There is no completely satisfactory way of comparing admissions strategies. Ideally, one would want to select a freshman class randomly from last year's high school graduates and let the chips fall where they may, so to speak. With a full range of students, one could get a truer picture of the relationship between information in the applicant's folder and how that student later does in college. That is good experimental design but quite impractical in the real world. First, self-selected applicants to a given selective college are certainly not random and are typically far from representative of high school graduates. Second, even if a selective college were interested in such an experiment—and few colleges have been—there would be no way to ensure a representative group of enrolled students or to avoid the experiment's significantly changing the learning context.

We are left with triangulating the problem as best we can. One possibility is to "accept" applicants hypothetically, using several methods, and compare the resulting groups (as in Wing and Wallach 1971). This simple approach has the great advantage of revealing immediately what effect different selection strategies have on the characteristics of the selected group. Working with the full range of applicants is another advantage. There are disadvantages. Who knows which of the students hypothetically selected will actually enroll and persist to the senior year or which ones will succeed in what ways? Students so "selected" cannot be followed up to find out because most do not enroll.

Another possibility is to use the same alternative selection strategies to identify the "most promising" half of the enrolling class. This method is similar to the familiar validity study and has the same disadvantage of working with a selected group. But there is the advantage of knowing who stayed in school and succeeded in what areas. Baird and Richards (1968) used this approach, though they followed the students only through the freshman year and so had very limited data on different types of success. To compensate for the strengths and weaknesses of these two approaches, we have used both.

SELECTION STRATEGIES DEFINED

The analyses to follow are based on three alternative selection strategies. The first is the *actual selection,* that is, those applicants who were actually accepted by the college. The actual selection of applicants is included as a basis for comparing the effects of alternatives. The objective here is not to analyze the selection decision of the colleges; that was done in some detail in *Personal Qualities.*

A second method of selection we might call the *academic strategy,* in which students are selected purely on the basis of who had the highest (equally weighted) average score for HSR and SAT. Various other methods could be used, of course, in defining a strategy that puts heavy emphasis on traditional academic measures. An equally weighted composite of HSR and SAT was suggested by the *Personal Qualities* finding that these two had heavy and essentially equal weight in selection as well as equal validity in predicting freshman grades.

The third selection method is called here the *academic-plus strategy*. Its purpose is to simulate what happens when HSR, SAT, plus other supplementary achievement measures are used to optimize the selection of students who are successful overall on a variety of criteria. Constructing this selection strategy involves two steps. First, how to define "overall success"? We dealt with that question in Chapter 4, where overall success was defined as a linear model (i.e., a composite) of eight types of success, each weighted according to how much value these institutions placed on different marks of success when they chose their most successful students (see section on The Most Successful Group in Chapter 4). This procedure gives an "overall success" score for each senior—as it happens, a score that places approximately equal weight on scholarship, leadership, and accomplishment.

The next step was to predict who did well on overall success, using the same six best predictors employed in numerous analyses in Chapter 5 (HSR, SAT, high school honors, follow-through, personal statement, and school reference). Finally, that predicted score (actually a weighted composite of the six preadmissions measures) was used as a basis for the academic-plus strategy. The weight on each of the six measures varied somewhat from college to college; the average weights were as follows (see note 1 for Chapter 8 in Appendix C):

High school rank	.89
SAT	.59
High school honors	.33
Follow-through	.44
Personal statement	.31
School reference	.34

As a result, the academic-plus strategy has these characteristics as a selection device: It puts weight on traditional academic measures as well as supplementary measures of personal achievement—about half and half. The amount of weight on each measure is not arbitrary. It depends on how useful each measure was in forecasting the kinds of success the colleges emphasized in picking their best students. The question now is how different is this academic-plus strategy from the academic strategy and how much can one hope to gain by giving careful attention to this additional evidence in the applicant folder?

In evaluating these alternative strategies, we should be alert to several questions. How many different students are selected in the trade-off of one strategy against another? Quantitatively, what is the potential impact on an institution? To what extent and in what respects does an alternative strategy result in a larger number of successful students? In what other ways might the characteristics of students differentially selected affect the nature of the student body or ancillary objectives of the college? These questions are useful in broadening the issue. They also suggest an important caveat.

This chapter focuses primarily on one particular aspect of admissions policy—what a college might gain in more successful students by emphasizing one admissions strategy as opposed to another. While such information is pertinent and useful, the social and institutional utility of an admissions policy must be considered on a much broader basis than a marginal increment in the number of students who are outstanding performers. In determining sound admissions policy, colleges also take account of other essential interests—e.g., meeting enrollment objectives, developing a balanced class, maintaining institutional ties, and sending a useful message back to secondary schools about what achievements are important. Much of the data in the following sections are relevant to these broader issues, but to a considerable extent they must be independently weighed, and we do focus here primarily on the issue of marginal improvement in the number of successful students identified. Furthermore, in implementing admissions policies that reflect multiple institutional objectives, colleges typically weigh a variety of factors that may be relevant in the case of individual candidates. Few colleges would compute a composite score based upon all such factors and then select those applicants above a given score. Thus the analytic procedure employed here is not intended to mirror an actual admissions process. Rather it evaluates how much difference alternate strategies could make if, for the sake of examining the question, one assumed that all decisions were driven by one or the other selection strategy.

ANALYSIS OF APPLICANTS

The original group of applicants to the colleges numbered some 25,000 students. Since it was neither possible nor necessary to carry out for this total group all the extensive analyses planned, several samples were drawn for different purposes. One was a random sample of 500 applicants to each college. Since records for this sample include all research ratings and other information necessary for the analysis of alternative admissions strategies, it forms the data base for this section. After deletion of foreign students and other students with some missing data, the total applicant sample used in this analysis was 4,125.

Our objective was to examine questions about alternative admissions strategies and educational outcomes in selective colleges generally, not to describe results for individual institutions. Consequently, the results have been aggregated across the nine colleges, though we have examined differences between more and less selective institutions. All of the analyses were carried out initially within individual colleges. For example, predicted scores used in the academic-plus strategy were computed college by college on the basis of equations developed with individual senior classes. And within each college sample, the number of applicants selected by an alternative strategy matched exactly the proportion actually accepted by that college.

Another important point requires explanation. As noted earlier, one shortcoming of any analysis of applicants is that there are no college performance data for most students. Only about a quarter of this random sample of 4,125 applicants actually enrolled. For this reason, past analyses of applicants selected under different strategies (Wing and Wallach 1971) have been limited to a description of the preadmissions characteristics of those hypothetically selected, especially the trade-off groups selected by one strategy but not the other.

In the present analysis we have to some extent gotten around that limitation. No one can know several years before the fact whether individual students will subsequently demonstrate one or another outstanding performance. But evaluating an admissions strategy does not require knowing what a particular individual will later do. It is sufficient to know what proportion of a large group of applicants would likely succeed in one respect or another.

Such group estimates of success can be readily obtained. Recall from Chapter 5 that logistic regression equations based on preadmissions information were used to estimate the probability that an individual student would be outstanding in, say, leadership. These estimates were then accumulated (in so-called residual analyses) in order to compare the actual number of leaders in any particular group of students with the number expected on the basis of their preadmissions characteristics. The same technique can be used to estimate the success rate for any group of applicants—whether or not they enroll. Such estimates appear in tables to follow. There is no certainty that applicants alternatively accepted will enroll and perform in accordance with predictions based on a restricted group admitted, but that is an uncertainty shared by all college prediction work.

Outcome of three strategies

Table 8.1 shows what happened when 64 percent (the overall accept rate) of the applicants were selected by each of the three alternative strategies. Entries in this table represent the proportion of the selected group that had each of the characteristics indicated. The column headed "actual selection" is simply a nose count based on real acceptances in this sample; it reflects some important aspects of the admissions process at these colleges. For example, it is evident that the colleges tended to select the most academically able students and gave relatively little attention to extracurricular accomplishment. But the purpose of this table is not to illuminate the basis for actual admissions decisions, and the interesting dynamics of the process remain largely obscure here. For much more on that, readers should consult Chapter 6 in *Personal Qualities*.

The purpose of including the actual selection strategy is rather to examine in what respects its outcome is similar or dissimilar to the alternative strategies. One thing is immmediately apparent. As presented in Table 8.1, the outcomes of the three strategies appear to be much the same. All three clearly reflect a preference for the academically able applicant. There is some difference in the number of high scores on follow-through, personal statement, and school reference. That is to be expected because these measures had quite different weights in the alternative selection composites. The other achievement measures and background characteristics differ little. The overall impression is that the group "accepted" is much the same, regardless of selection strategy.

This result seems counterintuitive. Is one to believe that it makes little practical difference whether applicants are chosen solely on HSR and SAT or with balanced emphasis on these measures plus other evidence of achievement? As with most complicated matters, the answer seems arguably yes and no. As an aid in understanding admissions decision making, Table 8.1 is both revealing and deceptive. To appreciate why, it is useful to examine two reasons for the generally small differences in the outcomes of the three strategies.

One reason for the similar outcome is that the selection strategies are highly correlated. When the strategies are highly correlated, the number of students selected by one strategy and not the other—which one might call the trade-off group—is not large. In other words, not many students are affected. For example, in selecting the same number of applicants (2,655) on the basis of either the *academic* or the *academic-plus* strategy, we find that 87 percent of the decisions are identical! This means only 275 in each of the two trade-off groups—i.e., 275 applicants accepted by one method, a different 275 accepted by the second method. A second reason for the small differences in Table 8.1 is that the trade-off group constitutes only a modest fraction of the group selected.

Table 8.1 Profile of Preadmissions Achievements and Characteristics for All Applicants, 2,655 Actually Selected, and a Like Number Selected by Two Alternative Admissions Strategies

	All Applicants	Actual Selection	Selected by	
			Academic Strategy	Academic + Strategy
High achievement on				
HSR (top decile)	29%	35%	38%	36%
SAT (600+)	27	30	32	30
High school honors[a]	10	12	13	13
Leadership[a]	17	18	17	19
Community achievement[a]	06	06	07	07
Athletic achievement	31	29	28	30
Creative achievement[a]	13	14	13	14
Follow-through[a]	43	43	41	47
Work experience[a]	23	22	21	22
Personal statement[a]	28	28	26	30
School reference[a]	37	39	39	43
Characteristics				
Woman	47	49	51	52
Aid applicant	40	42	43	42
Minority	04	04	03	03
Alumni parent	04	05	04	04
Percent				
College graduate	25	24	24	24
Parent prominent	09	08	08	08
Private high school	26	24	22	22
Close-tie school	24	25	23	24
Local resident	10	13	12	13
Distant resident	29	32	31	31
N	4,125	2,655	2,655	2,655

a. Rating of 4+.

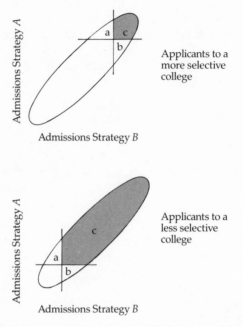

Admissions Strategy A

Admissions Strategy B

Applicants to a
more selective
college

Admissions Strategy A

Admissions Strategy B

Applicants to a
less selective
college

Figure 8.1 Effects of two admissions strategies in more and less selective colleges when the alternative strategies are highly correlated.

Comparison of trade-off groups

One implication is that the differential nature of two ways of selecting students is best understood by examining the characteristics of the trade-off groups—where those selected are actually different students. Another implication is that the differential impact of two selection strategies depends on the selection rate. All this is illustrated in Figure 8.1.

In this figure the ellipse represents a group of applicants. The lines through the ellipse represent cut scores used in selection. In comparing selection strategies, the cut score is set at the same level so that it segments an identical number of applicants—those in areas *a* and *c* according to Strategy *A* and those in areas *b* and *c* according to Strategy *B*. Since those in area *c* are the same in either event, it is by examining characteristics of students in the trade-off groups *a* and *b* that one can best detect any difference in the nature of the strategies. Since the correlation between the two strategies is quite high, the plot looks more like a loaf of French bread than a basketball, and the trade-off groups *a* and *b* are small.

Even though *a* and *b* are small, the choice of one or the other could make a significant difference in the freshman class of a more selective college because the trade-off group is a consequential portion of the group accepted. In the less selective college, on the other hand, the trade-off group is swamped by the much larger group *c* admitted by either strategy. In the group of more selective colleges (BUC, COL, WIL) in this study, for example, the trade-off group was 31 percent as large as the group accepted. In the group of less selective colleges (HAR, KAL, KEN, OCC, OHI, RIC), the trade-off group was only 6 percent the size of the total group accepted.

Table 8.2 shows several types of information for the two trade-off groups associated with each pair of strategies. For example, the first column (*A not B*) is based on 337 students selected by strategy *A* but not by strategy *B*. The bottom section of the table indicates the degree of similarity of the strategies; the higher the correlation and the percentage of identical decisions, the smaller the trade-off groups. The academic and academic-plus strategies were somewhat more closely related to each other than either was to the actual selection process. No doubt this is because the actual selections reflected a variety of institutional objectives (see *Personal Qualities,* Chapter 6, for details).

All other entries in Table 8.2 compare the outcomes of the selection strategies, but only with respect to differences between the trade-off groups. We will come back to the question of how large these differences are in the total groups accepted.

The first six lines of this table are all based on preadmissions information. They indicate to what extent these trade-off groups may represent different types of students at entry—different in the sense of having shown different patterns of achievement in secondary school. It is no surprise that the academic trade-off group selects up to twice as many students who are high on HSR and SAT as is true of the other two strategies. Both the academic and academic-plus strategies favor students who have won high school honors.

Other measures of personal achievement (follow-through, personal statement, school reference) got more weight in the actual selection process at these institutions than they would have in a strictly academic selection strategy. This was doubly true of the academic-plus trade-off group. It identified some twice as many students high on these measures as did the actual selection, and three to four times as many when compared with the academic trade-off group.

How many will succeed?

How do these different qualities at entry translate into later success? We described earlier the prediction procedure for estimating the pro-

Table 8.2 Pattern of Preadmissions Achievement and Preselected College Success for Trade-off Groups Accepted by one Admissions Strategy and Rejected by Another

	Selection Strategies A. Actual vs. B. Academic		Selection Strategies A. Actual vs. C. Academic+		Selection Strategies B. Academic vs. C. Academic+	
	A not B N = 337	B not A N = 337	A not C N = 353	C not A N = 353	B not C N = 275	C not B N = 275
% Achievement in high school						
HSR top decile	20	42	18	30	33	21
SAT of 600+	21	37	26	27	38	19
High school honors[a]	06	11	05	14	04	09
Follow-through[a]	45	37	26	56	17	67
Personal statement[a]	34	23	22	35	16	46
School reference[a]	39	34	24	52	19	60
% Expected in college success group						
Scholarship	16	24	14	24	18	21
Leadership	28	31	23	35	22	36
Accomplishment	23	23	19	28	20	31
Most successful	12	16	10	17	10	15
Correlation between strategies (ϕ)	.64		.63		.71	
% of applicants who were accepted or rejected by both strategies	84%		83%		87%	

a. Rating of 4+.

portions expected to excel in scholarship, leadership, accomplishment, and most successful. Those predictions are based on the same preadmissions measures shown here. On these four success criteria, the academic strategy was equal to or better than the actual selection process; it clearly yielded more scholars.

The more important point is the superiority of the academic-plus method of selection. It outstrips the actual selection process more consistently than does the academic method. When the academic and academic-plus strategies are compared directly, the latter is clearly superior. The academic-plus trade-off group (C not B) is predicted to yield half again as many students who would be identified as outstanding in leadership, accomplishment, or most successful. It is even marginally better with respect to scholarship.

Contrary to the doubtful impression at the outset of this discussion, these alternative selection strategies do pick students who have quite different track records and significantly different prospects for success. These differences between the trade-off groups were comparable for the more and less selective colleges, but the trade-off groups were only a limited segment of the applicants. The question now is how much of the difference gets translated into a difference between the full groups accepted by more and less selective colleges?

The very different effect in more and less selective colleges shows up in Table 8.3. In the less selective group of institutions, there is almost no difference in the *total* group accepted by the three methods. In the more selective colleges, however, there are differences. In a study of their qualifications at entry, the alternative accepted groups clearly differ in their strength on traditional academic measures compared with other indicators of achievement. For example, in a comparison of the groups accepted by the academic-plus and the academic methods, the latter group has about one-fifth more students who are high on HSR and SAT. On the other hand, the group selected by the academic-plus method has a fifth more students who were leaders or athletes in high school or had records of unusual creative accomplishments.

As for selecting students who succeed in college, both the academic and the academic-plus methods came out ahead of the actual selections. The two hypothetical methods were about equal in picking scholars, but as we have seen previously, academic-plus was otherwise somewhat better. The largest difference was between the actual and the academic-plus. Proportionately, the success rates of the latter were some 10 to 15 percent higher, depending on which success criterion is compared.

In a sense these differences in college success rates are hypothetical because most of these students never entered. We turn now to a similar

Table 8.3 Profile of Preadmissions Achievement and Expected College Success for Groups Selected by Three Admissions Strategies—In More and Less Selective Colleges

	In Less Selective Colleges[b]			In More Selective Colleges[c]		
	Actual Selection	*Academic Strategy*	*Academic+ Strategy*	*Actual Selection*	*Academic Strategy*	*Academic+ Strategy*
% Achievement in high school						
HSR top decile	30%	30%	31%	59%	79%	66%
SAT of 600+[a]	24	24	24	63	74	62
High school honors[a]	10	10	10	23	27	28
Follow-through[a]	39	39	41	60	57	74
Personal statement[a]	25	24	25	42	39	53
School reference[a]	38	36	40	47	49	60
% Expected in college success group						
Scholarship	31	31	31	33	38	38
Leadership	37	37	38	34	35	38
Accomplishment	21	21	22	31	32	35
Most successful	23	23	23	19	21	22

a. Ratings of 4+.
b. HAR, KAL, KEN, OCC, OHI, RIC: 82% accepted.
c. BUC, COL, WIL: 31% accepted.

comparison among the freshmen who were admitted. This group does not permit an analysis of admissions decisions, but it has the advantage of detailed information about actual performance in college.

ANALYSIS OF ENROLLED STUDENTS

In the previous analyses the "most promising" applicants were defined in three ways, and then groups "accepted" on that basis were compared. The same logic is now applied to enrolled students—three-fourths of whom are different persons. The freshman class in each of the nine colleges was sorted into a top and a bottom half according to the same two alternative selection strategies used previously—academic (HSR and SAT) and academic-plus (a weighted composite of HSR, SAT, plus four additional measures of achievement). The four resulting groups were 1,854 students selected as most promising (high) on both the academic and academic-plus definition, 1,847 who were low on both counts, and two trade-off groups numbering 405 each that were high on one method and low on the other. This result again reflects a high correlation (ϕ = .64) between the two definitions of promise. The college performances of these four groups are compared in Table 8.4. Three questions are of particular interest:

- Is there a similar pattern of difference in the four main measures of success for the trade-off groups as was found for applicants?
- Is that difference characteristic of less selective as well as more selective colleges?
- Does the more detailed information on educational goals and on actual performance further illuminate these alternative definitions of promise?

The first line of Table 8.4 shows the persistence rate for entering students in the four categories as indicated. Consistent with earlier analyses, retention was not much related to promise, by either definition. The remaining lines in the table are based on seniors. The largest differences are between the first and fourth columns—the freshmen who were consistently more or less promising. The trade-off groups in the second and third columns represent, one might argue, a narrow and a broad view of talent.

The percentage of students attaining the four major types of success—scholarship, leadership, accomplishment, and most successful—does vary substantially according to whether the student was more or

Table 8.4 Percentage of Students in Various College Success Groups—Classified as High or Low on Two Definitions of Promise When Freshmen

	Classified as Freshman			
	I *Low Academic* *Low Academic +*	II *High Academic* *Low Academic +*	III *Low Academic* *High Academic +*	IV *High Academic* *High Academic +*
% Persisting to senior year	73%	75%	78%	81%
% of seniors in success group				
College honors	09	16	21	44
Dept. honors	06	10	13	16
Appt. leader	15	17	25	31
Elected leader	15	13	20	22
Science accomp.	01	03	04	06
Artistic accomp.	04	03	06	05
Commun. accomp.	02	04	03	05
Physical accomp.	06	02	09	04
Organiz. accomp.	05	03	07	08
Other accomp.	06	06	12	14
Grad. on time	85	88	93	92
Double major	12	15	18	19
Advanced study	06	12	10	16
Scholarship	13	20	27	48
Leadership	27	26	39	43
Accomplishment	18	16	30	30
Most successful	11	11	20	31
Number of seniors	1,348	305	317	1,493

less promising at entry. For example, students high on both definitions of promise were almost four times as likely to win academic honors as were those low on both counts (48 percent versus 13 percent). For the present discussion, the two middle columns are the more interesting. Looking here at the actual performance of enrolled students, we see that the pattern of differences between the trade-off groups is quite similar to that found for applicants, though here the differences are typically somewhat larger (compare with Table 8.2). On each of the four success criteria, students identified as high academic-plus/low academic (column III) outperformed those identified as high academic/ low academic-plus (column II).

Much the same pattern of differences between these two trade-off groups was observed in the more selective and the less selective colleges (see Table D.8 in Appendix D). That is to say, a broader definition of talent is a superior predictor of success in more as well as less selective colleges, and the seemingly inconsequential difference between admissions strategies in less selective colleges (see Table 8.3) was, in fact, only the result of their high acceptance rate. Thus, the broader definition of talent is equally relevant in the less selective colleges. They are simply much less able to affect the balance of talent in the freshman class through different selection decisions.

Results for the additional, more specific types of success listed in Table 8.4 give a picture generally similar to that previously described. The trade-off group in column III was generally more successful than its counterpart in column II. That was true of both categories of academic honors, both forms of leadership, and most types of accomplishment. There were two interesting reversals, perhaps representing an extreme form of academic-extracurricular differentiation. Outstanding physical accomplishment was the only success achieved much more often by the less rather than the more academically able students (slightly true of artistic accomplishment as well). Note, on the other hand, that while students in column III were generally superior to those in column II, they were not more likely to be accepted for advanced study.

This discussion has focused on differential success of trade-off groups. Another important question is what differential effect does one have on the student body by giving preference to one view of talent or another? In the analysis of applicants, we compared the background characteristics and achievements of students differentially accepted. Some additional data relevant to this question were available for enrolled students: what educational goals the students considered to be very important and the major in which they eventually landed.

These data can be summarized briefly (see Table D.9 in Appendix D for details). To a considerable degree, more able and less able students seem to share generally similar educational goals. For example, comparing the students in columns I and IV of Table 8.4, one finds that in both groups almost half the freshmen stressed the importance of a liberal education, and in both groups about one-quarter thought that developing practical skills was very important. There was a small but interesting pattern of differences between the two trade-off groups. Typically, some 8 to 10 percent more of the students in the academic-plus trade-off group believed that these goals were very important: getting a good liberal education, being active in extracurricular activities, developing social competence, and giving special attention to moral and ethical issues—in sum, a broad perspective of higher education. With respect to college major, there were two significant differences between the trade-off groups. Students who were mainly talented academically were more likely to major in physical science; students in the more broadly talented group were overrepresented in the arts.

PRODUCTIVE FOLLOW-THROUGH

We have seen that a college can more effectively identify promising students if it gives heed to evidence of achievement beyond high school rank and admissions test scores. From a practical standpoint, how does one go about doing that? In the analyses presented here such supplementary evidence has been incorporated in a composite score that optimally weights honors, follow-through, references, etc. It is unlikely that many colleges have the resources and the patience to undertake the detailed ratings and computations that would be necessary to replicate that procedure in the actual operation of an admissions program. The results of Chapter 5 suggest a practical alternative.

Earlier correlational analysis indicated that in the prediction of who will succeed in college, most of the gain from the supplementary achievement measures could be realized by focusing on the more objective measures—namely, follow-through and high school honors, which were based largely on public and verifiable information. Also, we found that students identified as outstanding on the particular accomplishments upon which follow-through was based (by admissions staff flags or high research staff ratings) were more likely to succeed than their HSR and SAT scores would indicate. These findings suggest a useful way of looking for promising students: Seek out the young people who have demonstrated *productive follow-through* in secondary school.

Accordingly, for our purposes here, we have defined such a group of extracurricular producers as all students who got a top rating on follow-through, or on any of the four accomplishments upon which it was based, plus any students who were flagged by the admissions staff in the same areas. Academic honors are certainly another form of productive follow-through but are highly related to HSR and SAT. Academic honors were not included here so that producers in this analysis would constitute more clearly an alternative to academic talent (see note 2 for Chapter 8 in Appendix C).

The independence of these two types of talent in this sample is illustrated in Figure 8.2. These extracurricular producers are almost equally represented at each level of the academic composite. There is, in fact, no correlation between the two ($\phi = .01$). The same relationship held in the applicant sample. There were, then, a substantial number of students who were producers but below average on the academic measures—i.e., sections G and H of the figure. Are such students an attractive recruiting alternative to those with high rank and test scores but no such strong evidence of extracurricular accomplishment? The analysis of admissions decisions in *Personal Qualities* would indicate that the latter groups (sections A and B of the figure) are much more sought after.

Figure 8.3 compares three such alternative strategies of identifying promising students. In each comparison, the bars indicate the proportion of students in the alternative groups who succeeded on the four criteria listed. These data are based on seniors, but differential retention

		Extracurricular producers in high school	
		NO	YES
	1	A 633	E 496
Academic composite quartile (HSR + SAT)	2	B 701	F 429
	3	C 675	G 449
	4	D 666	H 462

Figure 8.2 Number of freshmen in each academic composite quartile who were and were not extracurricular producers.

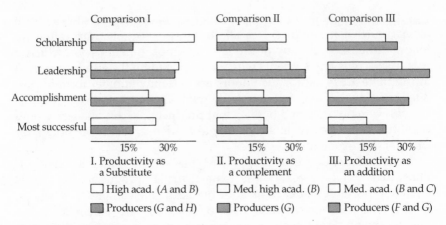

Figure 8.3 Comparison of the percentage of successful students identified when extracurricular productivity is used as a substitute for, complement to, or addition to evidence of academic ability. (Letters identifying groups compared refer to areas in Figure 8.2.)

was not an important factor. Persistence rate varied no more than 3 percent for any comparison.

Comparison I in Figure 8.3 contrasts producers who are below average on HSR and SAT with nonproducers who are high on the academic measures. In other words, what is the differential probability of success when an extracurricular producer is traded for a student who is more academically able? Looking at the groups in Figure 8.2, we see the trade-off is $(G + H)$ for $(A + B)$. This comparison treats extracurricular productivity as a *substitute* for academic achievement. The results indicate that the trade-off is not favorable. These high school producers were somewhat more likely to produce significant accomplishments in college (29 percent versus 22 percent), but they were far less likely to graduate with academic honors (16 percent versus 41 percent). And the substituted producers were less often named most successful.

Comparison II in Figure 8.3 works on a similar theory, but only in the midrange of ability. Here it is assumed that all students in the top quartile academically (A and E) are automatically selected as more promising, and those in the bottom quartile (D and H) are automatically selected as less promising. In this comparison of selection strategies, students in areas B and G are possible trade-offs because those are the two areas among the four in the midrange, where a different decision would be made depending upon whether it is based on the academic or the productivity qualification. Thus, extracurricular productivity *com-*

plements the academic measures by trading producers for academically more able students as before—but only within a limited range. The term *complement* is more appropriate here than *substitute* because productivity plays no role at all for students who are highly qualified or poorly qualified academically.

On all four success measures, the results show a shift favoring the producers. Here the trade-off groups are about equally represented in the most successful category, the gap is greatly narrowed with respect to scholarship, and the producers do better on leadership and accomplishment. These results illustrate the potential usefulness of extracurricular productivity as a complement to academic measures—that is, a means of exercising a limited trade-off of scholarship for other high performance.

Comparison III takes a further step in the same direction. Here we assume that there is a substantial number of students in the midrange where there is a choice between two students having essentially the same rank and test scores. Here the question is how much difference it makes if one can enroll an extracurricular producer in place of an applicant who was not a producer, but has essentially the same academic qualifications. Productivity is used as *additional* information to break a tie.

In this comparison the producer is a superior achiever in college on all counts—more likely to be a scholar and a leader, almost twice as likely to be cited for significant accomplishment, and picked as a most successful senior half again as often as the nonproducer with comparable HSR and SAT.

A final point on extracurricular producers may be obvious, but deserves examining nonetheless. There are producers, and there are producers. Some of these producers gained that distinction on the playing field, others in the student council, others in the art studio. What kinds of college performance can one expect of different types of producers in secondary school?

In the previous analysis three types of extracurricular producers were distinctive and fairly numerous: leaders, artists, and athletes. There were college success groups that represented similar achievement. Figure 8.4 tracks those three types of producers from school to college, with academic producers thrown in to round out the picture.

For each type of high school producer, this figure shows what percentage were outstanding in each of the four corresponding areas in college. The picture can be viewed in two ways. Looking at a particular kind of bar (e.g., the black bars) gives a college success profile for

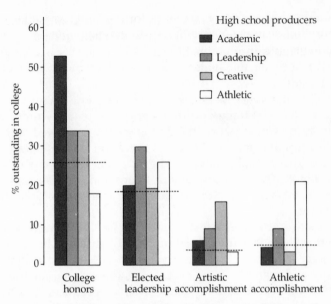

Figure 8.4 Incidence of different types of outstanding performance in college by different types of high school producers (------% for all students).

one type of high school producer. Looking at a cluster of bars indicates what types of students most frequently gain a particular recognition in college. The figure illustrates two important points.

First, within each area of outstanding college performance, the group most likely to excel had already produced in that area. The only instance where that rule is challenged is the strong showing of athletes on elected leadership in college. That linkage between sports prominence and political potential on campus was noted earlier.

Second, each type of producer tends to exceed the college class average (in percentage outstanding) primarily in the area of demonstrated excellence. This is clearly true of the scholars, and mostly true of those who won athletic or creative (mostly artistic) distinction in high school. Leaders are the exception. That leaders were high in all four areas of college success may reflect the fact that in high school, students often win leadership roles by virtue of, or in the context of, some other competence. In any event, leadership was often a shared characteristic of productive students. This analysis of extracurricular producers can be summarized as follows:

- Recruiting producers without regard for HSR and SAT is likely to be a poor enrollment strategy. Extracurricular productivity is *not a substitute* for academic qualification.
- When it is a matter of choosing between two students of equal academic ability, the producer is clearly the better choice. Extracurricular productivity is clearly favorable as an *additional* qualification.
- Within limits, recruiting a producer may be a reasonable trade-off to a student who scores somewhat higher on academic measures. Extracurricular productivity can, in this sense, be useful as a *complementary* qualification.
- Producers are not exchangeable. They are likely to produce in college in their area of interest and demonstrated competence, but not necessarily in other areas.

RECRUITMENT VERSUS SELECTION

A reasonable conclusion to draw from this analysis is that a broad interpretation of talent is preferable to one that focuses exclusively on traditional academic measures. In identifying promising students, the use of other evidence of competence to complement admissions test scores and the high school grade record does yield more students who succeed in college—succeed in ways that the colleges say they value. Productive follow-through in extracurricular activities appears to be a useful recruiting strategy if based on reasonably objective evidence and used as an addition or complement to, rather than a substitute for, academic competence.

These results unambiguously demonstrate one other fact. The differential effects on a freshman class of using an academic versus a broader-based selection strategy is obviously greater in a more selective as compared with a less selective college. There are two important aspects of this institutional difference.

One concerns the role and impact of selection strategy in a less selective college. It would be a mistake to conclude that method of selection is not important unless one can detect significant differences in the group accepted by alternative methods. Note that the proportion of applicants differentially selected by different methods was about the same in the more and less selective colleges here. Thus, the differential impact on students that comes from emphasizing one type of qualification or another is about the same. And the differential message being sent to students, parents, and schools as to what achievements are important is about the same.

Also, the less selective college has a mirror-image advantage over the more selective college in one respect. The less selective college is more efficient in identifying applicants who would do poorly because its small rejected group is farther below the academic ability of the typical admitted student than is the rejected group at a more selective college. For that reason, it is more important to identify them in the selection process.

A second important aspect of the institutional difference concerns the role of selection versus recruitment. While it is true that a less selective college may be able to change the profile of the freshman class very little through altering its selection rules, the same does not hold true for recruitment. The fact that talents other than academic ability are demonstrably relevant to success in college considerably broadens the potential recruiting pool. Furthermore, it may well be easier to recruit good students who are otherwise productive than it is to recruit applicants who are particularly high on rank and test scores. If so, one could increase the size of that favorable trade-off group by modifying somewhat the recruiting targets. In any event, these data illustrate the commonsense fact that recruitment is a far more fertile ground than selection if a less selective college seeks a beneficial change in its admissions strategy.

Recruitment is intimately related to student self-selection. In *Personal Qualities* it was argued that self-selection is probably more important than institutional selection in determining the nature of the freshman class. The results described here strongly support that point of view. This means that in most colleges institutional policy on applicant selection is important mostly because of the indirect effect it has on self-selection through the institutional image that is created thereby and reinforced through recruiting practices.

Finally, it is important to remember that this analysis has been concerned with one institutional objective—enrolling students who are likely to do well. There are other utilities to consider. A selective college has other objectives in admissions that reflect social and institutional interests. Only the individual colleges can evaluate those objectives and balance them with the selection strategies discussed here.

Summary of Findings and Conclusions

Before the results of this study are summarized, it is useful to step back and ask briefly, "What were the main issues addressed and what have we learned?" The first phase of this project examined the role of personal qualities in admissions. The next question was how those qualities are related to success in college. From a great deal of past research we know that the combination of high school rank and admissions test scores does a moderately good job of forecasting academic performance in college, and that it is very hard to find other measures that add much useful information for predicting grades. It seemed clear that a satisfactory answer to the question of how personal qualities of students are related to success in college would require a more careful assessment of success through the four undergraduate years—an assessment that goes beyond the grade point average.

Looking beyond grades, one finds many cogent arguments for defining success broadly and for taking an equally broad view of talent when evaluating applicants for admission (see references and discussion in Chapter 2 and in *Personal Qualities*, the report on the first phase of this project). Studies have shown that if college faculty and staff are asked to describe successful students, they ascribe to those students a variety of desirable traits and achievements. Furthermore, studies have shown that different types of achievement in college are best predicted by corresponding achievements in high school, though such work has largely been based on student questionnaires administered in the freshman and sophomore years. This follow-up phase of the Personal Qualities Project has attempted to add to previous research by addressing three broad issues.

First, if one examines the accumulated record through four years, can one find substantial evidence of distinctive types of achievement other than grades that influence the institution's judgment as to who are its most successful students? Data provided in Chapter 4 indicate that the answer is clearly yes. To a surprising degree, students who were named most successful were those who had achieved recognition for leadership and other significant accomplishments, as well as scholarship.

Second, can a college effectively recruit and enroll students whom it is likely to regard as most successful four years later by evaluating applicants only on the basis of school rank and test scores? If the institution defines success broadly, as did each of these nine colleges, the answer is no.

Third, are there any useful new approaches to supplementing school rank and test scores with measures that are likely to be valid and reliable as well as practical? The results of this study suggest that evidence of *productive follow-through* in secondary school may be an answer. There is much to gain from giving productivity more emphasis in college admissions. We return to this possibility after a review of the findings of the study.

THE MAJOR FINDINGS

The following analyses were reported in Chapters 4 through 8, respectively: how this class performed through four years, to what extent different types of success were predictable before entry, predicting grades in the upper versus the lower division, how the students viewed their success, and implications for admissions policy and practice. The main results can be summarized under the following questions.

How did students sort themselves into academic majors?

There were 3,676 students in the Personal Qualities Project—76 percent of the entering freshmen—who were still enrolled after four years. Finding a suitable major was a common problem for many students. At matriculation one freshman in five indicated no preference. Among those who did have a preferred major and remained enrolled, the majority changed to another field. As a result, only about one senior in three was majoring in a field preferred as a freshman. In virtually every major those students who started and finished in that same field were an academically superior group of freshmen. In most academic areas a fairly steady 35 to 45 percent of entering freshmen migrated out, and in each area the out-migrants were a representative group as to freshman grades. Looking only at the students who remained enrolled for four years, we find significant changes from freshman to senior year in the number and academic ability of students in different majors. Those changes were due almost entirely to in-migration, i.e., students attracted to the major in the course of four years.

What was the incidence of different types of success and how were they interrelated?

The yearly grade average for the 3,676 students who remained enrolled for four years rose steadily from about 2.8 in the freshman year to 3.1 in the senior year. Most of these students graduated on time in June 1983. One senior in four earned grades high enough to graduate with college honors (i.e., cum laude). One senior in nine won departmental honors on the basis of a senior thesis or a research project. Overall, 30 percent of the seniors were recognized for one or both of these types of superior scholarship. There were not large differences in scholarship honors from one major to another. As of June of the senior year, 412 (11 percent of the seniors) had been admitted to a medical or law school or to a Ph.D. program.

Among the seniors 18 percent were elected by students to a major campus office; 23 percent were appointed by the college to a responsible position. More than one senior in three held one or both of these leadership roles during their college careers. Men and women were represented equally in elected offices; the college-appointed positions went more frequently to women. There were not large differences among academic areas, although students in arts were less likely to be leaders while those in biological science were overrepresented in this success group.

The colleges typically employed very high standards in nominating one-fourth of their students for one or more of these six types of significant accomplishment: scientific-technical (3 percent), artistic (4 percent), communications (3 percent), physical (5 percent), organizing (6 percent), other independent achievement (10 percent). Only one in twenty was nominated in two areas; one in a hundred was nominated in three. There was little sex difference. Significant accomplishments were well spread among students in different majors, although they varied, as one might expect, on the basis of student interest (e.g., arts versus science).

How were different types of success related?

Scholarship, leadership, and accomplishment were moderately correlated (r = .25 to .35). Comparing any pair of the three (e.g., scholarship and leadership), we find close to half the students in one success group were also in the other. Eight marks of success were examined within these three categories. Within scholarship, college and departmental honors were highly related. Elected and appointed leadership appeared similar in some respects, different in others. The former was evidently associated somewhat more with athletic fame, the latter more with scholarly reputation. Among the four areas of accomplishment, scholastic forms of achievement (artistic, scientific, communications) were predictably related more to scholarship, while organizing achievement was related more to leadership. "Other independent achievement" was a success category often used to designate students much admired by the college. It was related to both scholarship and leadership. Physical achievement was largely independent of all types of success except elected leadership.

In the view of the colleges, who were their most successful students?

Nine college committees worked independently to select their most successful seniors. The selection process varied from campus to campus, and individual colleges chose different percentages of the class. The achievements of this most successful group were examined to determine what factors influenced the choices. Regression analyses indicated that each of the eight marks of success listed in the previous paragraph received at least some weight, though not in each college. As a group, these nine institutions placed very nearly equal emphasis on scholarship, leadership, and accomplishment when they picked the best exemplars of success as they saw it on their campuses.

What measures predicted the most successful student?

A central issue in this study was whether there is supplemental information over and above HSR and SAT that can be helpful in identifying applicants likely to be "most successful" in the institution's eyes. The answer was clearly yes. Four types of information—high school honors, follow-through, the personal statement, and the school reference—were useful additions. These measures improved the prediction of "most successful" students by 25 percent. They improved prediction of leadership by 65 percent, accomplishment by 42 percent, but scholarship by only 7 percent.

Follow-through—a measure of persistent and successful extracurricular accomplishment—was the strongest addition. Among all six measures, it had the largest weight in predicting leadership and accomplishment and the second-largest weight in forecasting which students were likely to be most successful. Students who did well on follow-through were overrepresented by 20 to 30 percent in each of the three main success categories, even after HSR and SAT scores were taken into account.

Two of the four most useful supplementary measures were rated subjectively (the student's personal statement and the school reference). The other two were based largely on objective and publicly verifiable information (high school honors and follow-through in extracurricular accomplishment). These latter two measures accounted for most of the improvement over HSR and SAT in forecasting college success.

What measures best predicted particular types of success?

The two traditional academic predictors, high school rank (HSR) and admissions test score (SAT), were by far the best at forecasting the scholastic types of achievement. In a comparison of the two, HSR was a somewhat better predictor of college honors (based on cumulative grade average), while the SAT was a somewhat better predictor of departmental honors. The latter were based on independent scholarship, arguably more characteristic of preprofessional work in the discipline than is grade point average. Except for the somewhat heavier weight on the SAT, winning departmental honors appeared to depend on much the same abilities as getting high grades.

While supplementary measures in the high school record were not very helpful in predicting scholastic achievement, they were substantially better than HSR and SAT in predicting some other types of success such as elected leadership, physical accomplishment, and organizing accomplishment. As earlier research has indicated, corresponding accomplishments were linked between high school and college. For example, college success in athletics, leadership, and artistic endeavors was best indicated by previous success in those areas.

How well did the admissions staff identify successful students?

The admissions staff ratings, which took account of all information about each applicant, were better than HSR and SAT alone in forecasting which students would likely be successful in college. These admissions staff ratings were not quite so accurate in forecasting as was the best weighted composite of HSR and SAT and other research staff ratings of each applicant's record, but the two (admissions staff and research staff ratings) were complementary to some degree. The admissions staff's academic rating of each applicant did reflect some intelligence not found in HSR and SAT about who was likely to earn good grades. Similarly, HSR and SAT were useful in identifying the better academic achievers in college, even among applicants who received identical academic ratings from the admissions staff. Of all the research staff ratings, follow-through proved to be the most useful addition to admissions staff ratings.

There were two types of admissions staff ratings in addition to the overall academic and overall personal ratings. All applicant interviews were rated on a 3-point scale. Also, all applicant folders were flagged if they showed evidence of any special talent or attribute that might positively influence an admissions decision. Typically only small groups of students were flagged, but those flags often turned out to be valid indicators of performance over and above that predicted by HSR and SAT.

The interview rating was another story. In Phase I of the Personal Qualities Project, it was found that in some colleges applicants who had an outstanding interview were much more likely to be admitted than their HSR and SAT scores would indicate. Four years later we found no evidence at all that this group had performed any better—in scholarship, leadership, or accomplishment—than their rank and test scores alone would lead one to expect.

In what ways was student background related to success?

Women were more likely to graduate with academic honors than were men (35 percent versus 25 percent). About half of that difference was because the women were somewhat more able. Underrepresented minorities (black, Hispanic, and American Indian) were less likely to graduate with honors than was predicted on the basis of their HSR and SAT (9 percent versus 16 percent). In examining black and Hispanic students separately, however, we found that blacks were significantly overrepresented in the leadership and accomplishment groups (more than a third over the number predicted).

Some applicants had an apparent tie with the institution (i.e., close-tie school, alumni relations, etc.). They received preference in admissions either for that reason or in the expectation of higher performance than their record might otherwise indicate. In general, students with an apparent special interest in the institution did not perform better than their record would indicate. Alumni sons and daughters were a mild exception. They had average qualifications at entry, but their performance in college did exceed expectations somewhat, mainly in the area of leadership.

There were some substantial differences in the college performance of students coming from secondary schools with different control and college-going rate. These differences were almost fully accounted for, however, by corresponding differences in qualifications at entry. For example, in this sample the students from private schools were not so well qualified at entry as were the students from public schools that sent few graduates to college, and both groups performed at about the level that their qualifications would lead one to expect. Students from public schools with high college-going rates were somewhat of an exception. They were more frequently represented in the leadership and accomplishment success groups than would be expected on the basis of their record at entry.

How well could persistence, graduation, and admission to advanced study be predicted?

Substantial college-to-college differences in retention rates were highly related to institutional selectivity: where selectivity was higher, retention was higher. Overall, there was a moderately good relationship between retention and academic ability, but within individual institutions the tendency to drop out was largely unrelated to HSR and SAT. This was because for most students dropout was also largely unrelated to college grades. In both the more selective and less selective colleges, most dropouts were not in academic jeopardy at the time they withdrew.

The academically more able students were somewhat more likely to graduate on time and to complete requirements in more than one major, but both of these aspects of graduation were largely unpredictable from preadmissions information. Admission to advanced study (medical or law school or a Ph.D. program) by June of the senior year was moderately predictable from three and only three preadmissions measures: intention (at college entry) to seek such advance training, SAT, and HSR, in that order.

How did the prediction of upper-division grades compare with the prediction of lower-division grades?

There are two ways of evaluating how well preadmissions measures predict grade point averages year by year. One is to use the cumulative grade point average based on all coursework completed at the end of each successive year; HSR and SAT predicted this cumulative average essentially as well after the fourth year as after the first. There was little variation from college to college. Another method is to use grade point averages based only on coursework taken during each year. As has been demonstrated in previous research, such yearly averages became progressively less predictable. The average drop was .17 and all colleges showed the same progressive decline.

Declining correlations with yearly averages in the second, third, and fourth years were characteristic of all academic measures examined: HSR, SAT-V, SAT-M, high school honors, and freshman grade average. None of the numerous preadmissions measures included in this phase of the study showed any sign of improved validity for upper-division grades as compared with lower-division. Even though overall predictability was poorer in the upper division, there was no indication that any change in the choice of measures or how they were weighted would materially improve that situation.

What accounts for weaker prediction of upper-division grades?

Three hypotheses were examined with data from this study and the work of other authors—namely, that the lower predictability in the upper division is due to the fact that the students are changing, the task is changing, or the grading is changing. The students-are-changing hypothesis did not appear attractive because of the convincing results of earlier postdiction research and the failure here to find any evidence of motivational drift among groups of students. That no measures in this study were differentially useful in predicting upper-division grades argues against the task-is-changing hypothesis.

Several lines of evidence supported the grading-is-changing hypothesis. When validity coefficients were computed within departments instead of within colleges, the decline in predictability of yearly grade averages was considerably lessened. Two factors help to explain this effect: departmental grading patterns and student migration patterns. First, grades in some departments remained steady from freshman to senior year while grades in other departments increased substantially. Second, students who were weaker academically were more likely to change major and also more likely to change into a major where grades go up. Measures that were more closely related to student migration (especially SAT-M) also showed the greatest decline in validity computed within college and the greatest recovery in validity computed within departments.

The apparent joint effect of departmental grading patterns and student migratory patterns was to diminish the intrinsic validity of upper-division grade point average as a measure of academic performance. Confirming evidence came from correlating upper- and lower-division grades with three other indicators of overall student success: those nominated as most successful by the college and by their peers and those students admitted to advanced study. In all three the lower-division GPA was more highly correlated with membership in the success group. These results suggest that the diminishing quality of the GPA criterion is likely a principal reason for the decline in predictability of yearly grade averages.

How did the students rate their progress?

In rating the importance of educational goals, seniors put 12 goals in almost the same rank order as they had as freshman. The only large shift was in their view of a goal concerning professional training, the definition of which emphasized grades. About twice as many freshmen as seniors thought it was very important to "make the grades I need in order to get into a good school when I finish here." Seniors were more satisfied with their progress generally than they had been as freshmen. Typically four out of five seniors indicated satisfaction with what they had accomplished in areas that were important to them. The exception was career exploration.

How did students view success in college?

When seniors were asked whether their college career had been successful overall, five out of six answered "mostly successful," and two of those five said "very successful." The percentage of students considering themselves very successful did not vary significantly by sex, by major, or from college to college. In written comments about their achievements in college, students talked most frequently about their personal and educational development. In response to specific questions on what factors may have contributed to or detracted from a successful and satisfying college career, personal contacts with faculty and students were the big pluses. Financial problems and poor sense of direction were the worst detractors.

In comparing student ratings of success with objective evidence of success in college (i.e., scholarship, leadership, and accomplishment, the students' view of success was much like that of the faculty—when it was someone else's success being viewed. But when looking at their own performances, students expressed more of a developmental view of success that was self-referenced and future-oriented—i.e., how have

I changed for the better? Compared with their nominations of peers, students' self-ratings of success were much less dependent on the objective facts of achievement and—it is no surprise—largely unpredictable from preadmissions information.

If applicants are identified on the basis of preadmissions measures that best predict overall success in college, how much difference can such an optimal strategy make?

Two strategies for identifying promising students were compared. An academic strategy was based only on HSR and SAT. An academic-plus strategy was based on six measures that best predicted students who were most successful overall in college. The two strategies were highly correlated. As a result, 87 percent of admissions "decisions" based on the alternative strategies were the same. When the trade-off groups selected by one strategy and not the other were compared, the academic-plus strategy clearly identified more successful students. In selective colleges the academic-plus strategy had some beneficial effect on the total group actually accepted. In the less selective colleges the differential effect on the total group was inconsequential because the trade-off group was a small fraction of those accepted. An analysis of enrolled freshmen showed that students identified by the academic-plus strategy were more likely to be successful in the more selective and also in the less selective colleges. This result demonstrated that the academic-plus strategy of identifying promising students can be equally useful in recruitment for both types of institutions.

Identifying "extracurricular producers" in high school (those who demonstrate productive follow-through in achieving outstanding accomplishments) appears to be a useful way of moving toward an academic-plus strategy, although its value depends on how the measure is used with HSR and SAT. Extracurricular productivity was a poor *substitute* for academic qualifications. Depending upon an institution's overall situation regarding recruitment and enrollment, extracurricular productivity can be a useful *complementary* qualification—i.e., possibly a useful trade-off to a somewhat higher HSR or SAT score. It was clearly favorable as an *additional* qualification when a choice was made between two students of equal academic ability.

A SUMMARY ASSESSMENT

The project started in the fall of 1978. Although it takes time to complete a longitudinal study, one advantage of such a lengthy process is the time it affords to think about the data and the issues and to profit from discussions with colleagues. Facts and ideas that seem straightforward now were not so obvious a few years ago—not to the author, anyway. The findings of this follow-up phase of the study have added to, but do not appear inconsistent with, those of the admissions phase reported earlier. The purpose of this final section is to reflect on the full study and to state briefly what appear to be the main conclusions and implications of the follow-up phase. The findings suggest a variety of policy issues that colleges and universities might well examine. The report ends with further discussion on how admissions officers might improve their identification of promising students. First, it is useful to note some connections with the Phase I report *(Personal Qualities)*.

Three years later

This follow-up analysis goes considerably beyond that reported in *Personal Qualities*, and the two phases of the study are concerned with somewhat different topics, but there are important areas of overlap. In several respects, findings reported here modify or reinforce implications discussed in *Personal Qualities*. Predicting yearly grade averages is a problem riddled with interesting complications. Results in the first report indicated that one could largely ignore the student's intended major in predicting freshman grades, but that surely changed in successive years—along with the predictability of yearly grades. On the other hand, the analysis of upper-division grades did not, in itself, reveal any useful new predictors or recommend any different admissions strategy.

The analysis of overall success after four years, including additional criteria beyond grades, certainly did suggest the possibility of a different emphasis in admissions criteria—precisely in the area of a policy-practice contradiction reported earlier. One of the more interesting findings of *Personal Qualities* was that colleges gave relatively little credit to applicants with important extracurricular accomplishments even though it was their stated policy to do so. The follow-up data iced the cake when it turned out that this is exactly the information that is the most useful supplement to school rank and test scores.

There is an interesting sidelight. It took the four-year follow-up to demonstrate the essential validity of that policy favoring extracurricular accomplishment even though it was not being followed very well. When this study was designed, the colleges were convinced (no doubt rightly) that freshmen would not have had sufficient time to demonstrate achievement in various aspects of college life. The only institutional success criteria available in the first year were grades and persistence. Suspecting that the students would have a good sense of their peers' capabilities by then, we asked them to nominate the most successful freshmen. As it turned out, the preadmissions measures that best predicted who would be selected the most successful by faculty and staff after four years were very much the same measures that predicted those freshman peer nominations. This finding suggests that peer nominations have good potential as a short-term surrogate criterion for institutional research (i.e., a broader criterion than GPA).

An added advantage of such use of peer nominations would be the opportunity to give more attention to leadership as a success criterion. These four-year results show that leadership is an extremely important form of success in the eyes of the institution. Leadership doesn't get a great deal of formal attention in the assessment of students' educational development in the upper division. It is all but invisible in freshman year studies that validate admissions measures. Most freshmen have not had time to move into leadership positions and many are not well known to faculty and staff. But other freshmen evidently do have a good sense of which classmates show leadership qualities.

Admissions officers put flags on some folders to indicate the applicants had demonstrated special talent and accomplishment. Those flags were more valid against four-year success criteria than they had been earlier—possibly because they were more relevant to the specific marks of success later identified. The flags stood in sharp contrast to the interview rating, which evidently had an influence on admission decisions but no discernible validity at all. The difference may have come from the fact that the flags were based on analysis of the student's record, while the interview was based on a limited face-to-face impression. This result dramatizes the dangers and potential inequities of personalism in admissions, but this is the mild and evidently unintentional form. Among experienced admissions officers, the extreme form is sometimes called "handshake admissions"—a snap judgment based largely on I-like-the-cut-of-your-jib.

The interview result is not atypical. Evaluations based on brief interviews seldom show any predictive validity (see other studies reviewed in *Personal Qualities,* Chapter 3). It has always been assumed, no doubt, that interviews would show some validity with the right criterion—that is, something like leadership or accomplishment outside the classroom. These results certainly give no support to that assumption.

This raises several interesting questions. If interviews have no predictive value, is it fair to allow them to influence admissions decisions?

Should admissions offices staff for individual interviews? How much value do interviews have for recruiting and counseling students? Are there better ways to serve those ends and better uses for the time and resources that interviews require?

One other implication of *Personal Qualities* gets added emphasis here. It was argued from earlier data that student self-selection has great influence on the applicant pool and that recruitment (compared with selection) has "greater potential for shaping the institution than is commonly realized." Table 8.3 shows what an understatement that was! Clearly, screening out those students who are not likely to make it academically is important for the student as well as the institution. But in a great many colleges the only way to materially change the student body is to change the body of applicants.

The main conclusions

In discussing conclusions, it is good to have in mind the limitations of a study. First, the definitions of success used here are certainly not complete and may even seem arbitrary in some respects. Are not all graduates successful? All do succeed in various ways that may be quite important to the individual. No general definition can accurately apply to the educational experience of a particular student. But the research purpose was to discriminate those who succeed to a greater or lesser extent. For that purpose the definitions are not arbitrary but are designed to identify achievement that the institutions considered important. It is certainly true that many students succeed in ways that are not visible—in ways that may even have great long-term significance. But it is only possible to study now what is visible now. Whether the particular types of success included here have long-term significance is an open question, but the findings are obviously limited to what has been measured.

Interpretation is limited in another important way. Research results can help inform policy discussion, but policy comes mostly out of experience, competing values, and compromise. Conclusions of a study like this do not apply automatically to any institution, though the findings should generalize to the substantial number of similar private colleges. Many of the implications can be as relevant to any institution, though it can not be assumed that specific findings would necessarily be the same in a group of public colleges. That caution is especially appropriate in looking at the results for students with particular background characteristics (e.g., ethnicity, type of secondary school).

It is important to remember that there are two ways of justifying and validating characteristics or measures used in admissions. One approach to admissions is to identify students who are likely to perform better in some sense. Measures used for that purpose are validated through prediction studies such as those reported here. Colleges also admit students because they fit other institutional objectives (diversity in the student body, maintaining effective ties with constituents, etc.). A measure that fails to forecast success is not necessarily inappropriate for use in admissions, although its use must be justified on other grounds. With these limitations in mind, the following conclusions seem warranted by the results of the study. They are based largely on this follow-up phase, but several are supported as well by analyses reported earlier. As will be evident from examining them, some of these conclusions are based on specific results, while others come from several related lines of evidence and an element of judgment.

1. Academic performance clearly lies at the heart of any evaluation of a student's college career. This study demonstrates again that the traditional academic predictors, school rank and test scores, were by far the best predictors of grade average, whether after one year or four years. But other types of excellence were often prominent when the faculty and staff of these colleges wrote about and nominated outstanding students. These colleges do not see success in college only, or even mainly, in narrow academic terms. The emphasis on leadership and accomplishment indicates a balanced concern not only for intellectual skills but also for other forms of personal competence important in adult life. The implication is that admissions policy should be broadly based to reflect the institution's view of the successful student.

2. There is some degree of inconsistency in the typical statement of broad educational goals and the facts of institutional practice. As *Personal Qualities* reported, an admissions policy of preference to applicants who have demonstrated significant extracurricular talent or accomplishment in high school was common; actual preference to such students was much less so. There is a corollary in the upper division. While leadership and accomplishment received very heavy emphasis when colleges identified their successes, those judgments of leadership and accomplishment were based in large part on activities that were not a formal part of the curriculum and were not assessed and recorded in any way remotely resembling the GPA on the transcript. The implication is that colleges subscribing to broad educational objectives need to give more attention to their actual practices in admitting students as well as the ways in which they structure learning experiences and recognize students who do well.

3. There are additional measures beyond school rank and admis-

sions test scores that are useful in identifying successful students. Of a large number of measures examined in this study, the best were high school honors, successful follow-through in extracurricular activities, a well-written personal statement, and a strong reference from the secondary school. How useful such supplementary measures might be to a particular college depends on how much importance the college attaches to leadership and accomplishments in addition to earning good grades. The important implication is that these other measures broaden the pool of talent in ways that were demonstrably relevant to educational objectives and can therefore provide additional information that is useful in recruiting and enrolling promising students.

4. Departmental grading patterns and student migration patterns considerably distorted the upper-division grade scales in these colleges. Otherwise, upper-division academic work appeared basically similar to lower-division work in terms of the types of skills and abilities required. The implication is that a validity study based on freshman grades likely gives as dependable results as one based on the grade average at graduation. The nature of academic performance through four years is an interesting research topic in its own right.

5. There is evidently a widespread human urge to speculate about and advance assumptions that students with a particular background characteristic—school type, family situation, some affiliation with the institution—are likely to do better or worse in college than their rank, test scores, and other qualifications would indicate. Data from this study provide almost no support for such hunches. The implication is that background characteristics may be a proper basis for preference in admissions if that serves other institutional objectives, but if the preference is based on some argument that "these students do better," there is a good chance it is incorrect and an unfair basis for preference in admissions.

6. Student statements of interests and goals do not appear to provide much useful new information regarding performance in college—that is, no information that is not already perceptible in their record of achievement. Student self-ratings of their progress and success in college do not appear to be useful in evaluating admissions policy because they are self-referenced and focus on development rather than achievement that is comparable from student to student. The implication is that student judgments about their interests, plans, and progress are likely more useful in admissions counseling, faculty advising, and program evaluation.

7. There can be strength in subjective assessment of applicants. These data indicate that admissions officers did a good job of evaluating

applicant folders. Careful ratings of the applicant's personal statement and the school reference also held up as useful additions to school rank and test scores—despite the obvious problems of interpreting studiously congratulatory prose. But there are hazards as well. Subjective judgments are often unreliable and are rife with possibilities of bias and unfairness despite the best of good intentions. There has been very little research on these problems and needs to be more. The interview is a prime example of subjective assessment that can inadvertently become influential in an important decision without real validity. The implication is that judgments about an applicant's potential should focus on what the student has actually done and on indicators known to be reliable and valid. Interview impressions should be separated from admissions decisions.

8. College selection decisions receive enormous attention because that is where the institution has direct control and that is the point at which students and parents focus their anxiety. But few institutions can much improve their destiny in that step of the admissions sequence. That is because even at a moderately selective college it is improbable that the freshman class would be noticeably different under any alternative selection strategy likely to be acceptable to the institution. The implication is that for most colleges it is more useful to think of admissions policy and strategy as a problem of what high school seniors to attract as applicants rather than what applicants to accept.

9. There are problems in giving added weight in admissions to student characteristics that are less strictly academic and objective than school rank and test scores. The so-called subjective factors or soft measures are often unreliable and may have a variety of undesirable side effects that make them impractical. Results of this study suggest a way to avoid the hazards and capitalize on the most valid core of the measures that add usefully to school rank and test scores. That valid core appears to be evidence in the student's track record that he or she can follow through to productive accomplishment. The following section discusses the rationale and ways that a college might look for signs of such productivity.

The merits of productive follow-through

A major purpose of this follow-up phase of the Personal Qualities Project was to look for new measures that would add useful information to school rank and test scores in identifying students likely to be successful in college. In the course of the search, more than 100 characteristics and qualities of applicants were compared with a number of success measures four years later.

A few measures survived that statistical analysis and came out looking quite attractive as indicators of success, broadly defined. But it is one thing to develop regression equations in a research context, and quite another thing to actually put substantial weight on an additional measure in recruiting and selecting students. A number of practical questions come up with any new measure. It it reliable? Is it too readily misrepresented or subject to bias of one sort or another? Would it remain valid if it were used widely in college recruiting literature and came to be seen as an important factor in the admissions decisions of many institutions?

Those practical problems were anticipated at the end of Chapter 8 when "extracurricular producers" were singled out to compare with academically able students. The purpose of that exercise was to examine an alternative way of identifying promising students based on information of proven validity but also potentially usable. What possible measures did we have to work with? The previous analyses had identified four:

- academic honors in high school
- follow-through (a measure of extracurricular accomplishment)
- a rating of the student's personal statement
- a rating of the school reference

The last two seem problematic as candidates for increased emphasis in undergraduate admissions in their present form. References are undoubtedly useful in individual cases. These results suggest that they do have promise and deserve further study on how to trade on their strengths and avoid their weaknesses. An escalation of emphasis on references would likely raise worries about possible prejudice and undue personalism in admissions. More emphasis on the personal statement would surely undercut its present usefulness. The statement is too subject to manipulation by applicants.

Both high school honors and follow-through are based largely on objective facts in the secondary school track record. Statistically, those two measures were almost as good as all four. One important conclusion of this analysis is that the most promising source of "other measures" is that track record. Since high school honors are a readily accepted and already widely used academic measure, we focused attention in Chapter 8 on follow-through in slightly expanded form. An extracurricular producer was defined as any student with a top mark on follow-through or any of the four types of extracurricular accomplishment upon which it was based. Since other analyses had indicated that the admissions staff had been just as accurate (and fallible) as research staff in identifying producers from the track record, a producer was also defined as anyone who got an admissions flag for "unusual talent and accomplishment."

As we have seen, the results were quite positive. Productive follow-through, thus defined, was clearly a useful supplement to school rank and test scores in identifying successful students. Analyses in Chapter 5 showing the validity of high school honors strongly suggest that such honors represent an academic form of productive follow-through. From a practical standpoint, how would one go about identifying producers (academic or extracurricular) and how can this identification be done fairly and reliably without undesirable side effects? A producer is a student who has accomplished something over and above earning good grades and test scores. The following three characteristics are useful in identifying productive follow-through:

1. *Clear Significance.* A critical dimension in defining valid productivity is the significance of the accomplishment, and significance implies importance as well as relevance. One avoids encouraging aimless activity in secondary school by refusing to reward it. By judicious reward of significant accomplishments, one can strengthen as well as expand the scope of excellence.

2. *Public Recognition.* Admissible evidence of productivity should be restricted to those accomplishments that are publicly recognized through formal awards and responsible positions. This key requirement solves two important problems. Publicly recognized accomplishments are more likely to be reliable and valid because they are locally assessed by those best informed to make the judgment. Their public character makes them also easily verifiable and less likely to be exaggerated by overeager applicants.

3. *Persistent Effort.* A developed skill or accomplishment that has taken time to achieve is more likely to be significant and to represent more commitment from the student. It also lessens the possibility of crediting accomplishments that the student has fallen into.

In this study both follow-through and leadership showed a consistent pattern of association with various types of college success four years later. These two indicators are similar in important respects. Follow-through was defined as a pattern of persistent and successful effort over time, preferably in more than one area of accomplishment. Leaders are typically selected because, over time, they have demonstrated the skills required of leaders, which almost always go beyond a particular expertise.

The connections between leadership and scholarship among successful college students demonstrate another fact about educational development that is too little appreciated. Sorting activities into academic and nonacademic categories is convenient and time-honored—and also very misleading. In this study, scholarship was often thoroughly tangled with leadership in the faculty's view of the truly effective and most admired students. Here too, at the criterion end, it often sounds much like productive follow-through when the college staff and faculty describe their very successful students.

As these data have demonstrated, productive follow-through has predictive validity and often identifies different applicants from the traditional academic measures. As defined, the measure can meet reasonable standards of authenticity and reliability. A main conclusion of this analysis is that looking for clear signs of productive follow-through is a useful way to mine the student's track record.

Does it really matter?

It is well known that the national cohort of high school graduates is declining and will continue to do so for the next several years. As a result, there are many fewer truly selective institutions than there were a few years ago. Most colleges look to the next decade as a time for maintaining enrollment, not turning away applicants or concentrating overly much on small differences in their likely success rates. This study has demonstrated the limited effect of alternative selection strategies on a freshman class. So accepting as fact that one can do a better job of identifying promising students by looking for signs of productive follow-through in their record, does it really matter? The question is not unreasonable. Some comments on reasons why it does matter are an appropriate way to end this report.

We note first that the wisdom and utility of an admissions policy must be evaluated on a much broader basis than the marginal increment in the number of students who are high performers in college. That is an important consideration, but from the standpoint of higher education generally, long-term effects of admissions policy on students and schools is a critical issue. An effective society calls for many forms of excellence. They need to be recognized and encouraged. It is equally important to give different groups of students—minorities, older students, those who are handicapped, men, women—every possible opportunity to put their best foot forward, to show what they can do.

From the perspective of the individual institution, maintaining enrollment and developing a balanced class in keeping with the objectives of the college are just as important as selecting the most able students. There is no reason to assume that the issues discussed in this report are relevant primarily to selective colleges. Quite the contrary. The finding that other talents are useful for success in college broadens the pool of admissible students. To the college concerned with maintaining enrollment, these results show that there are other places to look for able students besides the upper reaches of school rank and test scores.

Even if an alternative selection strategy has a marginal effect on the incoming class, there are important issues of equity to consider. The applicant, whether one of few or many, is concerned with fair treatment as an individual. If colleges typically announce interest in applicants who have done something significant with their time, the student has a right to expect that colleges will make selection decisions accordingly, that practice will be faithful to policy. If evidence of special productivity results in better identification of students who the college says are successful, what is the justification for *not* actively using the information—even if the effect is small?

But it is also a mistake to assume that the effect is necessarily small. A limited number of students in a particular area of accomplishment can have a leverage effect far out of proportion to their number because they provide leadership and a critical mass of quality performance in that area. In another very important respect the effect is not small. In secondary schools, students who have done something unusual are highly visible. If they are sought after by colleges, it is quickly apparent to other students and provides a signal as to what types of achievement are important.

Feedback from colleges can have either positive or negative effects on students in secondary school. On the negative side, if no one is paying attention, why bother? Why work hard to win an academic prize, or gain recognition as a debater, or write for a newspaper, or lead a community service group? It is essential first for young people to develop their minds—their intellectual abilities, their academic skills, their store of knowledge. It is also essential that they learn how to apply that knowledge and skill in socially constructive and personally satisfying ways. If they are taught to strive and produce and see that successful efforts are rewarded, they will do so. Young people are much influenced by what colleges say is important. That is perhaps the most compelling reason why admissions policy and practice do matter.

References

Aiken, L. R., Jr. 1963. The grading behavior of a college faculty. *Educational and Psychological Measurement* 23(2): 319–22.

American Association of Collegiate Registrars and Admissions Officers and the College Board. *Undergraduate admissions: The realities of institutional policies, practices, and procedures.* 1980. New York: College Entrance Examination Board.

Anastasi, A., M. J. Meade, and A. A. Schneiders. 1960. *The validation of a biographical inventory as a predictor of college success.* New York: College Entrance Examination Board.

Assessing Students on the Way to College. Vol. 1. 1973. Iowa City: American College Testing Program.

Astin, A. W. 1976. *Preventing students from dropping out.* San Francisco: Jossey-Bass Publishers.

Astin, A. W. 1978. *Four critical years: Effects of college on beliefs, attitudes, and knowledge.* San Francisco: Jossey-Bass Publishers.

Astin, A. W. 1962. "Productivity" of undergraduate institutions. *Science* 136: 129–35.

Astin, A. W., and R. J. Panos. 1969. *The educational and vocational development of college students.* Washington, D.C.: The American Council on Education.

Baird, L. L. 1976. *Using self-reports to predict student performance.* Research Monograph No. 7. New York: College Entrance Examination Board.

Baird, L. L., and J. M. Richards, Jr. 1968. *The effects of selecting college students by various kinds of high school achievement.* ACT Research Report No. 23. Iowa City: Research and Development Division, American College Testing Program.

Bejar, I. I., and E. O. Blew. 1981. *Grade inflation and the validity of the Scholastic Aptitude Test.* College Board Report No. 81-3. New York: College Entrance Examination Board.

195

Birnbaum, R. 1977. Factors related to university grade inflation. *Journal of Higher Education,* 48(5): 519–39.

Bowen, H. W. 1977. *Investment in learning: The individual and social value of American higher education.* San Francisco: Jossey-Bass Publishers.

Breland, H. M. 1979. *Population validity and college entrance measures.* Research Monograph No. 8. New York: College Entrance Examination Board.

Breland, H. M. 1981. *Assessing student characteristics in admissions to higher education.* Research Monograph No. 9. New York: College Entrance Examination Board.

Campbell, D. P. 1969. The vocational interests of Dartmouth College freshmen: 1947–67. *Personnel and Guidance Journal* 47(6): 521–30.

Campbell, D. P. 1971. Admissions policies: Side effects and their implications. *American Psychologist* 26: 636–47.

Chickering, A. W. c. 1969, 1972. *Education and identity.* San Francisco: Jossey-Bass Publishers.

Clark, M. J. and J. Grandy. In press. *Sex differences in the academic performance of Scholastic Aptitude Test takers.* New York: College Entrance Examination Board.

Cox, D. R., and D. V. Hinkley. 1974. *Theoretical statistics.* London: Chapman & Hall.

Davis, J. A. 1964a. *Faculty perceptions of students: I. The development of the student rating form.* College Entrance Examination Board RDR-63-4, No. 7; ETS RB-64-10. Princeton, N.J.: Educational Testing Service.

Davis, J. A. 1964b. *Faculty perceptions of students: II. Faculty definition of desirable student traits.* College Entrance Examination Board RDR-63-4, No. 8; ETS RB-64-11. Princeton, N.J.: Educational Testing Service.

Davis, J. A. 1964c. *Faculty perceptions of students: III. Structure of faculty characterizations.* College Entrance Examination Board RDR-63-4, No. 9; ETS RB-64-12. Princeton, N.J.: Educational Testing Service.

Davis, J. A. 1964d. *Faculty perceptions of students: IV. Desirability and perception of academic performance.* College Entrance Examination Board RDR-63-4, No. 10; ETS RB-64-13. Princeton, N.J.: Educational Testing Service.

Davis, J. A. 1965a. What college teachers value in students. *College Board Review* 56: 15–18.

Davis, J. A. 1965b. *Faculty perceptions of students: V. A second-order structure for faculty characterizations.* College Entrance Examination Board RDR-64-5, No. 14; ETS RB-65-12. Princeton, N.J.: Educational Testing Service.

Davis, J. A. 1966. *Faculty perceptions of students: VI. Characteristics of students for whom there is faculty agreement on desirability.* College Entrance Examination Board RDR-65-6, No. 15; ETS RB-66-28. Princeton, N.J.: Educational Testing Service.

Dawes, R. M. 1975. Graduate admissions criteria and future success. *Science* 187: 721–23.

Dressel, P. L., and L. B. Mayhew. 1957. *General education: Exploration in evaluation.* Washington, D.C.: American Council on Education.

Duran, R. P. 1983. *Hispanics' education and background: Predictors of college achievement.* New York: College Entrance Examination Board.

Family Educational Rights and Privacy Act of 1974. Department of Health,

Education and Welfare Final Rule on Educational Records, 45 C.F.R.S. (a).(6) 41 *Federal Register* 24662 (June 1976).

Feldman, K. A., and T. M. Newcomb. 1969. *The impact of college on students: Vol. 1. An analysis of four decades of research.* San Francisco: Jossey-Bass Publishers.

Fishman, J. A., and A. K. Pasanella. 1960. College admission-selection studies. *Review of Educational Research* 30(4): 298–310.

Fleishman, E. A., and W. E. Hempel. 1955. The relation in a visual discrimination reaction task between abilities and improvement with practice. *Journal of Experimental Psychology* 49: 301–10.

Forrest, A., and J. M. Steele. 1982. *Defining and measuring general education knowledge and skills.* College Outcome Measures Project Technical Report 1976–81. Iowa City: American College Testing Program.

Goldman, R. D., and B. N. Hewitt. 1975. Adaptation-level as an explanation for differential standards in college grading. *Journal of Educational Measurement* 12(3): 149–61.

Goldman, R. D., and R. E. Slaughter. 1976. Why college grade point average is difficult to predict. *Journal of Educational Psychology* 68(1): 9–14.

Goodman, L. A. 1976. The relationship between modified and usual multiple-regression approaches to the analysis of dichotomous variables. In David R. Heise (ed), *Sociological methodology,* 83–110. San Francisco: Jossey-Bass Publishers.

Guilford, J. P., and B. Fruchter. 1978. *Fundamental statistics in psychology land education.* 6th ed. McGraw-Hill Book Company.

Haberman, S. J. 1976. Generalized residuals for log-linear models. In *Ninth International Biometric Conference Proceedings,* 104–22. Raleigh, N.C.: Biometric Society.

Hackman, J. D., and T. D. Taber. 1979. Patterns of undergraduate performance related to success in college. *American Educational Research Journal* 16(2): 117–38.

Holland, J. L., and R. C. Nichols. 1964. Prediction of academic and extra-curricular achievement in college. *Journal of Educational Psychology* 55(1): 55–65.

Holland, J. L., and J. M. Richards, Jr. 1965. *Academic and non-academic accomplishment: Correlated or uncorrelated?* ACT Research Report No. 2. Iowa City: American College Testing Program.

Hoyt, D. P. 1966. College grades and adult accomplishment. A Review of Research. *Educational Record* 47: 70–75.

Humphreys, L. G. 1960. Investigations of the simplex. *Psychometrika* 25: 313–23.

Humphreys, L. G. 1968. The fleeting nature of the prediction of college academic success. *Journal of Educational Psychology* 59(5): 375–80.

Humphreys, L. G., and T. Taber. 1973. Postdiction study of the Graduate Record Examination and eight semesters of college grades. *Journal of Educational Measurement* 10(3): 179–84.

Juola, A. E. 1966. Prediction of successive terms performance in college from tests and grades. *American Educational Research Journal* 3: 191–97.

Lenning, O. T., Y. S. Lee, S. S. Micek, and A. L. Service. 1977. *A structure for the outcomes of postsecondary education.* Boulder, Colo.: National Center for Higher Education Management Systems.

Lenning, O. T., L. A. Munday, O. B. Johnson, A. R. Vander Well, and E. J. Brue. 1974a. *Nonintellective correlates of grades, persistence, and academic learning in college: The published literature through the decade of the sixties.* Research Monograph No. 14. Iowa City: The American College Testing Program.

Lenning, O. T., L. A. Munday, O. B. Johnson, A. R. Vander Well, and E. J. Brue. 1974b. *The many faces of college success and their nonintellective correlates: The published literature through the decade of the sixties.* Research Monograph No. 15. Iowa City: The American College Testing Program.

Lin, P. C., and L. G. Humphreys. 1977. Predictions of academic performance in graduate and professional school. *Applied Psychological Measurement* 1(2): 249–57.

Lindquist, E. F. 1963. An evaluation of a technique for scaling high school grades to improve prediction of college success. *Educational and Psychological Measurement* 23: 623–46.

Linn, R. L. 1966. Grade adjustments for prediction of academic performance: A review. *Journal of Educational Measurement* 3: 313–29.

Linn, R. L. 1973. Fair test use in selection. *Review of Educational Research* 43(2): 139–61.

Lins, L. J., and A. P. Abell. 1965. *Attendance patterns of fall 1958 new freshmen for twelve semesters after entrance.* Madison: University of Wisconsin, Office of Institutional Studies.

Lunneborg, C. E., and P. W. Lunneborg. 1970. Relations between aptitude changes and academic success during college. *Journal of Educational Psychology* 61(3): 169–73.

Manning, W. H. 1977. The pursuit of fairness in admissions. In *Selective admissions in higher education* (19–64). San Francisco: Jossey-Bass Publishers.

Moll, R. 1979. *Playing the private college admissions game.* New York: Times Books.

Nerlove, M., and S. J. Press. 1973. *Univariate and multivariate log-linear and logistic models.* R1306 EDA/NIH. Santa Monica, Calif: The Rand Corporation.

Nichols, R. C., and J. L. Holland. 1963. Prediction of the first year college performance of high aptitude students. *Psychological Monographs: General and Applied* 77(7 Whole No. 570, 1963): 1–29.

Pace, C. R. 1979. *Measuring outcomes of college: Fifty years of findings and recommendations for the future.* San Francisco: Jossey-Bass Publishers.

Peng, S. S., and W. B. Fetters. 1978. Variables involved in withdrawal during first two years of college: Preliminary findings from the national longitudinal study of the high school class of 1972. *American Educational Research Journal* 15: 361–72.

Pounds, H. R., S. L. Brown, and S. Astin. 1970. *Normative data for the 1969–70 freshman class, University System of Georgia.* Atlanta: Regents of the University System of Georgia.

Powell, L. F. J. 1978. Opinion in *Regents of the University of California v. Bakke,* 438 U.S. 265, 98 ct. 2377, 57 L. Ed. 2d 750.

Press, S. J., and S. Wilson. 1978. Choosing between logistic regression and discriminant analysis. *Journal of the American Statistical Association* 73: 699–705.

Ramist, L. 1981. *College student attrition and retention.* College Board Report No. 81-1. New York: College Entrance Examination Board.

Ramist, L. In press. *Validity of the ATP Tests: Criterion-related validity.* Chapter 7 in Advanced Testing Program Technical Manual. New York: College Entrance Examination Board.

Reilly, R. R. 1974. *Factors in graduate student performance.* GREB Professional Report No. 71-2P and ETS Research Bulletin No. RB 74-2. Princeton, N.J.: Educational Testing Service.

Reilly, R. R., and G. T. Chao. 1982. Validity and fairness of some alternative employee selection procedures. *Personnel Psychology* 35: 1–62.

Richards, J. M., Jr., J. L. Holland, and S. W. Lutz. 1967. Prediction of student accomplishment in college. *Journal of Educational Psychology* 58(6): 343–55.

Rogers, A. L. 1925. Mental tests for the selection of university students. *British Journal of Psychology* 15: 405–15.

Rubin, D. B. 1974. Characterizing the estimation of parameters in incomplete-data problems. *Journal of American Statistical Association* 69: 467–74.

Schrader, W. B. 1971. The predictive validity of College Board Admissions Tests. In W. H. Angoff (ed.), *The College Board admissions testing program: A technical report on research and development activities relating to the Scholastic Aptitude Test,* 117–45. New York: College Entrance Examination Board.

Skager, R. 1982. On the use and importance of tests of ability in admission to postsecondary education. In A. K. Wigdor and W. R. Garner (eds.), *Ability testing: Uses, consequences, and controversies. Part II: Documentation section,* 286–314. Washington, D.C.: National Academy Press.

Taber, T. D., and J. D. Hackman. 1976. Dimensions of undergraduate college performance. *Journal of Applied Psychology* 61(5): 546–58.

Tinto, V. 1975. Dropout from higher education: A theoretical synthesis of recent research. *Review of Educational Research* 45(1): 89–125.

Walker, S. H., and D. B. Duncan. 1967. Estimation of the probability of an event as a function of several independent variables. *Biometrika* 54:167–79.

Wallach, M. A. 1976. Psychology of talent and graduate education. In S. Messick and Associates (eds.), *Individuality in learning,* 178–228. San Francisco: Jossey-Bass Publishers.

Webb, S. C. 1966. Changes in student personal qualities associated with change in intellectual abilities. *College and University* Spring: 280–89.

Wechsler, H. S. 1977. *The qualified student: A history of selective college admissions in America.* New York: John Wiley & Sons.

Werts, C. E. 1967. The many faces of intelligence. *Journal of Educational Psychology* 58(4): 198–204.

Werts, C., R. L. Linn, and K. G. Jöreskog, 1978. Reliability of college grades from longitudinal data. *Educational and Psychological Measurement* 38: 89–95.

Whitla, D. K. 1977. "Value added: Measuring the outcomes of undergraduate education." Cambridge, Mass.: Harvard University, Office of Instructional Research and Evaluation.

Whitla, D. K. 1981. "Value added and other related matters." Cambridge, Mass.: Harvard University, Office of Instructional Research and Evaluation. ERIC Document Service No. ED 228 245.

Wickenden, J. W., Jr. 1979. Memorandum to all Princeton alumni on the admissions process. *Princeton Alumni Weekly,* October 22.

Willingham, W. W. 1962. *Longitudinal analysis of academic performance.* Evaluation Study No. 62-5. Atlanta: Georgia Institute of Technology.

Willingham, W. W. 1963a. *The effect of grading variations on the efficiency of predicting freshman grades.* Research Memorandum 63-1. Atlanta: Georgia Institute of Technology.

Willingham, W. W. 1963b. *Intramural migration and selective retention of students.* Research Memorandum 63-9. Atlanta: Georgia Institute of Technology.

Willingham, W. W. 1963c. Adjusting college prediction on the basis of academic origins. In M. Katz (ed.), *The twentieth yearbook of the National Council on Measurement in Education,* 1–6. East Lansing, Mich.: NCME.

Willingham W. W. 1973. *The source book for higher education.* New York: College Entrance Examination Board.

Willingham, W. W. 1980. The case for personal qualities in admissions. *College Board Review* 116: A1–A8.

Willingham, W. W. 1983. Measuring personal qualities in admissions: The context and the purpose. In R. Ekstrom (ed.), *Measurement, technology, and individuality in education: Proceedings of the 1982 ETS invitational conference,* 45–54. In M. Kean (ed.), *New directions for testing and measurement,* No. 17, March 1983. San Francisco: Jossey-Bass Publishers.

Willingham, W. W., and H. M. Breland. 1977. The status of selective admissions. In *Selective admissions in higher education.* San Francisco: Jossey-Bass Publishers.

Willingham, W. W., and H. M. Breland. 1982. *Personal qualities and college admissions.* New York: College Entrance Examination Board.

Wilson, K. M. 1970. Increased selectivity and institutional grading standards. *College and University* Fall: 46–53.

Wilson, K. M. 1983. *A review of research on the prediction of academic performance after the freshman year.* College Board Report No. 83-2 and Educational Testing Service Research Report No. 83-2. New York: College Entrance Examination Board.

Wing, C. W., Jr., and M. A. Wallach. 1971. *College admissions and the psychology of talent.* New York: Holt, Rinehart and Winston.

Appendixes

Appendix A. Senior Questionnaire

PERSONAL QUALITIES IN ADMISSION

RESEARCH QUESTIONNAIRE

Dear Class of '83:

Our college is participating in an important research study involving nine private colleges throughout the country. Your class is in the study group. You may recall completing one of the questionnaires when you were a freshman. The study is concerned with what role student characteristics, accomplishments, and goals play in admissions and how such qualities are related to subsequent achievement and progress in college.

The first phase of the study has been concerned mainly with the analysis of admissions decisions. The next step is to gather information about the activities and achievements of members of your class so that we can see how characteristics and goals of students at entry are related to a productive and successful college career. The purpose is to improve admissions practices, understand better how to advise students, and develop better college programs. We are collecting information from college records and from faculty and staff about many types of student achievement in your class. We are also especially interested in knowing your reactions as you reflect on your years of college and how you feel about your experiences here.

We urge your frank answers to the questions that follow, though your participation is voluntary. Fill in your name and birth date below only for identification in this study. Your responses will remain *strictly confidential*. Please return your completed questionnaire in the envelope provided. This study and your participation are very important to the college.

Thanks very much for your help.

Last name

First name   Middle Initial

Birthdate
month   day   year

If you entered college under a different name, please give us both names and indicate below (a) which name is new, and (b) which name is currently used by the college.

1 Listed below are 12 common goals of college students. These are stated with exactly the same wording as they were presented on a questionnaire to your class in the freshman year. Given your experience in college, how do you view them now? Consider each one and circle one of the numbers 1–5 to indicate, from your perspective, how important you think each goal should be in college. Then go to question 2 at the right.

2 To what extent do you feel satisfied with the progress you have been able to make on these particular goals? Please circle + or – at the right of each goal as you feel appropriate. Mark each item. If you are not sure, circle the ?.

Very Important
  Important
    Some Importance or Not Sure
      Minimally Important
        Not Important

Dissatisfied
  Not Sure
Satisfied

5 4 3 2 1 01. My main goal in college will be to get training for the work I want to do, or make the grades I need to get into a good school after I finish here. **+ ? –**

5 4 3 2 1 02. I see college as my great opportunity to read a lot, exchange ideas, learn about the significant cultures of the world, and generally to become an aware and more sophisticated person. **+ ? –**

5 4 3 2 1 03. I'm an active person. I like sports and other outdoor activities. Developing my talents and interests in this area is important me. **+ ? –**

5 4 3 2 1 04. I view college as a place where a person can learn practical skills valuable through a lifetime. I am especially interested in developing specific skills such as foreign language competency, computer programming, reading and math skills, good work habits, etc. **+ ? –**

5 4 3 2 1 05. I don't want to just learn a lot of facts in college; to me it's very important to learn how to deal with those facts. For example, learning how to reason, evaluate information, and construct a defensible argument are high priorities for me. **+ ? –**

5 4 3 2 1 06. Extracurricular activities appeal to me because they are a good way to get a lot out of your education; especially learning how to organize resources, work with others, and take the lead in achieving an objective. I hope to participate fully in this aspect of college life. **+ ? –**

5 4 3 2 1 07. I am not at all sure what I want to do for a career. To me it seems important that I get a better sense of direction and I hope to do that in college. **+ ? –**

5 4 3 2 1 08. I am especially concerned about ethical, moral, and religious issues. In the next year or so I would like to get a better sense of my own values in this area. **+ ? –**

5 4 3 2 1 09. I would very much like to develop a meaningful relationship with another person while I'm in college. If it's lasting, good; if it's not, that's OK too. **+ ? –**

5 4 3 2 1 10. I like to express myself creatively. I already have some talent in an area of interest to me (for example, theatre, music, painting, crafts, writing) and want to develop it further in college. **+ ? –**

5 4 3 2 1 11. I am very interested in community and social problems and would like to learn more about what's going on in the world. The opportunity to get personally involved in some sort of significant community service activity or environmental project would be important to me. **+ ? –**

5 4 3 2 1 12. In the next few years I would like particularly to develop more skill and confidence in dealing with different kinds of people. I think the social side of college is very important. **+ ? –**

3 In this study we are particularly interested in learning how students view "success" in college. Looking at these twelve goals on the previous page, in which area would you say you have made your MOST significant achievement or accomplished something for which you are especially proud? Indicate by circling ONE number.

01   02   03   04   05   06   07   08   09   10   11   12

Could you please describe the achievement and indicate why you think it was significant?

_____

_____

_____

_____

_____

_____

_____

_____

_____

_____

_____

_____

_____

_____

_____

_____

We would like to quote some examples of significant achievement—altering names and facts as necessary to protect privacy. If you have no objection to our using your answer in this way, please check (✓) here . . . . ☐

4 In your case, which of the following have significantly *contributed to* or *detracted from* a successful and satisfying college experience overall? Check (✓) all that apply.

Contributed to
↓   Detracted from
↓   ↓

☐ ☐ Ability to organize tasks and use my time effectively

☐ ☐ Availability of financial resources

☐ ☐ Health, attitude, eating and drinking habits, other personal factors

☐ ☐ Personal contacts with faculty and staff

☐ ☐ Personal contacts with students

☐ ☐ Sense of direction, knowing why I am in college and what career I would like to work toward

☐ ☐ Social life on campus

☐ ☐ Time I have spent on special interests and activities out of class

☐ ☐ Work experience during college or in the summer

5 Which students do you feel best exemplify success in college? Print below the names of up to five students in your class whom you consider, overall, to have demonstrated the knowledge, skills, and qualities of an especially successful college student.

_____

_____

_____

_____

_____

6 Objectively, how successful do you think your college career has been, overall? Check (✓) one.

1 ☐ Very succesful
2 ☐ Mostly successful
3 ☐ Mixed
4 ☐ Not particularly successful

7 Please circle how many college courses you have taken in each of the following areas.

0 1 2 3 4+   Biological Science
0 1 2 3 4+   Computer Science, Math, Statistics
0 1 2 3 4+   Economics, Political Science
0 1 2 3 4+   Foreign Languages
0 1 2 3 4+   Literature, History
0 1 2 3 4+   Music, Art, Drama
0 1 2 3 4+   Philosophy, Religion
0 1 2 3 4+   Physical Science
0 1 2 3 4+   Psychology, Sociology, Anthropology

8 What types of work experience have you had since fall 1979? Check (✓) all that apply.

☐ Internship, full-time for 2 months or more
☐ Full-time job for 2 months or more, experience of limited long-range value
☐ Full-time job for 2 months or more, valuable experience but not related to my career interests
☐ Full-time job for 2 months or more, valuable experience and training related to my career interests
☐ Teaching or research assistantship in department
☐ Other part-time or temporary job

9 What do you expect to be doing in fall 1983 (a year from now)? Check (✓) one.

1 ☐ Completing my undergraduate degree
2 ☐ Going to graduate or professional school
3 ☐ Working at a job related to my long-term career
4 ☐ Taking a break (work, travel, etc.) while I decide what direction I prefer
5 ☐ Serving in the military
6 ☐ Homemaking
7 ☐ Uncertain at present

10 What is your probable long-term career? Circle one.

1   Accountant, actuary
2   Actor, entertainer
3   Advertising, public information
4   Architect
5   Artist, designer
6   Athlete, coach
7   Banking, finance
8   Business manager
9   Business owner, proprietor
10 Business sales, marketing
11 Clergyman, other religious
12 Clinical psychologist
13 College teacher
14 Communications, radio/TV
15 Computer specialist
16 Dentist
17 Dietitian, home economist
18 Ecologist, forester
19 Editor, publisher
20 Engineer
21 Farmer, rancher
22 Foreign service
23 Homemaker (full-time)
24 Interior decorator
25 Interpreter, translator
26 Law enforcement officer
27 Lawyer
28 Librarian
29 Medical technician
30 Military service
31 Musician, composer
32 Nurse
33 Personnel work
34 Pharmacist
35 Photography, graphics
36 Physician
37 Politics
38 Public Administrator
39 School counselor
40 School administrator
41 Scientist (researcher)
42 Social worker
43 Statistician
44 Student personnel (college)
45 Therapist (physical, speech)
46 Teacher (elementary)
47 Teacher (secondary)
48 Veterinarian
49 Writer, journalist
50 Skilled trades, crafts
51 Other
52 Undecided

11 Have you investigated the characteristics and types of jobs likely to be available in fields of interest to you? Check (✓) one.

1 ☐ Not much yet
2 ☐ I have picked up some information but not in a systematic way
3 ☐ I have spent a good deal of time seeking out specific information about types of jobs that interest me
4 ☐ I already know of a specific job or company I am likely to go into

12 What is the highest degree you intend to obtain? Check (✓) one.

1 ☐ B.A., B.S.
2 ☐ Master's or equivalent
3 ☐ Ph.D., M.D., Law or equivalent

13 If you plan to go to graduate or professional school, in what field would it most likely be? Check (✓) one.

1 ☐ Art, Music, Drama
2 ☐ Biological Science
3 ☐ Business
4 ☐ Computer Science, Math, Statistics
5 ☐ Economics
6 ☐ Education
7 ☐ English, Journalism
8 ☐ Engineering
9 ☐ Foreign Languages
10 ☐ History
11 ☐ Law
12 ☐ Library Science
13 ☐ Medicine
14 ☐ Physical Science
15 ☐ Psychology
16 ☐ Social Work
17 ☐ Other Arts and Sciences
18 ☐ Other Professional & Technical
19 ☐ Uncertain
20 ☐ None Planned

14 Overall, do you feel that you have carefully chosen a career and made specific plans to enter it? Check (✓) one.

Yes	Not Sure	No
☐	☐	☐
1	2	3

Many thanks for your help. Please return the completed questionnaire in the confidential research envelope.

8400501 • RR52P9 5 • Printed in U.S.A.

Appendix B. Data Collection Guidelines for Leadership and Accomplishment

I. Instructions to Colleges on Identifying Leaders

There are two types of leadership roles to be identified separately, though it is assumed that some students will qualify on both measures. One type includes *responsible positions* on the campus to which students are appointed by faculty and staff; the other type includes *important offices* to which students are elected by student organizations, an entire class, etc. Students should be identified as filling either or both of these roles if they have held any position or office (for a normal length of time) that is judged to qualify according to the following guidelines:

A. *Appointed Positions*

These three standards should be used to determine whether an appointed position qualifies:

1. The job or function is considered to be an important role for students on the campus and selection is taken seriously.
2. In filling these roles, students are either *(a)* singled out or *(b)* selected from a surplus of applicants by a committee, faculty member, or administrator responsible for the particular appointment.
3. Selection is based primarily upon such personal qualities as maturity, interpersonal effectiveness, ability to get the job done, and ability to represent well the institution or serve as a role model for younger students. Financial need is not a major factor in selection. Specific experience or expertise may be a factor but is not sufficient without the personal qualities.

The following list illustrates the types of positions that might be considered. Include those positions that are judged to fit the three standards reasonably well.

- Dormitory counselors
- Peer advisers, mentors, tutors
- Admissions tour guides, campus hosts
- Key campus jobs, internships, or assistantships that depend on the qualities listed in paragraph 3 above.
- Graduation marshalls or other honorific roles
- Student representatives on faculty or trustee committees
- Group leaders for important projects, off-campus trips, foreign study, etc.
- Important student delegations or boards (e. g., judicial, media, etc.)

B. *Elected Offices*

These three standards should be used to determine whether an elected office qualifies:

1. It is an important elective office, either in terms of the honor attached to it or the responsibility it entails.

2. Election to the office is taken seriously by those students involved in the selection.

3. The position is a mark of some distinction in that not many attain it.

The following list illustrates the types of offices that might be considered. Include those that fit the three standards reasonably well.

- Presidents of social clubs, fraternities, sororities
- Presidents of campus organizations
- Vice Presidents or other top officers of such clubs or organizations if they are large or especially prominent
- Class officers (all years)
- Student Council officers (all years)
- Team captains (if prominent)
- Other group leaders (if prominent)
- Representatives to committees, boards (if elected and only if a limited number of students are so selected)

II. Instructions to Colleges on Identifying Students in Different Areas of Significant Accomplishment

A. There are *three bases for identifying* students who should be credited with one or more significant accomplishments. These include:

- *Competitions.* Winners or top contenders for important awards or college prizes, medalists in regional events or contests, individuals who have established some record or a significant "first," nominees for major fellowships (but *not* competitions based primarily on grade average).
- *Ex officio Evidence.* Individuals holding important jobs or positions because of their special talent and prior record of significant accomplishment. Examples include assistant coaches, managing editors, first violin, student instructor, leading actors. (Note that these are quite different from the appointed leadership roles in Task 2. Those were filled more on the basis of maturity and ability to represent well the institution, but the same individual might well hold both types of positions.)
- *Documented Nominations.* Individuals who have accomplished something significant in the consensual judgment of informed faculty and staff. Nominations are to be documented by written descriptions including such evidence of public recognition as having work exhibited, published, adopted, formally commended, etc.

B. A "significant accomplishment" represents student achievement in or out of the classroom that goes clearly beyond mastery of subject matter, carrying out course assignments, and making good grades on examinations. In order to qualify for the purposes of this study, an achievement should ordinarily meet the following *four standards.* Namely, a significant accomplishment:

. . . *involves independent initiative* on the part of the student.
. . . *requires persistent effort* over time, normally a term or more.

. . . *produces a tangible outcome* such as a developed skill, a finished product, or a completed project.

. . . *has unusual merit* due to its educational importance or high quality that is uncommonly attained.

C. Significant accomplishments should be identified in one of the following *six categories*. The following examples show the types of achievements that may qualify if they meet the four standards above; these illustrations are not intended to be inclusive.

1. Scientific/Technical Achievement
   - Recognized for design or construction of technical equipment
   - Carried out a complex scientific study or technical project with little supervision
   - Coauthor of a scientific or technical paper
   - Unusual level of competence in computer programming
   - Given an important job due to technical skill

2. Artistic Achievement
   - Won a prize for graphic art
   - Composed music that was performed publicly
   - Played important roles in local theater
   - Played first violin in school orchestra
   - Successful sale of art/craft products
   - A leading dancer

3. Communications Achievement
   - Regular announcer on local radio station
   - Published a literary work
   - A leading debater
   - A leading writer for the college paper
   - Gave an invited speech on an important occasion
   - A senior editor on a major college publication

4. Physical Achievement
   - Set a school or meet record
   - Carried out an exemplary program of physical development
   - Developed a notable expertise in outdoor activity
   - Selected on an all-star team
   - Consistent winner in an individual sport
   - Highly regarded instructor in sports or other physical activity
   - Reached an advanced level in martial arts

5. Organizing Achievement
   - Had an important role in an off-campus political campaign
   - Leader in a student movement
   - Recognized for a key contribution to an important service project
   - Organized a successful major event on campus
   - Founded a successful campus organization
   - Ran a successful business or entrepreneurial activity
   - Business manager for a major campus organization
   - Promoted to a responsible job due to demonstrated managerial competence

- Distinguished her/himself in an appointed or elected office through *specific accomplishment* far beyond what is normally expected in the role

6. Other Independent Achievement
    - Was a top contender for an important prize based upon specific achievements other than high grades
    - Carried out extensive field work in an exemplary manner with little supervision
    - Produced an unusually fine paper or project report based on substantial independent scholarly research
    - Was hired as an assistant because of special expertise or demonstrated competence
    - Any other significant accomplishment that clearly meets the guidelines but does not fit any of the above categories

Appendix C. Technical Notes

Chapter 3

1. Family Educational Rights and Private Act of 1974. Department of Health, Education and Welfare Final Rule on Educational Records, 45 C.F.R.S. (a).(96) 41 *Federal Register* 24662 (June 1976).

Chapter 4

1. Holland and Richard (1965) have argued, among others, that academic and nonacademic achievement are mostly unrelated, but Werts (1967) correctly points out that statistical artifacts account for part of this apparent lack of relationship. The correlations in Table 4.2 are tetrachorics, which avoid the problem of spuriously low product-moment (ϕ) coefficients due to discrepant marginal frequencies and course grouping. There are two other reasons that these coefficients tend to indicate a more positive relationship between academic and nonacademic achievement than seems indicated by the analyses of Chapter 8. In the latter instance relationships among different types of achievement are likely attenuated somewhat due to the tendency of self-selection and institutional selection to result in the enrollment of students who have one strength or another—the so-called Dawes (1975) effect. Another factor is that some of the coefficients in Table 4.2 may be elevated by experimental dependence and halo effect in the identification of successful seniors.

2. Figure 4.3 is a schematic representation in which the different areas were determined geometrically. The areas of the circles and the intersection of circles are accurate within drafting error. The area of dark centers is accurate if the variables are linearly related. If it is too large or small, the lightly shaded areas are correspondingly in error in the opposite direction. Visually they appear approximately correct.

3. The average within-college correlations from the senior matrix among scholarship, leadership (1), and accomplishment (a) were $r_{sl} = .25$; $r_{sa} = .30$; $r_{al} = .35$.

4. The six academic areas in Figure 4.2 represent a summarization of data for the 21 majors listed in Table D.6 in Appendix D; that is, migrate in or out refer to migration among the 21 majors, not among the six academic areas. This analysis disregards a few cases of migration within the 21 majors—e.g., from German to French, both treated here as foreign language.

5. The percentages of Figure 4.4 are on a normal probability scale so that differences are reflected more in keeping with Z score deviations. The departmental honors is probably depressed somewhat artificially because three colleges awarded few such honors. In the regression analysis immediately following in the text, the three types of scholastic accomplishment (scientific, artistic, and communications) were combined in order to make a large enough group to use as a variable in regression analysis.

6. To compare predictability of the composite "overall success" and the "most successful" nominated group, it was necessary to treat each as a dichot-

omous criterion with the same p/q split in each college. So computed, the two multiplies based on the six predictors used in Table 5.2 averaged .301 and .339. That is, using the linear model of most successful rather than the original nomination criterion improved predictability by 13 percent.

Chapter 5

1. There were several reasons for producing the "senior matrix." It was important to pool the data appropriately across colleges so as to determine the general trend of the results without the distraction of small sample fluctuations. Also, there were several important variables with significant amounts of missing data (departmental honors, interview rating, and school reference, in particular). Fortunately there is now a solution to that problem that does not incur loss either of variables or significant sample size (Rubin 1974). It would have been feasible but unreasonable to attempt to handle that missing-data problem college by college. Finally, having one large matrix with most variables of interest allowed far more efficient computation of the numerous multiple regression analyses required to examine different aspects of the data. In pooling the data it was important to avoid distortion that could result from possible—in some cases, clearly evident—arbitrary scale differences in college performance measures. Consequently, the individual college means of each measure were subtracted from each score.

The missing-data problem was handled by obtaining the maximum likelihood estimate of the variance-covariance matrix using the EM Algorithm (Rubin 1974). It was found that selecting 13 data patterns would retain 94 percent of the sample ($N = 3,442$). In obtaining the maximum likelihood estimate, indicator variables for the colleges were included so that adjusted college means for all variables could be obtained and removed from the data matrix. The full correlation matrix was then computed directly from the adjusted variance-covariance matrix.

2. Many of the success criteria used in this study were available only as dichotomous measures, i.e., success groups. This creates several problems. One is that correlations with continuous variables are systematically lower than would probably be the case if both measures were continuous. The point-biserials' upper limit of .798 is well known. Another associated problem is lack of comparability and interpretative confusion due to point biserials being interspersed with continuous scale product moments. In order to mitigate this problem, we have tried to compare similar types of measures (success groups) where possible. Also, point-biserials were systematically converted to biserials so that these coefficients would be more readily comparable to other correlation coefficients (Guilford and Fruchter 1978).

3. In the logistic model, the probability of acceptance of any given applicant is expressed as

$$P_a = \frac{1}{1 + e^{-XB}}$$

where X = the vector of independent variables and B = the vector of logistic coefficients. Maximum likelihood estimation procedures are then used to determine the logistic coefficients. The specific procedures used to determine the logistic coefficients follow those described by Walker and Duncan (1967). Multivariate normality was not assumed, and a conditional likelihood approach of the type advocated by Press and Wilson (1978) was used. For discussion of linear and logistic prediction of a dichotomous criterion, see Nerlove and Press (1973) and Goodman (1976). This method was used within each college to develop a predicted criterion score (probability of membership in the success group) for scholarship, leadership, accomplishment, and most successful. As described in the text, such predictions were based on HSR and SAT as well as on six predictors including these two. The predicted scores were put on file, thus facilitating use of a quite efficient residual analysis program for comparing predicted and actual membership in success groups for a wide variety of students.

4. The follow-through rating involved evidence of purposeful, continuous commitment to certain types of activities versus sporadic efforts in diverse areas. The rating guidelines were as follows:

5 Evidence of at least two instances of multiple-year involvement in an activity, with advancement and achievement (e.g., three to four years in student government going from representative to president, or sports participation up to team captain or notable achievement).

4 Evidence of at least two instances of multiple-year involvement with unusual success and/or advancement demonstrated in one of the instances.

3 Evidence of multiple-year involvement in at least two areas with moderate success (e.g., to varsity level in two sports).

2 Some evidence of multiple-year involvement but without indication of advancement and/or success.

1 No evidence of multiple-year involvement.

5. The p values in Table 5.2 are based on Fisher's standard method for combining probabilities (Cox and Hinkley 1974). Thus the significance test indicates that the pattern of p values for the beta weights across nine colleges was significantly different from zero.

6. Several points should be noted about Table D.7. The follow-through variable was omitted from this analysis even though it added slightly to most multiples. Follow-through created a linear restraint because of its similarity to (being largely based on) the measures of extracurricular achievement. Even though the N was large enough to produce stable results, inclusion of follow-through gave a misleading impression of the contribution of the individual extracurricular achievement measures. It is important to note that the weights in the table are reduced in size and are not comparable across criteria because they are based on point-biserial validity coefficients and the pq split varies from criterion to criterion. For that reason, analyses presented in this study place less emphasis on linear regression weights and more on logistic weights and associated residual analysis. The overall multiple correlation can be corrected to take account of the different pq splits by converting to biserial coefficients. That has been done routinely in the text. The last two lines of Table D.7 show the size of those corrections for the different criterion groups.

7. For these and other residual analyses reported here, the standard error for testing the significance of differences between predicted and actual group membership was $(\Sigma p_i q_i)^{-1/2}$. This test can be shown (personal communication, Paul Rosenbaum) to be conservative compared with the much more laborious exact test provided by Haberman (1976).

8. In Table 5.1 both HSR and SAT have small negative correlations with physical accomplishment. As Table D.7 and 4.2 indicate, that low negative relationship between academic and athletic achievement tends to run through the data. None of the other entries in the physical accomplishment column of Table 5.1 are negative, of course, because the remaining coefficients are multiple correlations which are necessarily positive.

9. Public schools with fewer than 100 seniors were defined as small, those with more than 500 as large. These accounted for 6 percent and 28 percent of the public school seniors. Of all seniors, 76 percent came from public schools. Among private school seniors, 90 percent came from schools that reported sending at least two-thirds of their graduates to college. Among public school seniors, 22 percent came from schools that reported sending two-thirds of their graduates to college. The same number of public school seniors (coincidentally) came from schools where only one-third went to college. The two-third and one-third splits were set arbitrarily. Since the two-third split includes 90 percent of all private school students here, results for that group are essentially the same as those for all private school seniors.

10. Previous studies of ethnic differences in academic performance have tended to indicate lower grades than predicted for black students (Breland 1979; Linn 1973). Interpretation of predicted versus actual grade achievement of Hispanic students is difficult since, as Duran (1983) has reported, college grades of Hispanic students are somewhat less predictable from previous grades and test scores.

Chapter 6

1. Even giving V and M optimal weights in each major in each year did not have a differential effect across years. This resulted in an increase in SAT validity of about .03 for each yearly GPA. Evidently students interested in areas that differ on the verbal-quantitative dimension tend to take more (or less) quantitatively oriented courses from the start.

2. Several writers have demonstrated grading variations and discussed their effects. During the 1960s particularly, there was a small but flourishing research interest in high school grading variations and their effect on the validity of high school grades (Linn 1966). Goldman and Hewitt (1975) and Goldman and Slaughter (1976) have reported data supporting their contention that college grading variations restrict the predictability of college grades—an argument clearly in keeping with the present analyses though their work was not connected to the issue of declining validity of yearly averages. Willingham demonstrated grading variations among instructors and courses (1963a) and the detrimental effect of departmental grading variations on the predictability of grades (1963b).

3. This analysis of departmental grading variations was also carried out by simply using the first major listed in the student's record if there were two. This procedure had the advantage of including most of the seniors, but the disadvantage of arbitrarily slotting one-sixth of the students in one major while their second would be just as defensible. Thus the presence of double majors should add noise to such a within-department analysis. This was the case. The decline in predictability was further lessened by within-department computation of validity coefficients when double majors were excluded.

4. There are two factors working to cause differences between the within-department and within-college coefficients. One is the restriction in the range of talent in the departments as compared with the college as a whole. As noted in the text, that restriction is constant across years because the same people are represented, and presumably there is a generally similar depressing effect on the validity coefficients from year to year. The effect on the validity of different predictors can be expected to vary, however, depending on what assumptions one makes about the role the measures may have had in the sorting of students into departments.

The other factor causing a difference between the within-college and within-department coefficients is variation in the grading standard among departments, which (as we see in later sections of the text) becomes more pronounced in successive years. The effect is to yield somewhat higher within-college validities for GPA1 because of the wider range of talent, but that advantage is progressively offset in later years by departmental grading variations that attenuate the coefficients pooled within colleges—the net effect being less overall decline in predictability within departments.

A secondary analysis that received little attention in the Humphreys and Taber (1973) postdiction study appears to have yielded results quite consistent with the findings reported here. Their postdiction of GPAs with GRE verbal and quantitative scores for a smaller group of seniors who had taken a GRE-advanced test was analyzed by advanced test area, a procedure more comparable to the within-department analysis here. Though one cannot be sure in the absence of a pooled control analysis for the same group, the decline in predictability was evidently reduced by about half. Humphreys and Taber speculated briefly that the different outcome in that analysis (the flatter decline) was due to differences in grading standards and quality of students from college to college that attenuate the correlation in *earlier* semesters—an explanation opposite from the rationale and supporting data presented here.

5. The reliability of the average gain score for 21 majors was .92 (based on random split halves of the total group, augmented by the standard Spearman-Brown formula). There were, of course, differences from college to college. The reliability of the gain score based on odd-even colleges was lower—but still .71. This figure suggests that fairly similar gain patterns would likely result if based on another generally comparable group of nine colleges.

6. Using gains for individual departments would more accurately reflect college-to-college variations within a major field, though this gain in precision would possibly be offset by the sampling fluctuations in the small groups this procedure would entail. A better estimate of the predictability of a discounted

GPA4 would require a Bayesian estimate of departmental gain that leans on other college data when the N of a particular department is small.

7. Presumably the predictability of the CGPA would go up over four years because of increasing reliability of the cumulative grade record, were it not for the fact that the yearly increments in the record have diminishing predictability. As a result the two factors balance one another and predictability of CGPA holds approximately steady from freshman to senior year.

8. To obtain another view of the effect of departmental grading variations, correlations of SAT-V, SAT-M, and HSR with GPA1 through GPA4 were computed with and without dummy variables representing the 21 college majors. To achieve stable results, all measures were converted to Z scores within colleges and pooled across colleges. Since this procedure does not take account of college variations in grading patterns within majors, it is only an approximation of the departmental analysis reported in Table 6.3. As expected, the validities did show less decline through the four years when the departmental dummy variables were included, especially in the case of SAT-M, which had the strongest association with selective student migration among majors. This dummy variable analysis also suggested that the lower validity coefficients within departments as compared to within colleges (Table 6.3) is due partly to restriction in range on preadmissions measures and partly to sorting over- and underachieving students by major (e.g., overachievers were more likely to migrate into natural science.). If those patterns of relative achievement vary systematically across years—an unlikely proportion—the within-departmental analysis would possibly overestimate the degree to which the validity decline is associated with departmental grading variations. These data do not provide any means of examining that possibility independent of the substantial variations illustrated in Figure 6.4.

Chapter 7

1. The following procedure was used to weight questionnaire responses for nonrespondents:

    a. Multiple linear regression with 47 predictors (including 8 college dummy variables) was used to determine which measures were significantly related to questionnaire response. The best predictors were college attended, whether the student responded to an earlier questionnaire, cumulative GPA, and peer nomination score. These variables gave an R of .32 with the response criterion.

    b. Product and power terms did not reveal any interaction or curvilinearity of regression on these predictors.

    c. A probability of responding PR_i was determined for each student through logistic regression within each college, using the best predictors identified in linear regression.

    d. Each respondent was assigned a weight, $W_i = 1/PR_i$.

Applying these weights to the group of respondents produced a group profile always accurate to within 1 percent of the full class. Because the response rate was quite good (70 percent), and the questionnaire items were evidently not highly correlated with nonresponse, the corrections in percent responding yes to particular items on the questionnaire were almost always quite small (i.e., 1 to 2 percent, at most).

2. These multiple correlations are comparable in the sense that both use the full-scale self-rating for a criterion. The R of .30 for the three types of success may be an underestimate, however, since the three success measures discriminate mainly at the top of the self-rating distribution. The corresponding biserial R was .38.

Chapter 8

1. These are logistic regression weights, standardized so as to assume equal standard deviations for the various predictors. The criterion group was those students who scored in the top third on the overall success criterion described in Chapter 5. This criterion varies somewhat from college to college, depending on how many students the college identified in each of the eight success categories that constituted overall success. The raw weight on each of the eight was consistent across colleges, however. Another approach would have been to use the group nominated as "most successful' as the overall success criterion. On the basis of analyses in Chapter 5 it was assumed that this would be a less stable criterion, but also less desirable as an alternative selection strategy because it would overestimate the number of most successful students that the "overall success" strategy would select. This definition of overall success was tried, nonetheless, and the results confirmed the assumptions; i.e., the selection strategy so defined was somewhat less effective than the overall strategy used, and overestimated beneficial selection of "most successful" students as compared with other types of success.

2. This particular way of defining *productive follow-through* is convenient for this analysis because it uses two lines of evidence (research and admissions staff ratings) to identify a group of students who are undoubtedly outstanding in these areas of accomplishments. The standard in both cases was quite high— so much so that it seems improbable that a student would qualify without having persisted at the task for some time. In one respect, however, this way of defining the group may be inferior to the original definition of the follow-through measure; namely, it does not require that all of these students have shown accomplishment in more than one area.

Appendix D. Tables

Table D.1 Senior Profile by Sex and College Major—Percentage of Seniors Who Considered Particular Goals Very Important

| | | Sex | | | | College Major | | | | | | |
Goal	All Seniors	M	F	Min. Stud.	Alum. Par.	Arts	Human-ities	Phys. Sci.	Biol. Sci.	Soc. Sci.	Bus.	Two Majors
Intellectual												
Liberal education	45%	40%	50%	39%	44%	50%	58%	34%	39%	48%	22%	48%
Intellectual skills	57	56	57	58	58	56	60	53	54	60	54	61
Moral values	14	12	17	26	16	15	19	12	08	14	06	14
Social awareness	11	08	14	18	10	04	10	06	07	15	06	11
Creative talents	16	14	18	17	21	63	23	12	09	09	06	16
Personal												
Physical development	19	22	16	21	20	16	13	20	18	20	26	18
Leadership training	33	30	36	30	36	40	31	27	29	34	45	36
Personal relations	17	19	16	21	22	23	17	17	16	18	15	18
Social competence	48	46	51	44	52	44	46	45	40	52	56	47
Career												
Professional training	23	23	23	28	20	16	13	27	34	22	32	23
Practical skills	16	14	18	19	11	13	16	25	13	12	21	19
Career exploration	27	23	31	31	29	35	27	25	26	26	29	25

Table D.2 Senior Profile by Sex and College Major—Percentage of Seniors Who Were Satisfied with Progress toward Particular Goals and on an Overall Basis

	All Seniors	Sex		Min. Stud.	Alum. Par.	College Major						
Self-Rating of Progress		M	F			Arts	Human-ities	Phys. Sci.	Biol. Sci.	Soc. Sci.	Bus.	Two Majors
Intellectual goals												
Liberal education	76%	75%	78%	70%	80%	75%	85%	64%	74%	83%	62%	82%
Intellectual skills	74	76	73	67	77	72	75	73	77	75	70	71
Moral values	54	49	60	58	50	59	60	50	55	55	43	56
Social awareness	38	36	40	36	32	32	36	34	38	42	37	41
Creative talents	40	38	42	40	41	78	45	34	40	34	33	39
Personal goals												
Physical development	63	66	60	48	70	62	61	65	65	63	68	60
Leadership training	64	63	66	58	64	69	63	61	68	64	72	69
Personal relations	60	57	64	60	64	64	62	57	60	60	62	60
Social competence	79	78	79	63	84	78	77	73	80	82	83	78
Career goals												
Professional training	61	59	63	56	56	57	57	71	60	58	72	63
Practical skills	60	56	64	57	56	58	57	70	62	57	65	62
Career exploration	55	55	55	61	55	59	48	61	55	54	59	55
Overall Self-ratings												
"Very successful" college career	30	30	31	14	33	29	32	34	34	29	31	37

Table D.3 Senior Profile by Sex and College Major—Percentage of Seniors Indicating Various Experiences in College

Type of Experience	All Seniors	Sex		Min. Stud.	Alum. Par.	College Major						
		M	F			Arts	Human-ities	Phys. Sci.	Biol. Sci.	Soc. Sci.	Bus.	Two Majors
Factors contributing to success and satisfaction												
Ability to organize	73%	69%	77%	68%	71%	66%	68%	72%	73%	73%	85%	75%
Financial resources	52	52	51	47	56	52	48	50	54	53	56	50
Health, personal factors	63	66	60	64	66	55	58	64	65	63	70	59
Faculty contacts	78	73	83	76	78	82	80	77	80	76	76	80
Student contacts	89	86	91	79	88	85	88	88	86	90	92	90
Sense of direction	56	55	57	65	55	61	43	62	57	51	74	55
Social life	62	61	63	38	64	56	58	59	60	63	77	60
Educational interests	76	72	81	73	82	81	79	71	76	75	76	76
Work experiences	72	68	76	80	75	69	69	70	75	71	74	70
One year + coursework in												
Biological science	31	27	34	20	30	20	23	24	99	24	20	28
Computer science, math	61	66	54	52	59	19	37	94	75	60	88	58
Economics, political science	63	69	57	60	64	35	64	45	29	81	100	65
Foreign languages	47	43	52	47	38	44	55	35	46	48	50	51
Literature, history	78	77	79	69	82	78	94	60	77	76	78	80
Music, art	38	34	43	42	48	88	49	31	34	34	17	38
Philosophy, religion	34	36	32	31	31	21	44	22	28	38	26	31
Physical science	41	48	33	33	44	22	24	86	84	30	18	40
Psychology, sociology	55	49	62	61	60	55	50	34	64	64	48	49
Significant work experience												
Internship, full-time	24	20	27	32	22	25	21	14	18	31	17	22
Full-time job, valuable exp.	52	52	53	51	54	56	58	46	46	56	46	52
Full-time job, career related	35	34	36	29	34	31	28	41	31	34	42	36
Teaching or research asst.	17	15	18	18	17	16	14	26	36	13	06	19

Table D.4 Senior Profile by Sex and College Major—Percentage of Seniors Indicating Various Educational and Career Plans

Education or Career Plan	All Seniors	Sex		Min. Stud.	Alum. Par.	College Major						
		M	F			Arts	Human-ities	Phys. Sci.	Biol. Sci.	Soc. Sci.	Bus.	Two Majors
Plans for next fall												
Complete undergrad. degree	03%	04%	01%	04%	01%	07%	03%	03%	02%	02%	03%	03%
Attend graduate school	27	31	23	36	26	22	24	37	50	25	10	31
Work at career-related job	44	38	51	43	49	44	36	43	23	46	77	43
Take a break, work, travel	12	12	13	05	10	14	18	06	13	13	04	10
Uncertain	13	14	11	09	13	14	19	08	12	12	07	13
Highest degree intended												
Master's	48	45	52	39	51	63	45	52	26	49	57	50
Ph.D., M.D., or Law	34	38	30	49	30	13	37	34	63	35	12	38
Degree of job investigation												
Not much yet	12	14	11	15	11	13	15	10	11	12	09	10
Some, not systematic	46	43	48	54	47	43	50	42	42	49	39	47
Good deal of time on this	31	31	31	17	32	33	28	38	33	28	34	32
Know of a specific job	12	12	11	13	11	11	08	11	14	11	17	12
Probable career area												
Artistic	10	08	13	11	12	51	24	01	03	03	01	13
Business	27	29	24	28	28	15	17	12	06	35	83	24
Human service	11	06	17	14	12	09	09	02	12	13	02	10
Law	09	11	07	14	06	03	15	01	01	14	04	12
Medicine	05	07	04	07	08	02	02	09	26	02	00	04
Science, technology	14	17	10	08	10	04	03	56	31	03	01	12
Undecided	13	12	14	14	13	11	19	11	09	15	04	13
Made specific career plans												
Yes	51	51	51	65	50	53	39	60	57	46	66	52
No	19	18	20	09	18	20	29	11	16	20	09	19

Table D.5 Senior Profile by Sex and College Major—Percentage of Seniors Achieving Success

Type of Success	All Seniors	Sex M	Sex F	Min. Stud.	Alum. Par.	College Major[a] Arts	Human-ities	Phys. Sci.	Biol. Sci.	Soc. Sci.	Bus.	Two Majors
Four-year cumulative GPA	2.95	2.86	3.04	2.60	2.95	2.93	2.99	3.00	3.10	2.95	2.90	3.09
Significant accomplishment	24%	24%	25%	28%	22%	37%	30%	25%	27%	23%	09%	32%
Scientific/technical	03	03	04	01	02	01	01	10	12	02	01	05
Artistic	04	04	05	06	05	26	07	03	02	02	00	07
Communications	03	04	03	02	03	02	07	01	01	03	01	05
Physical	05	07	04	06	05	05	04	06	05	07	02	06
Organizing	06	06	07	06	04	05	10	05	04	07	02	08
Other independent	10	09	11	15	12	08	15	09	10	11	04	15
Leadership role	35	33	37	37	41	31	32	37	46	35	35	40
Elected office	18	18	18	23	23	18	17	16	21	20	19	21
Appointed position	23	20	26	30	27	17	21	28	34	22	22	28
High scholarship	30	25	35	09	27	33	33	31	42	26	24	42
College honors	26	21	31	06	22	25	29	30	36	22	23	37
Dept. honors	11	11	11	03	10	18	14	10	17	11	00	16
Nominated most successful												
By college	20	18	23	21	24	29	20	21	26	18	20	27
By peers	18	18	18	15	21	15	17	19	23	17	23	21
Freshmen persisting 4 years	76	77	76	63	82	—	—	—	—	—	—	—
Seniors graduating by 6/83	89	85	93	81	92	87	89	86	93	90	94	91
Double major	16	15	17	10	15	31	34	20	17	25	06	100
Accepted in law/med/Ph.D.	11	13	09	11	09	05	12	16	27	10	04	16
Top third overall	34	30	38	25	38	34	36	35	45	31	35	45
Percentage of all seniors	100	54	46	03	09	07	26	17	09	38	09	16

a. Percentage of students in the six majors sum to more than 100 percent because students majoring in more than one area are included twice.

Table D.6 Number and Average Freshman Grade of Students Who Followed Various Patterns of Affiliation with 21 Majors from Freshman to Senior Year

		Freshmen[a] N/GPA1	Drop[b] N/GPA1	Migrate Out N/GPA1	Migrate In N/GPA1	Stay N/GPA1	Seniors N/GPA1	% Two Majors[c]
Arts	Art/music/drama	157/2.82	48/2.71	39/2.83	189/2.65	70/2.90	259/2.72	29%
Business	Accounting	107/2.70	25/2.65	47/2.56	56/2.83	35/2.91	91/2.86	12
	Bus. admin.	534/2.62	140/2.38	267/2.59	123/2.82	127/2.94	250/2.88	4
Biol. sci.	Biology	632/2.79	147/2.49	263/2.77	123/2.97	222/3.01	345/3.00	16
Humanities	English	345/2.82	89/2.63	106/2.87	297/2.80	150/2.90	447/2.84	30
	Foreign lang.	87/2.93	22/2.88	28/2.80	161/2.95	37/3.07	198/2.97	59
	History	122/2.76	25/2.45	56/2.84	236/2.74	41/2.83	277/2.75	30
	Philosophy	31/2.88	5/2.64	20/2.93	93/2.79	6/2.92	99/2.80	38
Phys. sci.	Chemistry	138/2.89	18/2.55	70/2.77	82/3.12	50/3.17	132/3.14	17
	Engineering	294/2.64	54/2.23	109/2.63	29/3.00	131/2.81	160/2.84	2
	Geology	31/2.71	7/2.80	12/2.84	93/2.70	12/2.54	105/2.69	16
	Math	187/2.85	31/2.59	80/2.65	106/3.05	76/3.17	182/3.11	27
	Physics	77/2.78	16/2.29	37/2.80	43/2.95	24/3.07	67/2.99	21
Social sci.	Economics	200/2.66	32/2.24	87/2.66	525/2.67	81/2.82	606/2.69	29
	Int. study	—	—	—	68/2.96	—	68/2.96	18
	Polit. sci.	358/2.82	60/2.63	191/2.83	222/2.72	107/2.90	329/2.78	33
	Psychology	228/2.63	61/2.29	101/2.68	216/2.67	66/2.85	282/2.71	24
	Sociology	58/2.78	24/2.84	20/2.67	160/2.45	24/2.83	174/2.48	29
Other	Education	120/2.69	37/2.51	55/2.72	26/2.62	28/2.88	54/2.75	28
	Health	85/2.49	30/2.31	28/2.44	37/3.01	27/2.74	64/2.90	9
	None	988/2.65	234/2.31	728/2.75	45/2.79	26/2.80	71/2.80	23
Total		4779/2.72	1105/2.45	2344/2.73	2930/2.77	1330/2.93	4260/2.82	25

a. Freshmen with no major were uncertain at the time.
b. Drop refers to withdrawal before the senior year.
c. Each major includes all of its students; as a result, double majors are doubly represented in the last four columns.

Table D.7 Standard Regression Weights for 11 Achievement Measures in Predicting 8 Types of Success in College

Predictor	Success Criteria							
	Col. Honor	*Dept. Honor*	*Elect. Leader*	*Appt. Leader*	*Scholas. Accomp.*	*Phys. Accomp.*	*Organ. Accomp.*	*Other Accomp.*
High school rank	.22	.08	.07	.11	.08			.06
SAT	.20	.15		.07	.10	−.09		.06
High school honors	.11	.05						
Community achievement			.05	.08			.04	
Athletic achievement			.08			.19		
Leadership			.06	.05			.05	.06
Creative achievement				.04	.09		.06	
Work experience								
Pers. statement, writing	.06	.06						
Pers. statement, content	.06	.05		.06	.05			.07
School reference								
% in success group	26%	11%	18%	23%	11%	05%	06%	10%
R_{pb}	.44	.24	.14	.23	.20	.24	.14	.18
R_{bis}	.60	.40	.20	.32	.34	.50	.28	.31

Note: N = 3,442.
* Weights shown are significant at .05 level. (See note 6 for Chapter 5 in Appendix C.)

Table D.8 Percentage of Students Achieving Four Types of College Success for Trade-Off Groups High on One Definition of Success and Low on Another—by More and Less Selective Colleges

	More Selective Colleges		Less Selective Colleges	
	High Academic / *Low Academic+*	*Low Academic* / *High Academic+*	*High Academic* / *Low Academic+*	*Low Academic* / *High Academic+*
Scholarship	22%	25%	17%	30%
Leadership	23	33	29	45
Accomplishment	19	41	13	21
Most successful	09	14	13	25

Table D.9 Percentage of Freshmen Who Considered Various Educational Goals Very Important and Percentage of Seniors in Different Majors—Classified as High or Low on Two Definitions of Promise at Entry

	Classified as Freshmen			
	I *Low Academic* *Low Academic+*	*II* *High Academic* *Low Academic+*	*III* *Low Academic* *High Academic+*	*IV* *High Academic* *High Academic+*
Educational goal considered very important				
Liberal education	44%	42%	51%	44%
Intellectual skills	64	58	63	53
Moral values	09	08	12	11
Social awareness	13	11	10	11
Creative talents	24	26	27	25
Physical development	31	18	25	20
Leadership training	36	28	39	35
Personal relations	21	18	17	17
Social competence	48	38	48	45
Professional training	53	57	52	55
Practical skills	25	25	25	23
Career exploration	36	33	32	32
Senior major				
Arts	09	02	09	07
Humanities	26	31	30	27
Physical science	12	22	13	24
Biological science	07	12	11	12
Social science	45	40	44	32
Business	10	08	07	11

Table D.10 Predictability of Yearly Grade Point Averages for Contrasting Groups of Students

Group	N	*Multiple R* (HSR, SAT)[a]			
		GPA1	GPA2	GPA3	GPA4
Sex: Male	1,713	.47	.43	.40	.35
Female	1,483	.48	.46	.44	.38
Miles from Home: < 400	818	.47	.46	.43	.38
400 +	2,378	.49	.46	.42	.38
Interviewed: Yes	1,518	.45	.44	.39	.36
No	1,679	.52	.47	.45	.40
Aid applicant: Yes	1,280	.54	.51	.48	.43
No	1,560	.44	.42	.37	.34
Major: National science	815	.48	.46	.41	.37
Social science	787	.47	.42	.37	.37
Humanities	1,099	.51	.48	.46	.40
Uncertain plans at entry: Yes	1,163	.49	.47	.42	.35
No	2,034	.49	.46	.43	.40
Respond to questionnaire: Yes	1,779	.50	.46	.43	.37
No	1,418	.45	.44	.41	.37
Student/faculty contact good: Yes	1,554	.50	.47	.44	.39
No	589	.49	.44	.40	.30
Cited detractions: Yes	1,411	.49	.47	.44	.39
No	1,786	.48	.45	.42	.38
Progress ratings above average: Yes	981	.52	.49	.45	.38
No	1,142	.47	.45	.41	.37
Nominated by peers: Yes	1,514	.53	.49	.45	.40
No	1,683	.42	.40	.36	.32
Cited for leadership or accomplishment: Yes	1,283	.53	.51	.48	.39
No	1,569	.42	.39	.36	.33
Total	3,197	.49	.46	.43	.38

a. All measures were standardized within departments.

Table D.11 Average Preadmissions Measures and Grade Point Averages for Seniors Grouped by Major

Major	N	HSR[a]	SAT	Acad. Comp.[b]	Yearly Averages[c]				4-Year GPA
					GPA1	GPA2	GPA3	GPA4	
Arts									
Art/music/ drama	162	48.5	532	48.2	2.71	2.80	2.99	3.07	2.89
Business									
Accounting	79	53.0	550	52.5	2.95	3.16	3.01	2.93	2.99
Business admin.	235	50.0	533	49.3	2.88	2.93	2.85	2.89	2.87
Biological science									
Biology/zool- ogy/botany	277	55.4	584	56.1	3.00	3.05	3.11	3.20	3.09
Humanities									
English	280	51.2	571	52.7	2.76	2.88	3.05	3.14	2.95
Foreign lan- guage	57	53.4	553	52.9	2.79	2.89	2.98	3.06	2.91
History	172	50.6	568	52.2	2.73	2.82	2.98	3.00	2.87
Philosophy and religion	54	5.14	595	54.7	2.77	2.83	3.03	2.98	2.91
Physical science									
Chemistry	104	57.9	604	59.2	3.13	3.06	3.12	3.14	3.11
Engineering	140	56.8	600	58.4	2.86	2.88	2.90	2.92	2.88
Geology	79	51.1	580	53.3	2.68	2.73	2.78	2.91	2.77
Mathematics	117	57.0	609	59.2	3.09	3.03	3.10	3.16	3.10
Physics	48	53.5	611	57.1	2.99	3.01	3.09	3.05	3.04
Social science									
Economics	396	49.3	550	50.0	2.64	2.78	2.89	2.99	2.81
Internat. stud- ies	51	50.9	588	53.8	2.94	3.02	3.13	3.21	3.07
Political science	196	51.1	562	52.1	2.70	2.82	2.98	3.06	2.89
Psychology	199	52.8	550	52.2	2.73	2.86	2.99	3.14	2.93
Sociology	103	48.5	507	46.6	2.44	2.67	2.87	2.99	2.75
Other									
Education	37	49.8	503	47.1	2.64	2.84	3.15	3.32	3.01
Health	55	53.3	522	50.7	2.81	2.93	2.96	3.13	2.96
Undesignated	43	49.7	525	58.6	2.72	2.76	2.90	3.07	2.87
Total	2,884	51.9	562	52.5	2.79	2.89	2.98	3.05	2.92

a. HSR was standardized to a mean of 50 and S.D. of 10.
b. Academic composite was an equally weighted sum of HSR and SAT, scaled as HSR.
c. Double majors are excluded.

Table D.12 Percentage of Seniors in Different Four-Year GPA Ranges—by Type of Success

Type of Success	N	Percentage in Four-year GPA Range				
		3.5+	3.0–3.4	2.5–2.9	2.0–2.4	< 2.0
Any scholarship	1,090	51%	45%	4%	1%	0%
College honors	944	58	42	0	0	0
Dept. honors	415	45	44	10	1	0
Any leadership	1,280	25	39	27	10	0
Elected	669	21	35	31	12	0
Appointed	841	30	42	22	6	0
Any accomplishment	886	30	39	24	7	0
Scientific	127	58	31	11	1	0
Artistic	158	21	44	30	6	0
Communications	124	30	48	21	2	0
Physical	188	15	30	34	20	1
Organizing	225	26	47	21	7	0
Other	373	42	38	18	2	0
Advanced study	412	42	41	14	3	0
Most successful	741	44	39	14	2	0
Any of the above	2,145	26	43	24	8	0
Double major	586	21	43	27	9	1
Grad. on time	3,268	16	39	32	13	0
Seniors in each N	3,676	550	1,341	1,167	572	46
GPA range in %	100	15	36	32	16	1

Appendix E. College Profiles

Bucknell University is a private institution founded in 1846. It is located in Lewisburg, a small town in the Susquehanna Valley in central Pennsylvania.

The university enrolls 3,100 undergraduate students from around the world. While incorporating a basic liberal arts curriculum in fine arts, humanities, social sciences, mathematics, and science, Bucknell offers the presence of a professionally accredited engineering program and management and education departments.

Bucknell also offers special programs such as the interdepartmental major, the college major, freshman advisory seminars and humanities semesters, independent study, an honors program, study abroad, and a unique cross-generational program.

Colgate University is an independent, nonsectarian, liberal arts institution founded in 1817 as the Baptist Education Society of the State of New York. As Madison University, it was granted the right to confer degrees in 1846, and in 1890, its name was changed to Colgate University. It is located on a 1400-acre campus in the rural village of Hamilton, New York.

The university enrolls 1,500 undergraduate men and 1,100 women. In addition, there is a small graduate program leading to the M.A.T. degree. Majors are offered in 37 concentrations, including interdisciplinary options.

Colgate has an academic calendar (4-1-4) of four fall and four spring courses, and a January course. Also, students can take advantage of some 20 "study groups" which travel throughout the world. Almost every department offers a specially designed freshman seminar of 15 to 20 students.

Hartwick College is an independent, coeducational, liberal arts institution founded in 1928. It is located on a 175-acre campus overlooking the city of Oneonta, New York, and the Susquehanna River Valley. Pine Lake, a 1,100-acre second campus, is an ecological preserve that serves as a resource for biological and ecological studies.

The college enrolls approximately 1,400 students from 30 states and 12 foreign countries. Majors are offered in 26 areas of study, including programs in management and nursing. In addition, the college offers each student the option of designing a personalized concentration that may be interdisciplinary or career oriented.

Many Hartwick students participate in the college's off-campus programs and may study in a foreign country, in an urban center, or in the field biology program in the Bahamas. Academic departments encourage participation in off-campus internship programs.

Kalamazoo College, an independent, residential, liberal arts institution founded in 1833, maintains its historical connection with the American Baptist Church. It is located on a 160-acre campus in Kalamazoo, Michigan.

The college enrolls 1,450 students from the United States and other countries. The Bachelor of Arts degree is offered in 19 departmental majors and 6 interdepartmental concentrations.

In addition to liberal arts study, Kalamazoo's curriculum includes a quarter spent in career development through positions with businesses, agencies, or communities. One or two quarters are reserved for foreign study at no additional expense to the student. During one quarter of the senior year, the student works off campus on a project of his own choosing.

Kenyon College is a residential liberal arts institution founded in 1824 as an all-male seminary. It remained a men's college until 1969, when women were first admitted. It is located in Gambier, Ohio, about 50 miles northeast of Columbus.

The college enrolls 1,450 students from all sections of the United States. Kenyon's traditional liberal arts curriculum offers 18 majors in the classical academic disciplines, including humanities, sciences, and fine arts.

Kenyon's Bolton Theater is considered one of the finest collegiate drama facilities in the United States. Also, the Integrated Program in Humane Studies offers a series of lectures, seminars, and tutorials. Each spring the college sponsors the Public Affairs Conference Center, a four-day forum at which contemporary issues are debated by political thinkers, educators, journalists, and business executives. The *Kenyon Review* is published on campus.

Occidental College is a liberal arts institution founded in 1887. It is located on a 120-acre residential campus 8 miles from downtown Los Angeles, California.

The college enrolls 1,700 students from 40 states and 30 foreign countries. The student–faculty ratio is less than 14 to 1. Occidental offers 30 majors, including the Independent Pattern of Study, which allows students to design their own majors. The liberal arts core program is interdisciplinary, encompassing natural sciences, humanities, social sciences, and fine arts.

In addition, Occidental offers a diplomacy and world affairs major and a marine biology program that makes use of the college's 85-foot oceanographic research vessel. There are 17 intercollegiate teams and over 100 clubs.

Ohio Wesleyan University is an independent, liberal arts institution founded in 1842 by the Methodist Church, with which a beneficial relationship continues. It is located on a 200-acre campus in Delaware, Ohio, 30 miles north of Columbus.

The university enrolls 2,250 students from the United States and 30 other countries. There are an almost equal number of men and women; one-third of the students are from Ohio. Majors are offered in more than 60 fields, including the liberal arts, sciences, and programs leading to professional degrees in fine arts, music, and nursing. The faculty consists of 160 full-time members.

Through cooperative programs with the Great Lakes Colleges Association (GLCA) and other arrangements, Ohio Wesleyan students may pursue a wide range of opportunities in international education. The university administers a New York Arts Program for the GLCA in New York City in which students apprentice with artists, publishers, theater groups, and broadcasters. Other off-campus apprenticeships are available in a number of fields. The 400,000-volume Beeghly Library is unusually comprehensive for a college of Ohio Wesleyan's size.

The University of Richmond is an independent, privately endowed institution founded by the Virginia Baptists in 1830. It is located on a 350-acre campus in the suburban west end of Richmond, Virginia. The University includes Richmond College, Westhampton College, the Coordinate Colleges for men and women, the E. Claiborne Robins School of Business, the T. C. Williams School of Law, the Graduate School, and University College.

The university enrolls 2,500 undergraduate students and offers 36 majors through 22 departments, and special programs include undergraduate research, independent study, internships, university scholars, and study abroad. The School of Business combines liberal arts study with a professional business curriculum. A full range of extracurricular activities complements the academic program.

The gift of $50 million from the E. Claiborne Robins family in 1969 has enabled Richmond to retain the character of a small college while developing the educational resources of a major university.

Williams College is a privately endowed residential liberal arts college founded in 1793. It is located in Williamstown in the Berkshire mountains of northwestern Massachusetts.

The college enrolls 2,000 students from the United States and more than 40 other countries. Approximately 55 percent of the students are men and 45 percent women; the student–faculty ratio is 12 to 1. The liberal arts curriculum has been enriched by the addition of several interdisciplinary programs, area study offerings, a program of critical languages, and two Master's degree programs: development economics for civil servants from Third World countries, and art history, which is offered in collaboration with Clark Art Institute.

Since 1967, Williams has been on a 4-1-4 calendar. The winter study program, a January term during which each student pursues one project or subject in depth, is a distinctive curricular feature.